Narrative Irony
in the Contemporary
Spanish-American Novel

Narrative Irony
in the Contemporary
Spanish-American Novel

Jonathan Tittler

CORNELL UNIVERSITY PRESS

Ithaca and London

THIS BOOK HAS BEEN PUBLISHED WITH THE AID OF A GRANT FROM
THE HULL MEMORIAL PUBLICATION FUND OF CORNELL UNIVERSITY.

First published 1984 by Cornell University Press.
Published in the United Kingdom by Cornell University Press Ltd., London.

International Standard Book Number 0-8014-1574-8
Library of Congress Catalog Card Number 83-21074
Printed in the United States of America
*Librarians: Library of Congress cataloging information
appears on the last page of the book.*

*The paper in this book is acid-free and meets the guidelines for permanence and
durability of the Committee on Production Guidelines for Book Longevity of
the Council on Library Resources.*

FOR SUE,
who shares in all my
joys and uncertainties

CONTENTS

PREFACE

Irony's value as a critical tool, especially with respect to the novel, is by now widely accepted. In this book I attempt to explore the ways in which irony, as a figure of speech, a paradoxical turn of events, and a state of mind, helps explain several outstanding works of current Spanish-American fiction. I introduce in addition the concept of "narrative irony"—the distance between and among novelistic elements—and employ it to study the spatial dimension of these structurally complex and highly self-conscious texts. I contend that, perhaps because of the erratic modernization and political volatility peculiar to the region, irony, in all its senses, is a characteristic property of the contemporary Spanish-American novel, a factor without which no understanding of the phenomenon can be complete. At the same time, the formalistically charged nature of the novels examined provides an extraordinary opportunity to show the method's potential for producing coherent readings. That potential is far from exhausted by this demonstration of mutually supportive literature and criticism.

Roughly the first half of the book applies the narrative-irony approach to four widely respected novels: Carlos Fuentes' *Death of Artemio Cruz* (Mexico, 1962), Juan Rulfo's *Pedro Páramo* (Mexico, 1955), Manuel Puig's *Betrayed by Rita Hayworth* (Argentina, 1968), and Guillermo Cabrera Infante's *Three Trapped Tigers* (Cuba, 1967). The second part of the analysis, as it gives commentary on three more novels—*Aunt Julia and the Scriptwriter* (Peru, 1977) by Mario Vargas Llosa, *A Manual for Manuel* (Argentina, 1973) by Julio Cortázar, and *The Fragmented Life of Don Jacobo Lerner* (Peru, 1978) by Isaac Goldemberg—challenges language's

9

signifying and referential capacity and thus, in a couple of words, ironizes irony. The work concludes with a summary of findings, a reflection on the intimate connection between irony and the novel, and an outline for future investigation into the relation between irony and the Spanish-American neobaroque.

My intellectual debts are innumerable. Unfortunately I must limit my expressions of appreciation to three friends and colleagues who, among all those who gave of themselves generously, have made a major impact on my thinking. First is Roberto González-Echevarría, whose broad and profound knowledge of Latin American literature and culture fundamentally informs this book. I also thank John W. Kronik, a paragon of professionalism with a rare talent for diplomacy and exigency. I have often sought and always valued his counsel. Philip E. Lewis painstakingly read portions of my manuscript and served unflaggingly as a model of articulate erudition.

I am also grateful to Dora Velasco, who retyped the final version of the manuscript with accuracy and speed, and to the Hull Memorial Publication Fund at Cornell University, which underwrote a large portion of its publication costs. I literally could not have done without the help of either. Irony aside for once, I extend to all these people and institutions my heartfelt gratitude.

Portions of Chapter 3 appeared in the article "Order, Chaos, and Re-order: The Novels of Manuel Puig," *Kentucky Romance Quarterly* 30, no. 2 (1983). An earlier version of Chapter 4 appeared under the title "Intratextual Distance in *Tres tristes tigres*" in *Modern Language Notes* 93 (1978). *MLN* is published by the Johns Hopkins University Press. I am also grateful to the following for permission to reproduce copyrighted material: to Farrar, Straus & Giroux, Inc. and Martin Secker & Warburg Ltd. for passages from *The Death of Artemio Cruz* by Carlos Fuentes, translated by Sam Hileman, copyright © 1964 by Carlos Fuentes; to Grove Press, Inc., for quotations from *Pedro Páramo* by Juan Rulfo, translated by Lysander Kemp, copyright © 1959 by Grove Press, Inc.; to E. P. Dutton, Inc., and International Creative Management, Inc., for material from *Betrayed by Rita Hayworth* by Manuel Puig, translated by Suzanne Jill Levine, copyright © 1971 by E. P. Dutton, Inc.; to Guillermo Cabrera Infante and Harper & Row, Inc., for passages from *Three Trapped Tigers* by Guillermo Cabrera Infante, translated by Donald Gardner and Suzanne Jill Levine in collaboration

JONATHAN TITTLER

Ithaca, New York

Narrative Irony
in the Contemporary
Spanish-American Novel

The world is too much with us; late and soon,
Getting and spending, we lay waste our powers:
Little we see in Nature that is ours;
We have given our hearts away, a sordid boon!
                              —William Wordsworth

Introduction:
An Approximation to Irony

It is thought that "irony" originated as a colloquial term of derision in ancient Greece,[1] acquired legitimacy in Roman times,[2] and passed into English in written form in the sixteenth century.[3] The concept assumed unprecedentedly privileged status with the German Romantics[4] and enjoyed currency among American New Critics a generation ago.[5] Today, although displaced somewhat by the concerns of deconstructive criticism, irony remains a key element in contemporary literature, literary criticism, and theory.

Apparently inexhaustible as a means of suggesting meaning, irony is equally fecund when it comes to engendering confusion. Rarely do we use the word twice in exactly the same sense. When Stanley Fish states, "Irony and ambiguity are not properties of

1. The most thorough study of the history of irony—its origins and role in classical literature—is J. A. K. Thomson, *Irony: An Historical Introduction* (Cambridge: Harvard University Press, 1927). See also Norman Knox, *The Word Irony and Its Context, 1500–1755* (Durham: Duke University Press, 1961); and G. G. Sedgewick, *Of Irony, Especially in Drama* (Toronto: University of Toronto Press, 1948).

2. According to Knox (*The Word Irony*, p. 5), Cicero was flattered to be considered an ironist.

3. Knox (ibid., p. 7) documents the initial appearance of "yronye" in 1502, in *Thordynary of Crysten Men.*

4. See Hans Eichner, *Friedrich Schlegel* (New York: Twayne, 1970); D. C. Muecke, *Irony* (London: Methuen, 1970); and René Wellek, *A History of Modern Criticism* (New Haven: Yale University Press, 1955), vol. 2.

5. Cleanth Brooks, among many others, says in "Irony as a Principle of Structure," in *Literary Opinion in America,* ed. Morton Zabel (New York: Harper & Row, 1951), that "*ironical* is in danger of becoming a catchword of our own period" (p. 737; italics in original).

Introduction

language but functions of the expectations with which we approach
it,"[6] he is concerned with how meaning is determined by context;
his irony is the master trope that articulates severally and simultaneously. In the system of Vladimir Jankélévitch, who writes,
"Irony is the awareness of the revelation by which the absolute in a
fleeting moment is realized and in the same blow destroyed,"[7] irony
is not an objective event or phenomenon, but a volatile state of
mind in which truth, in the act of revealing itself, suffers a necessary
negation. Robert Sharpe's commentary, "Drama is of all the arts
the most ironic, the most dependent upon ironical effects and the
most capable of producing them,"[8] must be understood as a reference to the act of impersonation inherent in dramatic representation. The duplicity of acting perceived by the spectator, according
to Sharpe, sets drama apart from other potentially ironic art forms.
And Georg Lukács, who posits irony as "the normative mentality
of the novel,"[9] is speaking of a form-giving principle, a sense of lost
immanence which, when located within a mind determined to reflect literarily all of historical actuality, gives rise to a certain genre:
the novel. All these uses of the term are both informed and legitimate. So too would be the inclusion of another sense, that expressed by Wordsworth in the epigraph above. While he says nothing explicitly about irony, the poet does convey the quintessential
attitude of the Romantic artist, who sees life as a "sordid boon"
and mankind as the hapless plaything of a whimsical Fate. Rather
than reason, paradox and contradiction (Romantic irony) prevail.

If irony is not to be crushed under the weight of its own protean
polymorphism, it must be examined systematically. In suggesting
such an undertaking I am duly mindful of pronouncements such as
A. E. Dyson's that "no embracing theories or criteria are possible

6. Stanley Fish, "Normal Circumstances, Literal Language, Direct Speech Acts,
the Ordinary, the Everyday, the Obvious, What Goes without Saying, and Other
Special Cases," in *Is There a Text in This Class?* (Cambridge: Harvard University
Press, 1980), p. 277. The article originally appeared in *Critical Inquiry* 4 (Summer
1978): 625–44.
7. Vladimir Jankélévitch, *Irony or the Good Conscience* (*L'Ironie ou la bonne
conscience*) (Paris: Presses Universitaires de France, 1950 [1936]), p. 11. Unless
otherwise noted, all translations in this chapter are my own.
8. Robert Boies Sharpe, *Irony in the Drama: An Essay on Impersonation, Shock,
and Catharsis* (Chapel Hill: University of North Carolina Press, 1959), p. xii.
9. Georg Lukács, *The Theory of the Novel*, tr. Anna Bostock (Cambridge: M.I.T.
Press, 1971 [1916]), p. 84.

16

and that attempts to seek for them are invariably misplaced."[10] But even if totalization is impossible (because irony is the essence of unachieved totalization), we are at present so far from threatening that absolute limit that surely much can be gained from a rigorous failure. Our immediate goal is to lay a foundation for the concept or group of related concepts, and to expand its reach slightly for literary criticism. The theoretical part of our inquiry will take into account the following dimension of the question:

> definitions
> preconditions and purposes
> objective irony
> subjective irony
> narrative irony

In the chapters devoted to textual analysis, I propose to establish irony's credentials as a fundamental presence in fiction, particularly in the Spanish-American narrative. The conclusions I draw will concern the various forms and textual loci of irony in representative contemporary novels and the extent to which irony is a basic trait of Spanish-American writing today. The book is composed of two parts whose conceptual frameworks, while overlapping considerably, diverge sufficiently to be qualitatively different. In brief, parts I and II represent the notions of stasis and kinesis respectively. Kinesis is judged more nearly perfect a formal reflection of irony's operating principle and world view, whereas stasis is seen as a necessary precondition, a foundation on which to establish the contrast. In its very conception, then, this book emulates the interrogating, vertiginously self-correcting movement of ironic thought.

Definitions

It is possible to isolate two moments in irony, objective and subjective. There are also two types of objective irony, that commonly called *intended irony* (most often verbal) and another termed *accidental irony* (alternatively, irony "of events"). Roughly put, intended irony is that figure of speech in which the speaker's words have a meaning not totally in consonance with (often the

10. A. E. Dyson, *The Crazy Fabric: Essays in Irony* (London: Macmillan, 1965), p. ix.

opposite of, often more significant than) their straightforward literal sense. Accidental irony refers to a paradoxical circumstance, one that is contrary to expectations or to reason itself. *Subjective irony* is normally understood to refer to the state of mind induced by *objective irony*, either intended or accidental. It implies an apprehension of incongruity and the subsequent reactions to that perception. Although the distinction is not categorical and usage among scholars is far from uniform, throughout these pages the adjective *ironical* is applied to the purveyor of intended irony; *ironic* describes the incongruous circumstance come upon accidentally.

Preconditions and Purposes

Verbal irony can arise only in a social context, for it is a product of intersubjective communication.[11] Furthermore, in order for a dissembling ironist not to deceive altogether (since no irony results if the literal meaning of a locution is not soon rejected) the parties involved must accept a common frame of values.[12] The "victim" of verbal irony must therefore be a potential ironist as well and already embody the duplicity necessary to identify that of the ironist. As Kenneth Burke, who has perhaps most clearly seen irony's cooperative dimension, puts it: "True irony, humble irony, is based upon a sense of fundamental kinship with the enemy, as one *needs* him, is *indebted* to him, is not merely outside him."[13]

The apprehension of the irony of events, in contrast, may be a solitary experience. It stems from the perception of either incongruity, conflict, or contradiction.[14] Regardless of whether these discords are in one's own nature or in the surrounding world, they

11. René Schaerer, "Le Mechanisme de l'ironie dans ses rapports avec la dialectique," *Revue de Métaphysique et de Morale* 8 (1941): 181–209.

12. Søren Kierkegaard, *The Concept of Irony, with Constant Reference to Socrates*, tr. Lee M. Capel (New York: Harper & Row, 1965), p. 265: "The ironic figure of speech cancels itself . . . , for the speaker presupposes his listeners understand him."

13. Kenneth Burke, "Four Master Tropes," in *A Grammar of Motives* (New York: Prentice-Hall, 1945), p. 514. Italics in the original.

14. Haakon Chevalier, *The Ironic Temper: Anatole France and His Time* (New York: Oxford University Press, 1932), p. 37. See also Edwin M. Good, *Irony in the Old Testament* (Philadelphia: Westminster Press, 1965), p. 30; and Reinhold Niebuhr, *The Irony of American History* (New York: Scribner, 1952), p. viii.

cause the viewer to become detached from the situation in order to view it impartially.[15] These contradictions, however, are not in themselves the sole and simple cause of irony: necessary too is a sense of doubt. That is, an incongruity, conflict, or contradiction does not present itself to a tabula rasa, but rather appears only when a doubting mind looks for such phenomena to confirm its suspicions. Otherwise, the contrast would not be apprehended as such, but would be elided immediately into a synthesis on another level (for example, "God moves in mysterious ways" or "Exploitation of the worker leads to armed uprising and a classless society"). It would therefore never achieve the opacity necessary for its reification as an ironic event. Doubt and conflict, rather than a simple cause and effect, function in a way similar to the interaction between language and thought. Just as one cannot reason without language, neither can one speak without already having available the mechanism of conceptualization.[16] The factors are mutually determinative. Without existential conflict, there is no doubt; and without doubt, conflict does not appear as such to consciousness. The irony of events depends, therefore, on a certain kind of subject finding him- or herself[17] in a particular sort of context. These necessary components must enter into a reciprocal catalysis to bring about both the conflictive event and its apprehension.

The preconditions common to both the sort of irony sensed in observing events and in the kind practiced in dialogue are not so numerous as one might imagine. One condition is quite abstract and deals with what we might call a prime quality of reality, whereas the other seems in comparison almost trivial. As irony depends on apprehending a disparity between this and that, the first condition, what Palante calls "the generating principle of irony,"[18] is a dualism or basic twoness that can assume different forms and take the shape of diverse antinomies. These dichotomies may include

15. Georges Palante, "L'Ironie: Etude psychologique," *Revue Philosophique de la France et de l'Etranger* 61 (1906): 153; see also Sedgewick, *Of Irony*, pp. 13ff.

16. Kierkegaard himself cites this example (*Concept of Irony*, p. 264): "If I have the thought without the word, I do not have the thought; and if I have the word without the thought, I do not have the word."

17. Owing to the frequency with which I refer to ironists, victims, readers, and authors, I have settled, for purely stylistic reasons, on "he" and "him" as generic pronouns for human beings; the inadequacy of the term is regretted.

18. Palante, "L'Ironie," p. 148.

19

thought and action, the ideal and the real, intelligence and emotion, or cognition and intuition, to name a few contrasting pairs. As with ironic discord, it is not clear whether the duality is located in consciousness, in the world, or in both; omnipresent binarism may be no more than a projection of the Western mind.

The other, more historically determined precondition to irony is a certain degree of leisure. Jankélévitch has seen that "art, the comic, and irony become possible precisely at the point where *vital urgency* is relaxed."[19] Being ironical and seeing things as ironic are not the same as subsisting in strife and expressing a resultant dolorous vision. One must first have at least some ease and security in order (a) to reflect on a situation as being ironic (rather than merely experience it as catastrophic) and (b) to indulge in the circuitous and often time-consuming mode of interplay called ironical. Irony thus depends on a relatively advanced civilization, one that has evolved a degree of specialization and the institutionalization of dialogue to resolve differences. Irony is especially ill suited, it follows, to situations such as war or conflagration, where direct action is required. That such a historical "accident" may be prerequisite to "intended" irony, however, ought to give one pause about the sufficiency of labels in the universe of irony.

Intended irony may have as many different purposes as it has practitioners. When the ironist concentrates on his ingenuous interlocutor, asserts René Schaerer, the mechanism may carry out a pedagogical function: "Irony has but a preparatory value, in that it liberates the spirit of prejudice and disposes it to true research."[20] And just as irony of pure reason may train one to unearth latent absurdities, irony driven by an ethical impulse may serve to expose invisible scandals.[21] Regardless of the excellent ends to which it *may* be applied, however, I agree with Kierkegaard that "the purpose is none other than irony itself . . . merely to feel free."[22] It is a means of communication that may be used or abused, with varying degrees of skill, in order to achieve widely diverse goals. Ethically speaking, irony is inscrutable.

19. Jankélévitch, *Irony or the Good Conscience*, p. 1; italics in the original.
20. Schaerer, "Mechanisme de l'ironie," p. 195.
21. Jankélévitch, *Irony or the Good Conscience*, p. 90.
22. Kierkegaard, *Concept of Irony*, p. 272.

An Approximation to Irony

Objective Irony

Our basic definition of verbal irony is "a figure of speech whose intended implication differs from the literal sense of the words." The word derives from the Greek *eironeia,* which in Latin takes the form of *dissimulatio,* and in English is approximated by "dissemblance." Dissembling speech goes under many alternative names, such as *simple* irony, *rhetorical* irony, *direct* irony, and *normal* irony.[23] The simulation of ignorance, commonly called *Socratic* irony, includes gestures and other nonverbal signs, and may be considered the behavioral analogue of intended verbal irony.

All critics agree that intended irony implies a subject who is detached from his situation and reticent in his transmissions. While there is some debate over whether the resultant meaning of an ironical statement is the opposite of what the words might mean in another context, or merely somehow different, we need not rehearse the particulars of the issue here. A third alternative suggested in a theatrical example by Robert Sharpe appears to be preferable to either of these suggestions.[24] The essence of drama, Sharpe proposes, is impersonation. An actor impersonating a character encompasses simultaneously both nature and art; the audience is aware of a vital situation at the same time as it entertains a fiction. No one takes only the fiction to be real, nor does one sit through an entire evening of theater without granting some credence to the illusion enacted on the stage. The theater has the property of at once absorbing us in its simulacrum and repelling us from it. In much the same way does one grasp the meaning of verbal irony. The single meaning of the ironical statement has a forked, ramified quality. The literal meaning is not totally rejected or negated but rather partially effaced, leaving both literal and figurative senses to coexist in suspension. Not just an embellishment on prosaic, literal language, irony speaks a truth that encompasses an entire scene:

23. "Simple" and "direct" irony are favored by F. McD. C. Turner, *The Element of Irony in English Literature: An Essay* (Folcroft, Pa.: Folcroft Press, 1969 [1926]); Gonzalo Díaz-Migoyo, "El funcionamiento de la ironía," *Espiral* (forthcoming; quotations are from the author's ms.), prefers "normal" irony; Sedgewick, *Of Irony,* and Knox, *The Word Irony,* use "rhetorical" irony.
24. Sharpe, *Irony in the Drama,* p. ix.

actors and characters, words as well as meaning. The significance of an ironical utterance, moreover, must always include the motives for being ironical in the first place. Like much of postmodern literature, irony underlines language's opacity and compels one to dwell at least as much on the signifier as on the signified, and on the enunciation as well as the enunciated.

Theatrical illustrations of the nature of irony, of course, bring to mind the sort of irony called "dramatic." Dramatic irony, which "always depends strictly on the reader's or spectator's knowing something about a character's situation that the character does not know,"[25] is a pivotal concept. It occupies both the intended and accidental fields at once. When viewed through the dramatist's eyes it is assuredly intentional, as intentional as any aspect of a literary work can be. Seen from the viewpoint of the audience, however, dramatic irony approaches the irony of events, discussed below. If one suppresses the fact that a theatrical presentation is intended and illusory and accepts the conflictive situations simply as events in the world, the two terms merge into identity. Because of the detachment one experiences in the presence of contradictory situations, be they theatrical or vital, many critics favor this consolidation to some extent.[26] That dramatic and situational irony are analogous is beyond debate, but their equation seems equivocal owing to the problematical "suspension of disbelief" necessary to that perception. Presumably, in practice at least, the intensity of catharsis one would undergo when witnessing Don Alvaro shoot Doña Leonor's father[27] would differ from that felt upon squeezing the trigger oneself. *Dramatic irony* opens a space between its victim and the observer—a space which the *irony of events* (where the only observer of the irony is the victim himself) closes within the victim alone.

25. Wayne C. Booth, *A Rhetoric of Irony* (Chicago: University of Chicago Press, 1974), p. 255. A subgroup of dramatic irony, that which takes the form of an articulation of simultaneously incidental and portentous language, became known in the nineteenth century as "Sophoclean irony." See Bishop Connop Thirlwall, "On the Irony of Sophocles," in *Remains, Literary and Theological*, ed. J. T. Steward Perowne (London: Daldy, Isbister, 1878 [1833]), vol 3.

26. Sedgewick, *Of Irony*, Turner, *Element of Irony*, and David Worcester, *The Art of Satire* (New York: Russell and Russell, 1960 [1940]) are three examples.

27. In the Spanish romantic tragedy *Don Alvaro o la fuerza del sino*, by Angel Saavedra, Duque de Rivas (1833).

Focusing on dramatic irony with regard not to the author or viewer but to the characters inscribes a return to the very scene of irony's origin.[28] Any time there is a dissimulating *eiron* somehow confounding a boastful *alazon*, one finds intended irony (from the author's and *eiron*'s point of view) and accidental irony (from the *alazon*'s and spectator's perspective). What has not been delineated sufficiently, however, is that the intending *eiron*, in that he is conventionally unaware of his fictional status, misconstrues the "true" situation and incurs an unintentional irony of his own relative to the spectator.[29] The principle derived from this classical case, as Stanley Fish has remarked, is that irony depends on context, the ironist always conceiving a broader context than the victim. But the moment when the ironist's notion of the "real" context is relativized, as when he takes himself too seriously in a work of fiction, he reverts to the status of victim in a heightened ironic configuration. What appear to be fixed entities—the elements common to all ironies—thus manifest a marked instability.

Accidental irony has been labeled the irony "of events," "of fact," "of fate," and "of nature," as well as "situational" and "cosmic" irony. All these terms designate the incongruence between the actual result of a sequence of events and the virtual result that experience or theory would have one expect or desire. This sense of irony, the legacy of Friedrich Schlegel, Tieck, and the German Romantics in general, is quite pervasive in the everyday speech of our time and is relatively unproblematical. I would offer only one additional observation with respect to the causes and victim of accidental irony. As the impact of an incongruous event or chain of events depends as much on one's expectations as on the nature of the configuration itself, we would do well not to overlook the role of the victim in the *creation* of accidental irony. Branding a situation ironic implies an interpretation or reading on the subject's part. But a reader who looks exclusively for happy endings (Guillermito Nervo in Carlos Fuentes' *Holy Place* provides a ready in-

28. Kierkegaard, *Concept of Irony*, Knox, *The Word Irony*, Worcester, *Art of Satire*, and A. R. Thompson, *The Dry Mock: A Study of Irony in Drama* (Berkeley: University of California Press, 1948), all concur.
29. Such self-conscious works as Pirandello's *Six Characters in Search of an Author* and Unamuno's *Niebla* (*Mist*) elude the net cast here.

Introduction

stance) becomes the writer of an ironic plot by underlining every momentary setback in his desired scenario. Much as the *eiron* in dramatic irony can be seen as the spectator's *alazon,* the victim of accidental irony casts himself as the coauthor of his own uncanny fortune.

Subjective Irony

Irony does not appear devoid of agency but comes about during an interaction of mind and world. The relation of objective irony to the ironist assumes the triangular configuration below:

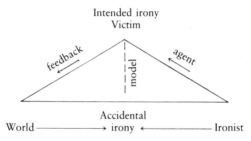

Beginning with the base of the triangle, one finds an interaction between the objective world and an ironist disposed toward fixating on incongruity. It is through the interaction of these elements that "events" are hypostatized and that accidental irony arises. That irony then serves as a structural paradigm for intended irony, whose agent is the undeceived, duplicitous ironist. The intended irony leaves its imprint on a victim and then adds to the irony already in the world, making it more likely that the forces of incongruity come to the attention of other potential ironists (ex-victims themselves), who would perpetuate the cyclical process. What merits underlining here is that objective irony, intended or accidental, is situated neither wholly in the world nor in the ironist, but in a zone of history somewhere between the two. My subsequent comments disclose in what sense subjective irony resides no more purely within the ironist than the objective sort lies completely without.

The apprehension and assimilation of irony can be characterized as a three-step process. The first stage entails the cooperation of the

24

ironist and the world in bringing about paradox, incongruity, or contradiction. As a reflex response to the perceived shape of events, the ironized mind enters a second phase, that of detaching or distancing itself from its immediate circumstance. The variety of terms critics have employed to describe that movement ("lack of identification," "aloofness," "reserve," "estrangement," etc.) need not distract us from its basically agreed-upon nature.[30] But the third step in the internal mechanism—whatever may happen to the ironist once emancipated from his surroundings or impulses—has produced a split among theorists. One school of thought, represented by Thompson, would have the ironist be something of a martyr; the effect of irony is seen as an emotional discord felt when something is both funny and painful.[31] At the opposite pole one finds critics like David Worcester, who envisages the hovering ironist as coping felicitously with the collision: "When the mind is paralyzed by conflicting drives, irony offers a way of escaping from the conflict and rising above it. The reason is saved from the shattering effect of divergent commands, and the mind regains equilibrium."[32] On a more general plane the question is this: Is the ironist a happy coward who realizes facile syntheses of irreconcilable propositions, or is he a tormented meditator trapped in a polemical tangle of double binds?

Rather than argue either side of the question, let us settle on the following determination. It is *how* one handles one's irony that forges the outcome of the process, and the results may be as dissimilar as Erasmus' exhuberant figure of Folly and García Márquez's pathetic and horrifying *patriarca*.[33] All irony can do is instill a moment of resonance when paradoxes are registered and competing factors are assessed. Instead of temporal, the mechanism may be best understood as a spatial moment, one which permits a simultaneity of visions from several perspectives. The custom of ironic

30. Here we are glossing the works of Chevalier, *Ironic Temper,* Jankélévitch, *Irony or the Good Conscience,* Sedgewick, *Of Irony,* Thompson, *Dry Mock,* and Maria Paiva, *Contribução para uma estilística da ironia* (Lisbon: Publicações do Centro de Estudos Filológicos, 1961).
31. Thompson, *Dry Mock,* p. 10.
32. Worcester, *Art of Satire,* p. 141.
33. Erasmus needs no introduction. The second allusion is to Nobel Laureate Gabriel García Márquez's titular protagonist in *Autumn of the Patriarch* (*El otoño del patriarca* [Buenos Aires: Sudamericana, 1975]).

apprehension, once acquired, ceases to interfere with what appears to be singleminded action. The installation of ironic circuitry, the redoubling of the self upon itself, of course, makes for an altered experience from the perspective of the ironist. In addition, it forges a different *kind* of deed from that which would ensue upon a more partial appraisal of events. By assuring what Jankélévitch calls a "justice of succession" and a "justice of coexistence" (the then as well as the now, the here as well as the there) in any given situation, the ironist may work on the world in a manner consistent with circumspect reflection.

It should be evident that I do not take sides in this polemic because I cannot. The only adequate response to a choice between irony as problematic openness and simple closure is Socratic *aporia*. Duly prefaced, of course. The taciturnity of the ironist is a statement, albeit absent, of the ironist's vision of truth as an ever-unfolding process of logical contradiction. In concrete terms that truth is inconceivable, much less susceptible of adequate representation in words. Verbalization is therefore minimized and channeled mainly interrogatively.

Thus, subjective irony is impossible to express symbolically and equally impossible not to convey asemically. As I have suggested, it is not simply subjective, for it is the very sense of the self as other, as part world and part self, part thou and part I, more a relationship or movement than an entity. As the ironist constitutes objective irony from the inchoate incongruency of the world, he is also aware of constituting himself as an ironical subject and ironic object. Subjective irony implies the freedom to conceive of oneself not just as a subject but as a function in an elusive and paradoxical system whose unnamability is named irony.

Narrative Irony

Irony as I have outlined it—objective and subjective, intended and accidental—may of course take part in the thematics of works of fiction, and identifying instances of ironic (and ironical) phenomena in existent novels will make up a considerable portion of my analysis. In addition to offering these reflections of life, however, narrative fiction bears in its interstices a potential form of irony that is fundamental to our enterprise. This property—distance—is inherent in every sort of classical irony. In the original case of dramatic irony between the *alazon* on the one hand and the theater-going public and dissimulating *eiron* on the other, one finds the distance between ignorance and knowledge. In objective intended irony, between the speaker who means the opposite of his words or who has plural senses in mind, and the listener who takes the words only at their surface value, there is again the remoteness of duplicity and innocence. And between an observer of accidental irony and the contradictory phenomena he criticizes—whether in theoretical debate, a work of art, or events in the world—again one notes the detachment implicit in the attempted or successful reconciliation of contraries by the subject. Given that irony is everywhere accompanied by distance, the deduction seems inevitable that distance is one of its essential characteristics. This invariant relationship has prompted my labeling the distance between or among constant elements in works of fiction "narrative irony."

The elements I scrutinize, particularly in the four chapters in part I, "Static Irony," are familiar enough: author, narrator(s), character(s), and reader. This model is suggested by Wayne C. Booth, who has contributed a major study on the way irony works on readers.[34] In *The Rhetoric of Fiction* Booth states with respect to the inner workings of narrative fiction: "In any reading experience there is an implied dialogue among author, narrator, the other characters, and the reader. Each of the four can range, in relation to each of the others, from identification to complete opposition, on any axis of value, moral, intellectual, aesthetic, and even physical."[35] Adding a temporal factor to Booth's list, we arrive at a complete repertory for the creation of static narrative irony. I prefer, however, the term *disirony* to Booth's metaphor of "identification" in referring to instances of zero intratextual distance. And *intra-elemental irony* is a refinement necessary to denominate a situation where the distance lies not between components but with-

34. I refer again to Booth, *Rhetoric of Irony*.

35. Wayne C. Booth, *The Rhetoric of Fiction*, (Chicago: University of Chicago Press, 1961), p. 155. Drama and lyric poetry, to be sure, may incorporate distance as we use that term here. But the customary absence of a narrator in the former, as well as the frequent fusion of author, narrator, and characters in the latter, set narrative apart where internal space is concerned.

Introduction

in a given component. In part II, "Kinetic Irony," I go beyond this framework in order to accommodate more complex forms of irony (that which separates one from structures or processes, from language or from literature) and in order to investigate the relation between irony and play as well as that between irony and fragmentation.

Our agenda, then, consists of incorporating the notion of narrative irony suggested by Booth with the more conventional senses in which irony is understood, and applying the entire ironic apparatus to a sampling of outstanding contemporary Spanish-American fiction. The novels studied, in the order of their appearance, are Carlos Fuentes, *The Death of Artemio Cruz* (Mexico, 1962); Juan Rulfo, *Pedro Páramo* (Mexico, 1955); Manuel Puig, *Betrayed by Rita Hayworth* (Argentina, 1968); Guillermo Cabrera Infante, *Three Trapped Tigers* (Cuba, 1967); Mario Vargas Llosa, *Aunt Julia and the Scriptwriter* (Peru, 1977); Julio Cortázar, *A Manual for Manuel* (Argentina, 1973); and Isaac Goldemberg, *The Fragmented Life of Don Jacobo Lerner* (Peru, 1978). They are all, in one sense or another, highly ironic works. Determining the various senses in which they are so, as well as identifying the specific textual coordinates of their respective ironic interplay, is a task reserved for the epilogue.

STATIC IRONY

1

The Death of Artemio Cruz: Anatomy of a Self

Mexican Carlos Fuentes' *The Death of Artemio Cruz* has received a great deal of critical attention in the more than twenty years since its first publication.[1] While such attention automatically bestows a certain status on any work, it is not for its prestige that the novel appears in this study. In many senses *The Death of Artemio Cruz,* densely populated by ironists and replete with multi-layered and occasionally mutually canceling ironies, may be considered a model ironical narrative. The general view of mankind and the world it projects, moreover, which would qualify as pessimistic if it were not so ambiguous, is also imbued with irony. But what crowns the novel as a masterwork of irony—what accounts for its indeterminacy and finally secures its primal position in this investigation—is its high formalistic valence. It displays the abstract

---

1. Page references, included parenthetically, are to the translation by Sam Hileman (New York: Farrar, Straus & Giroux, 1964). The novel was initially published as *La muerte de Artemio Cruz* (Mexico City: Fondo de Cultura Económica, 1962). Reactions among critics have been strong, although not always favorable. See, for instance, Manuel Pedro González's article "La novela hispanoamericana en el contexto de la internacional," in *Coloquio sobre la novela hispanoamericana* (Mexico: Tezontle, 1967), pp. 89–100, where the novel is attacked for lack of originality and excessive formal rigidity. Keith Botsford, in "My Friend Fuentes," *Commentary* (Feb. 1965): 64–67, is no more favorably impressed; indeed, his commentary runs to the vitriolic. For able defenses see Nelson Osorio, "Un aspecto de la estructura de *La muerte de Artemio Cruz,*" in *Homenaje a Carlos Fuentes: Varaciones interpretativas en torno a su obra,* ed. Helmy F. Giacoman (L. I. City: Las Américas, 1971), pp. 125–46, in which the structure is described as "organic, functional, and significant" (my translation), and Daniel de Guzmán, *Carlos Fuentes* (New York: Twayne, 1972), who observes that "the novel is remarkably well constructed, convincing, and moving" (p. 115).

totality (according to Lukács, incomplete totality) of its form in a prominent fashion and, through that form, makes as clear a negative statement (i.e., unarticulated statement) as one is likely to encounter in modern fiction.

The action of the novel, in at least one acceptable reading, takes place within the mind of a man in the hours just before he expires. The narrative is highly fragmented, both spatially and temporally. The three narrators, who represent different parts of the protagonist's psyche, or self, expound in a regular order on the protagonist and his world, past and present. In two-thirds of the narrative fragments or "episodes," the action is presented to the reader out of the chronology in which it presumably occurred in the protagonist's life. Only Narrator I—the voice of Artemio Cruz's conscious mind—who uses the first-person narrative perspective, follows a linear temporal order as he reveals the events that constitute the novel's present. The first episode and every third episode thereafter are his province.[2]

Narrators II and III resist such a univocal characterization. I shall investigate the nature of these narrators and offer an interpretation of their "personalities" later in this chapter. At this point it is sufficient to note that Narrator II functions at times like a subconscious,[3] a part of Cruz's self which, although it is in constant operation (it is aware of what the conscious knows, though in a different way), cannot—or at least does not—speak out until the conscious voice is silenced. This narrator uses the second person familiar form of address (you [tú]) and, with few exceptions, speaks in the future tense. Narrator III, whose point of view is the third person, speaks only after the other two narrators are finished. He maintains an apparently external perspective relative to the protagonist and narrates primarily in the simple past tense. The narra-

2. See Bienvenido de la Fuente, "*La muerte de Artemio Cruz:* Observaciones sobre la estructura y sentido de la narración en primera persona," *Explicación de Textos Literarios* 6, no. 2 (1978): 143–51.

3. Donald L. Shaw, "Narrative Arrangement in *La muerte de Artemio Cruz,*" in *Contemporary Latin American Fiction,* ed. Salvador Bacarisse (Edinburgh: Scottish Academic Press, 1980), 34–47, cites an interview with Fuentes and Mario Benedetti in *Letras del Continente Mestizo* (Montevideo: 1967), in which the author states his intention that "you" be the voice of the character's subconscious (164). Wimsatt's "intentional fallacy" notwithstanding, the device does function in the novel as at least Artemio's subconscious, in addition to a memory and a guilty conscience.

tive fragments related by Narrator III are the most extensive, comprising approximately two-thirds of the novel's length.

Since the narrational organization is complex, the following diagram may aid in conveying a sense of the novel's overall shape:

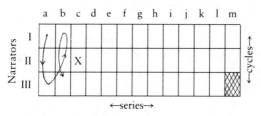

The reader experiences the text "vertically" before "horizontally," in this order: Ia, IIa, IIIa, Ib, IIb, IIIb, etc. (the first narrator speaks, then the second, then the third, then the first again, and so on). The chronology of events in the present, however, moves horizontally: Ia, Ib, Ic, etc., forcing the reader to piece the past episodes together in order to create the line one assumes a story to embody. For convenience of discussion the vertical dimension (Ia, IIa, IIIa) will be called "cycles," and the horizontal dimension, the domain of any given narrator (Ia, Ib, Ic), "series." Episode IIc, marked with an X in the diagram, would be the eighth episode in the book as experienced by the reader.

Series I: Ego Dismantled

The ironic dynamic in Series I is achieved through the presentation of a narrator-character whose amorality, passivity, and limited vision impede the reader from sympathizing with or trusting him. The movement is precipitated by a disintegration of the narrator-character's personality coincident with his process of physical decay. This internal irony (a distance contained within the character) is initiated in the following passage, which appears early in episode Ia: "I tighten the muscles of my face and open my right eye and see it reflected in the squares of silvered glass that encrust a woman's purse. I am this, this am I: an old man with his face reflected in pieces by different-sized squares of glass: I am this eye, this eye am I" (4). In the repeated use of the verb "to be" lies a preoccupation with ontology, with defining what constitutes one's being. The narrator focuses on parts of his face and calls those parts his whole being, and with this synecdoche he begins to fragment that whole. The fragmentation is made graphic by the choppy prose. The reflection he sees—part of him in the sense that it is an image of his face—is not the same as his face; metaphor is not identity. The reflection is an "other," based on messages the body sends to the brain (here it is through the sense of sight). This play of figures signals the protagonist's first awareness of his own dispersal and sets in motion a process of increasing estrangement between the self and the other. The process of internal disintegration continues throughout Series I and initiates the dynamic between the character and the reader.

As the first-person narrator of an interior monologue, Artemio is also a character in his narration. His predominant use of the present tense serves both to establish the present of the novel's action and to convey how he is locked between an irrevocable past and, with his imminent death, a nonexistent future. He is spatially confined as well. He lies on his deathbed and, with his failing perceptual capacities, tries to record what transpires both inside and outside his splintering self. Relative to the reader's expectations—built on experience with other narrators—Artemio's initial position is an ironic, distant one. The reader is put on guard to be critical of the narrator, who may not be consistently trustworthy or informed.

Artemio's shortcomings as a narrator are exposed even prior to the above passage, in the novel's opening sentence: "I wake . . . the touch of that cold object against my penis awakens me. I did not know that at times one can urinate without knowing it" (3). The first utterance is not quite correct. He amends it quickly and conveys more accurately his passivity (reinforced later in his words "I let them do what they will" [7]) and his vulnerability. He lacks control, both over what others do to him, and what he does to himself. Formerly a man who wielded great power, he comments frequently on his present weakness ("although it is not desired, something shimmers insistently near my face" [4]; "I ask: but I feel the hand that is caressing me, and I would like to escape it but don't have the strength" [5]; "I can't stand it, I can't, I didn't choose this" [7]). No less exasperating for him is his lack of self-control, first exemplified in the act of involuntary urination. In addition, his body inflicts great pain on him, and he is unable to escape the present by exercising his memory. His frustration at failing to regain the past is encapsuled in the line "I'd like to go back there, Catalina. But how useless" (6). Another step along the path toward disintegration is taken when Artemio comments that his granddaughter Gloria "must notice this stink of dead skin; she has to see my sunken chest, the gray tangled beard, the fluid dripping from my nose" (6). As he expresses his self-disgust he projects himself into her mind, dispersing the self once again and leaving it less whole, less integrated. The strangeness he feels toward himself leads him to see his reflection in the mirror as "his twin, Artemio Cruz, his double" (7). The reader knows that the narrator's observation is again not quite accurate. The "double" is not outside Artemio but within. The healthy, willful Artemio of former years cannot admit his present decrepitude. His prejudices about and expectations of himself deceive him into missing the largely temporal nature of his split. And as the breach widens, his ability to assess his situation is further impaired, causing his rapport with the reader to become even more distant.

Each episode in Series I corresponds to a period when Artemio awakens from a swoon or slumber. In Ib he rallies and feels more "like himself." The exact length of time he was unconscious is unknown (indeed, Series II and III may occur simultaneously with Series I, in spite of the inevitable sequential nature of their written representation), but it is at least sufficient for him to feel renewed. He mentions several times that his health seems better ("I don't feel so bad now. Maybe I'll recover" [26]) and can even joke about the thought of actually dying. Looking around at his despised wife and daughter, he quips: "Something more interesting than they ought to be within the sight of half-open eyes that are seeing things for the last time" (26). The period of severe illness, it seems to him, is now in the past, leaving him feeling slightly embarrassed at his momentary loss of dignity ("I would feel perfectly all right if it weren't for the stink rising from the folds of these sheets that I have stained with such ridiculous splotches" [25]) but otherwise in good spirits. Traces of insecurity about his identity still remain, however. Why else would he ask so vituperatively: "Why are they sitting here, ugly false old women, reminding me that I am not what I have been?" (27)? Why is he so emphatic that he is "still a living man who rules a home, the same as before, the same, the same" (27)? He appears to be trying too hard to convince himself that everything is all right, allowing, by his very efforts to the contrary, his doubts to surface.

In fact, there are many reasons for the reader to be more suspicious than ever of Artemio as a narrator. For one thing, he has a tendency to repeat phrases and words, as one who is not completely lucid might do. His thoughts upon seeing his faithful underling Padilla ("Today, more than ever, you ought to want me to think that everything goes along the same as always" [24]) are revealing of his inclination to play ironical games of mutual deception; they are also an exact duplicate of what he said in Ia, as is the cabalistic phrase that appears repeatedly throughout the novel: "We rode our horses across the river" (24). Artemio of Series I is probably unaware of these repetitions; he is in no position to waste words.

Most of the episodes in Series I continue according to the scheme set forth thus far. Except for isolated moments of apparent improvement in Artemio's condition, which show him to be magnanimous (54) or lucid (223–24), he continues to reject his present lamentable state. He is unable to make his bodily needs known and incapable of warding off pretenders to his wealth and power (135–36). As his senses gradually fail, his words tend to lose coherence (262–66, 297–99), and he sinks into an ever-deepening solipsistic pit. In contrast to the almost linear development of the character-narrator's approach to death, however, the reader's relation to the process is likely to follow an oscillating pattern. With the knowledge that Artemio speaks occasionally from within a drug-induced stupor (24) and, as death nears, with increasingly impaired memory and perception, the reader continues to view him as a highly unreliable narrator. That distance is amplified by some of Artemio's other characteristics: the perversity he exhibits in fantasizing about a repulsive Joseph raping the Virgin Mary (25) and the cynicism embodied in his machinations with Mr. Corkery, the representative of North American interests in Mexico (54), are two salient examples.

This epistemologically and ethically motivated breach, however, is attenuated to a large degree by other concerns. Artemio has certain qualities that tend to redeem him and even make him strangely attractive. In spite of his blatant selfishness, for instance, one cannot deny his ability to assess unflinchingly his own motives

("Who will have the honesty to say, as I say now, that my only love has been material possessions, sensual acquisition?" [132]; "They haven't understood. I did nothing for them. I never even thought about them. I did it for myself" [195]). Relative to the mediocrity and parasitism of those who surround him, Artemio is a paragon of virtue.

Equally impressive is his adamant unwillingness to concede defeat to death. With such statements as "I still have things to do" (156) and "I will learn to live with all this" (215), he demonstrates a fighting spirit that must be admired. But what ultimately bridges the character-reader chasm is the pathos inspired by the unrelenting solitude in which Artemio has lived and is now dying. As for his family, he says, "I have remembered you with the indifference of a cold business matter" (196). The only woman's love he ever received was that of Regina, but unfortunately, when she offered him everything, "I didn't take it. I didn't know how to accept it" (197). Love is such an unknown element in his life, in fact, that when Catalina takes his hand, his response is: "That will be love. I ask myself. I do not understand: will it be love?" (213).

The unabashed egoism for which it is easy to condemn Artemio, although unpardonable, seems more understandable in the light of his solitude. If he had not looked out for his interests, who would have? To be sure, Artemio never quite attains the status of a sympathetic character, even now that he suffers, lost and alone ("I don't know where to go . . . who to ask for help" [298]), but neither can he be simply dismissed as evil. He is obviously a complex personage full of contradictions and inconsistencies, both an ironist and an irony.

In the end it is the breakdown of the orderly cycle of narrative fragments that signals the utter decomposition of Artemio's personality and discloses the full anatomy of his psyche. At one point he describes himself from both the first-person and third-person points of view: "He vomits face up. He vomits his shit. It runs out over his lips, down his jaw. His excrement. They cry out, the women cry out, though I don't hear them" (237). Elsewhere, at the end of a drug-induced monologue, a voice informs the reader that "the stretcher runs out of the ambulance on little wheels" (266). It would appear that Artemio's condition and angle of vision preclude him from giving such a lucid relation of events; it cannot be he speaking, but there is no one else in this series. A plausible explanation is that another aspect of the self, the voice of generic consciousness that narrates Series III, has intervened to violate the narrative order. This interruption creates a psychic fragmentation of an entirely new dimension, for it signals a doubling of which Artemio is unaware. The reader can only watch in wonder as Artemio's selves proliferate.

Artemio himself is too close to death to clarify things. Hardly conscious, he rambles: "I don't know . . . don't know . . . I am he or if . . . you were he . . . or if I am the three . . . You . . . I carry you inside me and you will die with me" (305). His disintegration continues to be expressed through a breakdown in logic ("I am he," etc.), but it is not just "the other" outside him or in his past over whom he is now confused. He is suddenly aware of a "you" (the voice of his subconscious that narrates Series II) as well as the "he" (the generic consciousness alluded to above), also integral parts of his being. At his death, when present time ceases to exist for him, Artemio's temporal breach—an obsessive nostalgia that makes him a stranger to himself—is no longer an issue. At that moment he penetrates his defenses, confronts his true motives, and accepts his lot in history. In this respect, he finally manages to circumscribe his identity and, for a spasmodic instant, to achieve utter self-knowledge. It is, however, the very moment of his demise and therefore too late for him to do anything with this invaluable information.

His thoughts, just as he loses consciousness for the last time, are toward the future ("I carry you inside and with you I die" [306]) and reflect the animalistic spirit of self-preservation that characterized his whole life. Artemio has struggled with his ephemeral identity, only to have his antagonist removed by the failing health that instigated the crisis in the first place. This removal was accompanied by the simultaneous creation and destruction of a new schism at death (the subconscious and superconscious embodied in Narrators II and III), likewise unacceptable to Artemio, not for the disunity they represent, but because of the nothingness immanent in the unity of death. The reader must recognize at least the character's capacity for confronting his adversaries and his unconditional desire to survive. Their relation has run a course whose origin is the reader's ironic distrust of Artemio's multiple presence (narrator-character, body-mind, present-past, the one-the other) and whose conclusion is the reader's intimate embrace of his absence.

Series II: Mastering Desire by Remembering the Future

The ironic trajectory of Series II takes its first impulse from the following passage: "The cutting edge of memory that separates the two halves, life's solder that welds them together again, joins them and dissolves them, follows and finds them: fruit with two halves that today will be made one again, and you will remember the half you left behind" (12). The new narrator informs the character ("you") that he, like the fruit, has parts that will undergo a process of fusion. The method indicated will be to explore the memory—whose selective disuse has been the cause of the separation—and to use the resuscitated past to join the components. The narrator "I" speaks from within Artemio and has been characterized as a subconscious voice, but that is only one aspect of his multifaceted nature. He is also a voice of conscience, of circumspect restraint, of opposition to Artemio's public side: a voice of irony. Narrator II uses the familiar form of address (*tú*) to indicate the ties that link him with the character; they dwell within the same body-mind complex and depend on its existence for their survival. What distinguishes them—their respective notions of time—is manifested principally through the narrator's use of the future tense, even in relating events which from the standpoint of Artemio's conscious mind occur in the past. This is not to be dismissed as mere eccentric tinkering with verbal conventions. Narrator II's subversive role is to level the past, present, and future in such a way as to efface the privilege that the conscious unthinkingly grants to the present. It is through the conscious mind's gradual grasping of the past's role in shaping the present, of the significance of present events from the standpoint of the future, and of the destiny and identity constituted by the historical process, that the distance between the two novelistic elements diminishes until they eventually share the same point.[4]

4. Narrator II has been described by Luis Harss as "a curiously incongruous device consisting in a kind of voice of conscience that addresses the protagonist in the second person and the future tense, a disembodied accusative that tortures the syntax and disrupts the action" ("Carlos Fuentes, Mexico's Metropolitan Eye," *New Mexico Quarterly* 36, no. 1 [Spring 1966]: 48). Other critics have termed Narrator II "a lived future" (Juan Loveluck, "Intención y forma en *La muerte de Artemio Cruz*," in Giacoman, ed., *Homenaje*, 217 [my translation]); "the wiser and better man Artemio might have been in happier circumstances" (Anthony West, "*La muerte de Artemio Cruz*," *New Yorker* 40, no. 25 [8 Aug. 1964]: 88); and "the alter ego, the possibilities that Cruz has within himself" (A. González Arauzo, "No Other Ends Than Possession," *New Mexico Quarterly Review* 1, no. 4 [1962]: 269).

Static Irony

The "I" of this series is not exactly the same as the narrator of the previous one. In the unfolding of the novel, Narrator II may speak only when the other "I" (here addressed as "you") is silent, either asleep or comatose. This narratee, the listening part of Artemio, is thus paradoxically an "unconscious conscious." The narrating "I" of Series II does not suffer from the self-delusion to which the first-person narrator-character of Series I is susceptible. He exists beyond the defenses and blocks of the conscious mind and evokes the past, when the physically induced disintegration process had not yet begun. With the knowledge of Artemio's destiny and the temporal mobility to visit moments when that destiny was forged, the speaking part of Artemio enjoys a superiority of perspective over the listener. Like the classical ironist, "I" generously relinquishes that advantage during the course of the narration.

The difference in their vision of events is expressed in episode IIa: "You would prefer to remember . . . not what has happened already but what is going to happen" (7). The character can judge events only through hindsight, whereas the narrator's vision is as much metaleptic as proleptic. "I" also has the capacity to recall the narratee's actions and to penetrate into his most intimate thoughts and feelings. In the same episode the narrator establishes a policy of not permitting his listener what might have been blissful ignorance; painful though it may be, he demands a candid appraisal of motives: "You will not deceive yourself with ceremonious words: and the gentlemen will be convinced again, persuaded again, that is, bought again" (9). The admirable frankness that Artemio demonstrates in Series I thus finds its uncomfortable origin in Series II. The reader is called on here to activate the interplay of narrative fragments and to create thereby the illusion of psychological depth in the character.

The different temporal perspectives of "I" and "you" lead to disparate values. The narrator disapproves of the character at times and takes apparent pleasure in reminding him of his shortcomings. "I" queries: "Does that disturb you? Yes, it's troubling. How much more comfortable to be able to say: this is the good, and this is the evil. Evil: you will never be able to point it out" (28–29). Goading his listener, "I" observes: "You will prefer not to think about this. You will detest the I, the part of your you that calls it to your attention" (29). The strained syntax in the last sentence underlines their separation doubly: it signals the disagreement that exists between "you" and "I," and it states plainly that this voice is the "I," the *ego*, the more authentic identity with which "you" is out of touch. The external "you" is then reduced to the subaltern status of a mask, a façade that may mislead itself into believing it is what it covers. From his interior perspective, however, "I" is not taken in by the disguise; he declares his independence and establishes his position as observer of the relatively ignorant and amoral "you." In the lexicon of irony, Series II portrays a silent dissembler ("you"), whose actions have already spoken for themselves. His ironical observer ("I"), meanwhile, generates a discourse that neutralizes the intended duplicity of the aspiring ironist and actual victim.

Later, the narrator noticeably tempers his hostility toward "you" and moves from the role of antagonist to that of consultant. In the lines "You will close your eyes and you will see again" (55) and "going back, back, never forward, in order to be satisfied" (58), there is a beckoning to follow the narrator's lead, to visit the past, and to witness one's own image in the internal projection. The urgency of this flight into the past is conveyed by the final line of the scene: "Before chaos prevents memory" (58). The narrator not only has the ability to evaluate the character's motives but also keeps an eye on the stopwatch that ticks away his (their) life.

A decreased distance between observer and victim is perceptible in the lines "Awareness weakens us, we are changed into victims by awareness when we become aware of the pain that never consults us, being unaware of us" (56). This is the first time the first-person plural ("we") is employed, a significant move from the "you" and "I" divergence in the first episode of this series. The narrator here gives full recognition to his lack of control over external events. We see him sharing the fate of "you," but with the added burden of dramatic irony: like the spectator in a ritualized theatrical production, "I" knows what will happen at which juncture but is powerless to act in order to change it.

Using his superior reflective and analytical ability, "I" probes the differences in how they experience existence. He predicts that the involuntary bodily functions "will master and conquer you because they will require you to notice life's processes instead of merely living" (84). The "I" understands, the "you" acts: they must inevitably differ in knowledge and values as long as Artemio is alive.

41

The unity that "I" predicted at the outset will not take place quickly; it will not, in fact, occur at all during the protagonist's lifetime. The location of the unity at a receding limit-point is recognized in the line "You will become your own enemy, that the proud battle may go on" (86). The narrator must act as he is destined to do, reminding "you" of the equally inevitable vanity of the narratee's actions. They must differ, but their difference is the effect of a single cause: impersonal fate.

Activating Artemio's memory, the narrator takes the character back to review scenes of his life that expose his amorality and cynicism (117–18). In addition to chiding him before the reader, the narrator tends to play maliciously with the character. "I" evokes a particularly painful memory of Artemio's innocent youth, when he sat at his teacher's knee. "You will not want to remember that: . . . this memory does not come from me and will not reach you" (118). In this series the narrator has been evoking images in the character's mind by simply emitting key words. Here he continues the process, but then pretends that the thought will not leave the domain of "I" or enter the character's conscious mind. This can only be interpreted as a cruel joke with which the narrator vexes the dying old man. The sense of the line "This memory does not come from me" is nullified by the power of the very words that comprise it.

Language acquires more importance as the narrator becomes aware of the potency of his position. He probes the nature of linguistic symbols and their effect on the narrator-character relationship in a long passage that explores many uses of the verb "to fuck" [*chingar*] (137–38). Words are the means by which a literary text exists—a statement almost too obvious to make. If "you" and "I" exist at all, it is only through language in general, and through this word, "to fuck," in particular ("You are what you are because you knew how to fuck 'em without letting them fuck you" [138]). Yet the passage ends with "Murder the word that stands between us [. . .] so that it cannot be either our reply or our destiny" (139). The word that joins also separates because it has people deal with each other indirectly, through a system of verbal signs, themselves imperfect reflectors of extralinguistic reality. The verb "to fuck" especially separates them because its sense poses individuals as inevitable mutual adversaries. The ethic of "to fuck" forces the conscience to criticize the conduct of the character as both act out their fated roles.

As Artemio (the sum of the parts) nears death, the passive character is more and more able to grasp the relation of fate, history, and
identity as the conscience does. "I" prepares "you" by appealing to
the survival instinct; but this is only the first step in stripping away
the barriers to the listener's self-awareness. "You will survive," "I"
says, "[. . .] by the dark chance of a universe growing colder and
colder, in which survival is possible only to [. . .] those that can
elaborate that frontal neural mass and can foresee danger" (199).
The mind is the locale of this narrative series. It is what allows man
to invent the notion of time, to remember, and to take decisions
whose execution forges his destiny. In this episode "I" shows that,
although he has no capacity for action, his knowledge of the future
affords him a superior understanding of the meaning of the character's deeds and misdeeds. In his words: "You will choose from the
infinite array of mirrors only one, the one which will reflect you
irrevocably and will throw a black shadow over all other mirrors"
(200). The "other mirrors" are the destinies that Artemio did not
choose, embodied in such people as Gonzalo, Lorenzo, and the
unknown soldier, all of whom died so that he could survive.[5] It is
thus not a naive predeterminism that "I" preaches, but a dialectical
interaction of circumstance and human will, which gives rise to
destiny and identity. "I" shows also that it is the memory that is the
medium through which one gains access to the significance of one's
decisions, in terms both of history and of self-definition. Throughout this lesson, "you" remains passive, accepts the coaching, and
grows toward the vantage point of "I."

The benefits of the instruction are seen in the next episode (IIi),
where the subconscious asserts: "And when Lorenzo turns twelve
you will bring him to Cocuya to live and that, you will tell yourself,
will not be a mistake" (217). "You" is beginning to grasp the
notion of how every action has brought him to where he is and
made him what he is. Even though Artemio's bringing up his son in
his own image predisposed Lorenzo toward fighting in the war in
which he was eventually killed, Artemio ("you" and "I" thinking in

5. Narrator II's view is distinctly Bergsonian: "Our character is the result of a
choice that is continually being renewed. These are points . . . all along the way,
where we may branch off, and we may perceive many possible directions though we
are unable to take more than one." See Henri Bergson, *Laughter: An Essay on the
Meaning of the Comic*, tr. Cloudesley Brereton and Fred Rothwell (London: Macmillan, 1911), pp. 166–67.

accord) is not willing to regret his actions. He looks on rather with resignation: "And you [. . .] would like only to explain that here years ago, forty years ago, something was broken so that something else would begin, or maybe so that something even newer would never begin" (218–19). One could spend a lifetime fretting over what was not done or imagining what might have been. Artemio appears to understand that action changes the course of history, and affecting history is the key to defining one's identity.

This is not the same as to say ingenuously that joy will follow with certainty upon willful action. The shape of this episode shows something entirely different—that existence implies struggle and that the winner of each skirmish only qualifies to challenge the next opponent. Artemio's fond memories of the few moments he spent with his beloved son are constantly interrupted by the presence of his wife Catalina: "You will have awakened that morning, as every morning, happy for the day to be spent with him. 'I have always turned the other cheek,' Catalina will say, with the boy near her. 'Always. I have always accepted everything'" (217). But "you" wards off these incursions, just as he neutralized her influence in raising their son. He counters her theistic discourse with the offer of earthly freedom, symbolized by the sea. He gains ground; her image stops shattering his reveries of communion with Lorenzo.

The end of that scene and of their struggle, however, leads to Lorenzo's acting in accord with the laudable values which his father had espoused and then betrayed ("You would do the same, Papá, [. . .] It has been as though you were living your life over again. Do you understand?" [219]). The youth goes off to his death. Having defeated Catalina, Artemio must now deal with the pain of his victory. He struggles to awaken, to escape from his memory, but "they [those at his bedside] will compel you with physical force to go on remembering; and you will not want to, you do not want to, *ay* you don't want to" (219). The pain becomes unbearable; "you" suffers a major setback. The memory of the posthumous letter he received from Lorenzo precipitates in him the desire to have acted otherwise: "You will read and you will choose again: you will choose another life. . . . You won't push him to responsibility for himself, to that fatal destiny which could have been yours" (237). The wave of suffering spreads and makes him wish he had done countless things differently, until he arrives at the natural conclusion: "You will not be Artemio Cruz, you will not be seventy-one, you will not weigh a hundred and seventy-four pounds, you will not be five feet eleven and a half" (238–39). The message is clear: to reject the past is to obliterate one's identity. There is no viable alternative to resignation where history is concerned.

What allows the character to escape from a path of self-pity is the memory of the land that constitutes his country. He remembers it in its multiple forms ("It is not one; there are a thousand countries, with a single name" [266]), and it fills him with humility and awe. Only the patria is undying and significant. He evokes its "nature that refuses to be compared or controlled, that wants to live on in harsh loneliness and has granted men only a few outlying valleys and rivers for them to cling to her skirts" (267). He realizes that all those, like himself, who sought to conquer it "finally met exasperating defeat before mere reticence, deaf mockery, and indifference" (271).

With a sense of how vainly he has lived, "you" can accept the idea of his fast-approaching death (it is alluded to four times on pp. 266–68) and can appraise with surprising impassivity the legacy he leaves behind. The positive factors ("They will accept your legacy: the decency that you acquired for them: they will offer up thanks to bare-foot Artemio Cruz because he made them people of position" [268]) are more than counterbalanced by the negative ("You will bequeath this country: your newspaper, the hints and the adulation, the conscience drugged by lying articles written by men of no ability; you will bequeath the mortgages, a class stripped of natural human affection, power without greatness" [269]). He can admit that he was always afraid of the camaraderie that bound men who fought under the same banner ("You feared it all of the days of your power" [268]) and that, but for the fact that his personal position was put in jeopardy by it, he admired the revolutionary spirit ("You wait with three feet of earth above your head, wait until you feel the tramp of feet over your dead face, and then you will say 'They have returned. They didn't give up,' and you will smile"[269]).

As a hard man in a hostile world, Artemio Cruz has learned well how to dissimulate, how to function behind an ironical mask while waiting to seize the opportunity for self-advancement. To circumvent his cynical defenses it is necessary to return to a time before the barriers were erected. "You" is taken back to a moment when he first becomes aware of the vastness of the world. The normal ease with which one becomes intimate with a child in this case is enhanced by its being a moment of extreme openness ("your heart, open to life"[304]), of new revelation ("Your innocence will die, not at the hands of your guilt, but before your enormous surprise" [301]), and of optimism ("You will feel [. . .] better, more in control of your life and more serene" [303]). In this scene, the character "you" undergoes what we have termed "intra-elemental irony," for he is torn between wanting to be the innocent boy in the past and inevitably being the observer of that scene in the present.

Artemio's many facets thus constitute all the components—ironist, observer, victim, and object—of this ironical situation of extraordinary intensity. As the narrator evokes the memory, "you" in the present of course views this moment differently from the way he lived it as a child. He has an awareness of the relation between Cruz-niño, "freed from the destiny of birth and birthplace" (299), and the starlight that reaches his eye ("Dead in origin, it will still be alive in your eyes" [302]). His sense of time and space is also more highly refined. As a child he lived in an eternal present, absorbed in the immediate ("You will stop on the first rock platform, lost in your quaking incomprehension of what has taken place, the end of a way of life that you secretly believed to be eternal" [299]), with no sense of history ("You will not suspect that you stand upon new land risen from the sea only a few hours ago" [302]). The adult, under the tutelage of the voice of destiny, deals with the present in a historical context, that is, as if he stood at the end of time. This is most appropriate, as, except for his prostrate position, Artemio *does* stand at the end of time.

With full awareness of what lies ahead for all of Artemio Cruz, "I" invokes the notion of unity in abstract terms: "The boy-child, the earth, and the universe: one day there will be no life left for any of them, no warmth, nothing except forgotten nameless unity . . . when no one will be alive to speak a name: fused space and time, matter and energy. One day everything will have the same name: nothingness" (303). Existence entails contradiction, difference, and conflict; the attempted resolution of these is the stuff of existence, that which lends it meaning, albeit negative. At this point, the two disparate elements within Cruz have resolved their differences to such a degree that only one obstacle separates them from merging into one, that is, into none: death itself.

Death comes to Artemio on the operating table. The end is indicated by his final loss of consciousness (episode Im), and the subsequent inability of the subconscious to contact the conscious (IIm). The last hairline fissure between "I" and "you" is prophesied to fuse completely in the line "I who was he, I will be you" (305), where the pronouns manifest their essential identity by gathering around the verb "to be" as interchangeable predicate nominatives. The final sentences of the novel are "The three, we . . . will die. You . . . die, have died . . . I will die" (306). They evince a breakdown in syntax that signals not only a lack of distinction in sense between the various personal forms of the subject pronoun but also a unity of verb tense, perfect, present, and future. "You" and "I," now and then, are one at last: the merger is accomplished.

Series I explores the creation and resolution of a split in the conscious part of Artemio Cruz, which is aware only of itself. Series II reveals an ethically oriented subconscious, aware of itself and of the conscious. It is eager to consolidate with the latter, even at the cost of its own existence, and thus it is antithetical to the self-centered ethic announced in the verb "to fuck." With the completion of this process and the disappearance of the narrator, the novel is brought to an internally compelled halt.[6] The conscience has had its way in spite of itself: the *telos* of morality has defied and vanquished the *telos* of survival. Instead of propelling himself through an incessant present of insatiable desire, Artemio comes both to accept death as the only tomorrow and to desire finally what must be.[7]

6. For a brief explanation of the possible reasons for the novel's ending with the second narrator, see n. 12 below.

7. Fuentes has elucidated his notion of destiny in an interview in *Diacritics* 10, no. 4 (1980): 50: "I do not share the Marxist vision of the polarization between freedom and necessity. I think that what is necessary is what can be free. And it nevertheless shares something with fatality, but opposes it—freedom is the possibility of opposing fatality; and the result of this is what is necessary. It is not fatal, it is not totally free: alas, it cannot be. It is simply necessary. If we understood this I think we would be much saner people than we are."

Series III: The Anxiety of Reading History

The narrator of Series III enjoys a position of superiority relative to Narrators I and II. Unlike the first-person narrator, he is not limited in mobility or in sensory perception. His customary perspective is external to the characters, and his emotional state, impassive. He relates events in the past "objectively," with the interested indifference of an ideal historian. Unlike the second-person narrator, who views events as having a significance in the light of the inevitable moment of Artemio's death (in which the narrator himself participates), Narrator III is unimpressed by death. He maintains a godlike equanimity that enables him to treat every moment of the life he describes as having equal worth. He narrates in epic fashion—without commentary and with attention to detail—some moments in which history and Artemio Cruz acted on each other, and both came away from the encounter altered.[8]

The limitations to which Narrator III is subject are—and this is eerily consistent with earlier observations—temporal. Not that he cannot treat any moment in Artemio's life, from 1889 to 1959, but that he is not free to speak whenever he likes. He must await his turn in the narrative order. Both the conscious and the subconscious preempt him, leaving only the void of the moribund protagonist's psychic inactivity for Narrator III to fill. Within this limited span he closes some of the gaps existing in Artemio's biog-

---

8. René Jara C., in "Mito y la nueva novela hispanoamericana," in Giacoman, ed., *Homenaje*, pp. 147–208, sees the presence of Narrator III as an "optimistic" aspect of the novel, in that he perceives a hierarchy of events and chooses from it to present his story. This would imply, then, that the cosmos could be reduced to significant lines. Such a cosmic view would indeed be felicitous, but that is not necessarily indicative of the situation at hand. The Artemio Cruz who lies dying, trapped in the present, has no awareness of a hierarchy of values other than to survive. The same may be said of the Artemio of the past (described in Series III). It is only through a historical perspective (that of Narrator III) that cause-and-effect relationships and an order of significance emerge. The facts that this perspective is not achieved until the day of the character's death, and then reveals itself only during moments of unconsciousness, severely undercut any cause for rejoicing. The optimism is illusory and is disclosed as such by Narrator III's interplay with I and II. See Klaus Meyer-Minnemann, "Tiempo cíclico e historia en *La muerte de Artemio Cruz* de Carlos Fuentes," *Iberoromania* 7 (1978): 88–105.

raphy. In the process, he answers in no apparent order questions raised by the other two narrators.[9]

In what seems to be rancor over his limited freedom and status (the anthropomorphism is defended below), Narrator III is oddly reluctant to reveal information that would facilitate reading his text. A similar phenomenon can be observed in *Pedro Páramo* (see chapter 2 herein), where approximately the second half of the novel must fill the lacunae built into the first half, a transitionless, fragmented textual morass. If Narrator III were the only narrator, he would be playing the traditional role of the omniscient relator of anecdotes who gradually informs the reader, and he thus would be hardly worthy of commentary. But his unique relation to the other narrators, to the character he portrays, and to the reader, whom he keeps at an uneasy distance, constitutes a peculiarly complex narrative irony that demands attention.

In episode IIIa, the scope of this teller's powers are clearly in evidence. The inclusion of the date ("1941: July 6" [13]) that precedes the scene demonstrates the exact knowledge of fictional data with which he is endowed. Within the episode, which consists of scenes that alternate rapidly between a middle-aged Artemio, on the one hand, and his wife and daughter, on the other, it becomes apparent that the narrator also has all the spatial mobility he needs. He records the characters' conversations and gestures, switching back and forth without transition as they move through the urban setting. While suggestive of a technique proper to cinematography, these cuts tend to bewilder the reader. When juxtaposed with the narrator's potential telling ability, they give a clear indication of his peculiar "personality," which reveals itself with every word he chooses or omits. Just such an omission is the narrator's failure to use proper nouns to identify the principal characters in the episode. The women are referred to either jointly as "the two women" or simply "they," or separately as "the mother" and "the daughter";

9. For a thorough analysis of the order of the episodes in Series III, see Nelson Osorio, "Un aspecto de la estructura de *La muerte de Artemio Cruz*," in Giacoman, ed., *Homenaje*, pp. 125–46, and Donald L. Shaw, "Narrative Arrangement in *La muerte de Artemio Cruz*," in Bacarisse, ed., *Contemporary Latin American Fiction*, pp. 34–47.

the man is "he." The reader must deduce who "he" is through his rapport with Padilla, already identified in the previous episodes of this cycle (Ia and IIa) as Artemio's secretary. The identities of the women are only suggested, through reference to the man as "your papá." It is clear, then, from the first episode, that the narrator, who is capable of clarifying everything almost at once, is reluctant to be so forthcoming. He prefers instead to focus on isolated moments whose significance unfolds only gradually and partially.

This narrative reticence carries over into episode IIIb, which also begins with the pronoun "he" and temporarily disorients the reader, who cannot know for certain if "he" refers to the same character as in the previous scene. In fact, it is not until well into the episode that the protagonist introduces himself to Father Páez as "plain Artemio Cruz" (42). This presentation takes place in a flashback that follows a scene with Don Gamaliel, his daughter Catalina, and Cruz, and explains the events leading up to their encounter. Throughout the scene the reader is keenly aware of the ambition and opportunism that motivate Cruz and distance him from the other two. But it is not until later, in the flashback, that one realizes that the others are cognizant of Cruz's strategy but allow him to proceed anyway because they need his strength. The irony the reader apprehends is at most only one-third of the total irony present: on a second level there is duplicity between the Bernals and Artemio as they deceive him into believing they are taken in by his ruse. And a final dimension can be found in the aloofness with which the narrator treats the reader by not apprising him of the facts necessary for a full evaluation of the scene until after those facts are needed. At that time the reader stumbles upon a double revelation: he learns both the meaning of the events and the significance of his purposely having been kept ignorant of that meaning.

By the third episode, having perceived the pattern formed by the narrative technique, the reader should be somewhat accustomed to it. What was once strange is now routine. The love scene described undoubtedly involves Artemio at some time in his past (he is again denoted as "he") and Regina, who is identified by name almost at once. Her name appeared in episode Ia ("Regina, I hurt. I hurt, Regina" [7]); she only awaits further development. Here it is not disturbing that Artemio is not referred to by name until a third of the episode has elapsed ("Lieutenant Cruz!" [66]); the identities of the characters seem no longer to be a problem.

It becomes clear by the end of the episode, however, that knowing a character's name does not even approximate knowing his or her identity. In fact, the novel reinforces this notion every time an episode is narrated from a different perspective. In the early portions Artemio is portrayed as an idealistic young soldier, passionately in love for the first time ("Word of honor, he had never even slept with a woman" [65]). The story of the lovers' first meeting by the sea serves only to support the purity and freshness of their romance. Their intimacy is such that "both were the same and were saying the same words" (63).[10] But after they part and Artemio goes off to do chivalric battle, the pristine image is sullied somewhat. At one point he deserts out of fear; at another he refuses to aid a comrade whose life depends on his intervention. Later he is mistaken for a hero and does nothing to rectify the misconception. And finally it is disclosed that the lovers' original encounter, as first reported, is a lie that Artemio is unwilling to confront as such ("He ought to believe her pretty lie forever, until the end" [76]).

The truth, as revealed later, is that he grabbed the first female he laid eyes on and dragged her to the officers' barracks, where he raped her. The reader is reminded that in an earlier episode it was shown that after the Revolution Artemio renounced the causes for which he supposedly fought and, using Don Gamaliel, clawed his way to power. Artemio's identity is inseparable from the notion of dissemblance. Like its protagonist, the love scene with Regina is riddled with duplicity, for its surface tenderness and intimacy are undercut by a second sense. That is, the information necessary for assessing the scene's meaning is again concealed from the reader until the scene is over. Each new reassessment on the reader's part must of course be more tentative than the previous one, for each false step instructs him that he has judged prematurely, on the basis of an insufficiently determined context. After several such instances of victimization, the reader soon learns of the anxiety inherent in attempting to evaluate Artemio's (hi)story.

10. For commentary on this scene and those like it see Roger D. Tinwell, "*La muerte de Artemio Cruz:* A Virtuoso Study in Sensualism," *Modern Language Notes* 93, no. 3 (1978): 334–38.

After commencing each of seven episodes in this series with "he" or "his," pronouns that are now associated immediately with Artemio, the narrator breaks form. This time he uses the third-person singular to denominate Artemio's son Lorenzo ("He was on the roof with a rifle in his hands" [220]). It is only through observing the terms that come into play ("Fascist," "Republican," "Madrid," etc.), the date of the entry ("1939: February 3"), and the description of "he" as a young Mexican that one can deduce that this scene portrays Lorenzo's participation in the Spanish Civil War. The change in narrative format (the only one in the series) reflects again the complexity of Artemio's identity. Lorenzo is the Artemio who could have been if his opportunism had not overrun his ideals. By referring to the son by means of a pronoun proper to the father the narrator equates them, even though Lorenzo's destiny has marked him as an "other." Again, nonetheless, this doubling has been effected at the expense of the reader, who has been conditioned to expect one thing and been given another.

There is an explanation for the narrator's perversity in the character he portrays. One of the constants in the life of Artemio Cruz is his isolation. In Series I his loneliness is a factor that decreases the distance between him and the reader by inspiring pathos. In Series II Artemio learns that, by resisting making contact with his subconscious and his conscience, he has become his own worst enemy. Series III underlines his estrangement from other individuals—from his mate, his comrades-in-arms, and his business associates. In episode IIIa Artemio is shown separating from his wife and daughter, who live in a world of fashions and fattening desserts. The form of the episode—estrangement, followed by rapid scene changes from one character to the others—underlines acutely the distance between them. The episodes that follow—using Don Gamaliel, falsely claiming heroism, ingratiating himself with the President, etc.—present in a similar fashion the guarded, cynical way in which Artemio deals with others, whom he considers only obstacles to the attainment of his desires. Spiritual aloofness is expressed spatially in IIIg, which tells of Artemio's experiences as an army officer: "Several meters away from him lay eighteen men: he always slept or kept watch separated from them by such a strip of earth, always alone" (164). As he ages, and his power grows, so does his isolation. At one of his ostentatious New Year's Eve parties, which he admittedly holds in order to consolidate and demonstrate his might before his guests, he is approached by an ambitious young man, on whom he refuses so much as to cast his gaze ("The unwritten law: guests were never to come near him except to speak some hasty praise of the house or the dinner. They were supposed to keep their distance" [258]). Respect his distance is what the reader must do with the narrator, and in so doing, the reader must recognize how much the storyteller and his protagonist have in common. By keeping the reader at arm's length as he portrays the isolation in which Artemio lives, Narrator III acts in accord with the character he describes. The narrator's unrelenting standoffishness lends vigor to the hypothesis that the character and narrator are parts of the same whole.

In contrast with the novel's other two narrators, who appear to reside within Artemio, this one seems at first to be external to and independent of the character. He speaks of Artemio as if he were another individual, does not allow him a monopoly in psychological development (see, for instance, the stream of consciousness of Catalina in IIId), and relates his abominable acts with the same gusto as his admirable ones. His disinterested overview makes him appear to be as removed from Artemio as an omnipotent deity in heaven would be from man on earth.

But there are many good reasons to view them as one and the same. Their apparent separateness, to begin with, follows from the narrator's looking at a past Artemio, one who no longer is. In addition to this temporal factor, Narrator III is removed from the character spatially. That is, he exists as that part of the man which projects outward and participates in the energy of the cosmos: his is the voice of consciousness itself. As the link between the individual and the transcendental, he can discern the lack of importance of the former and can thus look upon death, even his own, with relative equanimity. The equanimity is only relative because, whereas Artemio's death leaves Narrator III unaffected, that of his beloved son moves him deeply. One can notice certain stylistic "lapses" that dispel the illusion of aloofness cultivated elsewhere. In the midst of a sentence narrated in the third person, in the Spanish version at least, there appears a first-person plural possessive ("a running soldier appeared, one of ours, a Republican") that wrenches the point of view to that of Lorenzo.[11] The narrator's concluding eulogy for Lorenzo, moreover, clearly bares his emotional ties: "Down, down, down, Lorenzo, and those old [sic; nuevas] boots upon the dry earth, Lorenzo, your gun to the ground, Mexican, and a whirling inside your stomach, as if you carried the ocean in your entrails and now your face upon the earth with your green eyes open and a half dream" (232). The narrator shares the pain with the character Artemio, his own appendage, who reads Lorenzo's letter along with the reader.

In the following episode (IIIi) the intimacy with the character is maintained, though by a different means.

> ". . . no, because cortisone makes me break out. . . ."
> ". . . haven't you heard about the spiritual exercises Father Martínez is giving? . . ."
> ". . . look at her. Who said it . . . ? And they say that they were . . ."
> ". . . Luis comes home so tired that all he wants is . . ." [255]

This description of the crowd of guests at Artemio's New Year's banquet is far from the impartial rendering of a circumspect observer. It represents instead the impressions the character receives as he mingles among the guests at his party. It bears the incompleteness and disorder one would sense while witnessing the scene in the present and lacks the ordering hindsight that is the hallmark of this series. Nowhere else in the novel is it so apparent that Narrator III and Artemio occupy the same point in time and space.

In later episodes, even when the narrator's focus returns to the world outside Artemio, the descriptions are not random. A passage that enumerates the luxurious furnishings of his house ("the elegant hangings, the rich inlays, the gold frames, the bone and tortoise-shell chests, the locks and hasps" [261]), for example, is a replica of the list that appears in another (subconscious) scene from Series II (241), to which this narrator is evidently privy. These objects of opulence represent all of Artemio Cruz's life; they are infused with his being. The knowledge that he possesses them and can manipulate them at will is his only incentive. Elsewhere in the same episode

---

11. My translation here only. The published English translation inexplicably omits this key element.

Artemio punches his mistress for reminding him of his advanced age (demonstrating the protagonist's pride), daydreams about the disgusting rats that inhabit the walls (his perversity), gloats as he exercises control over his guests (his power), and forbids his subalterns from approaching him (his demand for privacy). This narrative section shows most of Artemio's essential traits, and there is nothing in it that does not serve to elucidate who he is. It is as if the narrator's own being depended on a thorough delineation of the character.

The final two episodes of this series deal respectively with Artemio's childhood and his birth. The return to his origin runs counter to the direction of Series I, where he is on the verge of dying. After having been a reluctant revealer during much of the novel, Narrator III attempts to expose the character's whole identity, and in so doing, to witness his own emergence into being before time runs out. A quasi-identity that does emerge—in the juxtaposition of the words "he cried and cried and began to live" (305) and of Artemio's imminent demise—is that of birth and death. Both are moments that border on nothingness and, for the individual, annihilate history. At birth, one has no past, only a future; at death, the present stops its ineluctable movement into the future and likewise ceases to create the past in its wake. It has been the role of this narrator to recount history, and now, since the history of Artemio Cruz is no longer in the process of being forged, that role is eliminated. The narrator's voice is silenced.[12]

The death of Narrator III, simultaneous with that of the other narrators and aspects of the character, signals explicitly his part in

---

12. Only Osorio ("Un aspecto de la estructura . . .") has attempted to explain why, in a work where symmetry plays a preponderant role, the final cycle is left unclosed. His interpretation is that "The fragment of the past that would complete the parallelism from a formal point of view is missing because it is constituted in a sense by the entire work, by the last day of Artemio Cruz, that closes the whole cycle of birth and death" (133, my translation). A less contrived possibility should not be overlooked: in a work that shows thematically the pointlessness and vanity of a person's life (his fight for power and wealth appears foolish from the vantage point of the edge of death), openendedness and asymmetry are to be expected. An unproblematic, determinate form would suggest a decipherable cosmic order that this novel takes pains to question. See also Ileana Araujo, "Valores temáticos y estructurales en *La muerte de Artemio Cruz*," *Caribe* 2, no. 2 (1977): 69–75; and Gertrude Chermak, "The Image of the Labyrinth in *The Death of Artemio Cruz*," *Rackham Literary Studies* 2 (Ann Arbor, 1972): 124–26.

the totality of Artemio Cruz. Conceived narrowly, his silence represents the extinction of that portion of generic consciousness in which an individual participates. At the same time, it marks the end of the period in which Artemio interacted with the world, making history and shaping his own identity in the process. Narrator III's turning mute need not mean anything so sweeping as the death of God or the destruction of the universe. For Artemio Cruz, however, whose constituent parts are united, whose contradictions are finally resolved, and whose inter- and intrapersonal distance is reduced to nothing, it might just as well.

Our detailed analysis of the three narrative series at this point opens access to more general aspects of the novel. In all three series the narrators and protagonists are the same personage, yet somehow different, because of the internal distance of time (Series I), moral rectitude (Series II), or cosmic perspective (Series III) between the respective parts. The fact that all narrators and protagonists are in some sense Artemio Cruz serves to dramatize an aspect of his life that most effectively arouses the reader's compassion: Artemio's utter loneliness, which is no different from that of every person about to die. Furthermore, the plurality of narrative perspectives suggests a corollary of the ironic view: the multiplicity of the self. Artemio Cruz's identity is always partial and dynamic, depending on what fragment is being considered from which perspective, and at what moment in time. This instability of identity is reinforced by the recurrent appearances of various "others" whose destinies come so close to Artemio's (he can be said to "trade" destinies with them) that they contribute to the plurality of his already dispersed self.

Beyond any narrator or character lies the implied author, whose presence is inferred from his choice of narrators, the order and length of their appearances, the omission or inclusion of transitions, and the like. Any comments we might make on the perversity of Narrator III (the author's closest reflection, but certainly not his equal) are more applicable still to the author. The discontinuity that characterizes the text on so many levels is an instance of how the implied author's presence imposes itself *through* the work, as an absence *in* the work. Another example may be found in the fact that Series III, which deals with Artemio's actions in the past, constitutes approximately two-thirds of the novel's length. A factor in what Barthes calls the "readerliness" of the novel, this disproportion also may be taken as a tacit statement that an individual is defined principally from without, by his participation in history. As Booth says of the implied author, "He is the sum of his choices."[13] His choices in this case clearly indicate him to be aloof from his creation, neither embracing nor rejecting the character he evokes; he impersonally allows Artemio to expose his contradictory self at every turn. He leaves the reader little choice but to keep the novel at an equally substantial distance. Only at the end, when the reader is confronted with a solitary death that potentially reflects his own, may he be drawn into complicity. Whether or not he admires Artemio, he is compelled to recognize aspects of himself in the composite image before him. At the conclusion of this and any literary work, when the reader has all the information the author has deemed necessary to convey the fictional universe, he joins the author in a simultaneous convergence toward one central point on the axis of cognition.

But the reader of ironic fiction must beware of facile solutions. The contradictions within Artemio's identity are resolved because he has *no identity:* he is dead. As Narrator II says of a state of unity, "One day everything will have the same name: nothingness" (303). The equation of "the same" and "nothingness' shows that in *The Death of Artemio Cruz* the notion of resolving contradictions itself implies contradictions of another order. The author seems to be saying—Narrator II suggests it most emphatically—that living beings do not fit neatly into squares marked plus or minus. If these ideal notions are operative at all, it is only in the sense that they are extreme opposite poles that create the field of tension occupied by historical actuality. These antithetical forces pull the individual in several directions at once, creating "intra-elemental irony," a paradoxical psychic distance from oneself. Fuentes demonstrates with remarkably protracted restraint that the artist's function is not so much to show his allegiance to one set of values or another as it is to portray the irony-fostering tension in operation and to show the impossibility of its resolution within an existential framework.

13. Wayne C. Booth, *The Rhetoric of Fiction* (Chicago: University of Chicago Press, 1961), p. 75.

CHAPTER 2

Pedro Páramo:
The Structure of Death

Although Juan Rulfo's diminutive masterpiece *Pedro Páramo*[1] appeared in print seven years before *Artemio Cruz*, it follows Fuentes' novel in this analysis because in several senses it is the more ironic novel. To call it more ironic is to suggest, among other things, that the novel has a more estranging effect on the reader. The frequent instances of contradiction in *Artemio Cruz*, which cause the reader to hover somewhere between admiration and repulsion, here become a relentless and intransigent pessimism. This greater negative certainty is conveyed in the plot of *Pedro Páramo* through the interaction of characters whose only alternative to eternal solitude is mortal conflict.

The apparent disorder of its narrative composition also contributes to the novel's overall dismal outlook. Whereas Fuentes maintains a regular rotation of narrators and verb tenses, Rulfo vacillates erratically between the past tense and the present, and (apparently) between a first- and third-person narrator, in episodes

---

1. The first edition of *Pedro Páramo* was published in Mexico City (Fondo de Cultura Económica, 1955). Page references to Lysander Kemp's English translation (New York: Grove Press, 1978) appear parenthetically. *Pedro Páramo* is Rulfo's only novel to date. Besides some movie scripts (published as *The Golden Cock and Other Film Scripts* [*El gallo de oro y otros textos para cine*], ed. Jorge Ayala Blanco [Mexico: Era, 1980]), his only other fiction published outside of periodicals is the highly lauded short-story collection *The Plains in Flames* [*El llano en llamas*] (Mexico: Fondo de Cultura Económica, 1953). When questioned as to the relative sparseness of his literary production, Rulfo has said with laconic candor, "I have no obligation to write. . . . I don't feel compelled to do it" (Ivan Restrepo Fernández, "La cacería de Juan Rulfo," *Mundo Nuevo* 39–40 [1969]: 43; my translation).

of unpredictable length.[2] *Pedro Páramo* systematically excludes formal epiphanies of any sort, offering instead a vision in which all things are represented as equally amorphous and invalid. It is a calculated chaos that suggests a leveling of all values to an entropic degree zero.

Ironic also is the role of Rulfo's reader, who, compared to Fuentes', is given a paucity of linguistic signs. The reader of *Pedro Páramo* is forced to supply more of his own transitions and to fill in the many absent anecdotal details. In fact, the most recurrent typographical signal in *Pedro Páramo* is the blank space that separates the fragments of which the novel is composed.[3] Rulfo's frugal prose, as unadorned as the Jaliscan countryside it evokes, adheres to an esthetics of scarcity that allows the creation of a full-fledged novel within 122 pages. But it also constitutes a work whose intimate relation with nihilism threatens to transgress what irony can tolerate.

The disrupted chronological order and unannounced changes in narrative perspective are means by which Rulfo creates a timeless reality,[4] one where the dead and the living dwell side by side. This last aspect, part of the novel's dehierarchizing enterprise, is the most alienating thematic quality in *Pedro Páramo*. The reader must overcome his preconceptions and learn to view life and death as different phases of a continuum. It is life, with its transitory nature, which turns out to be the more illusory condition. And with the devaluation of life go myriad cherished institutions and practices that no longer enjoy the slightest privilege in this bleak realm. Until the reader grasps Comala's peculiar operant code and rejects those of other cosmos, fictive or real, *Pedro Páramo* remains mystifying. Once the system is deciphered, however, the puzzlement turns to unadulterated repugnance.

Other distinctions between Fuentes' and Rulfo's novels are best

2. Nancy Ann Abramoski, in "A Linguistic Approach to Literature: Three Modern Latin American Novels" (Cornell University: unpublished Ph.D. dissertation, 1972), presents the order and content of every fragment in chart form.
3. I am indebted to Wolfgang Iser's *The Act of Reading: A Theory of Aesthetic Response* (Baltimore: Johns Hopkins University Press, 1978). Both his discussion of the function of textual fissures and his critique of "good continuation" are essential to my reading of *Pedro Páramo*.
4. This is the gist of María J. Embeita's essay, "Tema y estructura en *Pedro Páramo*," *Cuadernos Americanos* 26, no. 2 (1967): 218–23.

approached through their similarities, such as the fact that the lives of both protagonists brush against the Mexican Revolution. For the indigent Artemio Cruz the Revolution provides the chaos necessary to break into the established order and rise to power. Pedro Páramo, already an oligarch when the Revolution sweeps through his region, is, for a time at least, on the opposite side from Cruz: he is the target of the rebels' uprising. Through bribery and deception, however, he avoids succumbing to their insurrection. Instead, he cunningly convinces the revolutionaries to take reprisals against the wealthy landholders in the neighboring village of Contla. Both novels, then, demonstrate how the Revolution failed to achieve its aim of an egalitarian redistribution of wealth and land, either—as with Pedro Páramo—allowing the old order to remain unscathed or—in the case of Artemio Cruz—simply substituting an industrial power elite for the agrarian structure. In Comala the Revolution serves only to accelerate the spread of its ally: death. The macabre structure of Rulfo's fictional universe is impervious to mere military or political measures in general. As we shall see, the problem is much more deeply seated than that.

The title of each novel bears its protagonist's name. Artemio Cruz is both narrator and character in all three narrative series of Fuentes' novel. The view projected of Pedro Páramo is much less internal. Although Pedro does have an incongruously lyrical side, his thoughts and sentiments are greatly overshadowed by his deeds. He dominates Comala the way Artemio Cruz never could dominate all of Mexico. Comala is an externalization of Pedro's principally hard (Pedro) and cold (Páramo) essence. Hence it is the interstices of the village of Comala, and not those of its *cacique,* that are explored most energetically in the novel, for to study the setting already implies an inquiry into the character. In this Mexican Inferno,[5] the ruthless Pedro languishes along with the other inhabitants whom he oppresses. The only bond joining them is the common denominator of death.

Despite its title, however, *The Death of Artemio Cruz* is about

5. Hugo Rodríguez Alcalá, *El arte de Juan Rulfo* (Mexico City: Instituto Nacional de Bellas Artes, 1965). Pp. 95–110 are dedicated to studying the parallels between Comala and Dante's Inferno. His observations coincide with D. C. Muecke's contention that the diabolical typically figures in the ironic world view and literary mode. See *The Compass of Irony* (London: Methuen, 1969).

the *life* of its protagonist. Because of the narrators' and characters' perspectives from within Artemio, his death is precisely the one thing the novel cannot show, except perhaps by the silence that brings the narrative to a halt. *Pedro Páramo*'s Comala is a village dead before the novel begins, despite the absence of any explicit mention of "death" in its title. Such a concrete signal is unnecessary, because Pedro himself embodies a death principle. A negative Midas, Pedro has a touch that reduces everything to dust. The mere mention of his name thus suffices to convey the novel's lugubrious and funereal impulse. In terms both of its location beyond the threshold of death and of the asymmetrical and irregular narrative technique that menacingly challenges the reader, then, it may be said that *Pedro Páramo* begins where *The Death of Artemio Cruz* leaves off.

We might even say that Rulfo's characters exist according to a principle that excludes "disirony."[6] In general, they enter into only adversary relations with other characters, although there are counted instances of mutual affinity. But these harmonious moments are inevitably undercut, either by inner turmoil with respect to one or more of the constituents or by the context in which the ostensible harmony appears. In one particular case, a character who threatens to broadcast excessive optimism, Father Rentería, is simply expelled from the novelistic scene.

The basic configuration of characters within this circle of discord has Pedro Páramo pitted against the rest of Comala. In truth, he is not entirely alone; as the plenipotentiary owner of the Media Luna ranch, he enjoys the doglike loyalty of both Damiana Cisneros, his chief domestic servant, and Fulgor Sedano, his administrator. He also indulgently raises one of his illegitimate sons, Miguel, whose early penchant for violence marks him as a grotesque reflection of his already deformed father. But these supporting characters either are so subject to the will of the *cacique* or resemble him so closely that, for the purposes of diagramming the novel's major forces, we may subsume them under the name of the leader of their camp, Pedro Páramo. He is at the center of the fictional world, surrounded by mortal enemies.

6. This economical neologism denotes a textual site where there is no significant distance between two or more elements of a novel.

61

But Pedro is no victim of circumstance. He comes to occupy this inimical position by perpetuating an impressive series of insidious deeds.[7] After the accidental death of his father, Lucas, Pedro assumes command of his inherited landholding and proceeds to ravage the people of Comala. He marries Lola Preciado, the daughter of his largest creditor, and incorporates that family's wealth into his own (36–37); he acquires the territory of Toribio Aldrete through a suit of dubious legality and has Toribio killed when he protests the tampering with the boundary markers (31–32); and he similarly appropriates (the details of the matter are unclear) the holdings of Galileo Fregosos (42). Once firmly entrenched, Pedro abandons Lola, who is pregnant with his legitimate child, Juan, and arranges to have Filoteo Aréchiga supply him with young girls for his carnal amusement. Among the numerous illegitimate children he sires are Miguel, whose killing and raping make him as much feared as his father, and Abundio, who eventually assassinates Pedro. When a band of revolutionaries kills his administrator and threatens the stability of his empire (this is the extent of the novel's fleeting contact with the Revolution), Pedro deceives the rebels into considering him an ally. He hires El Tilcuate to join them and have them dissipate their bellicose energy elsewhere. He manages meanwhile to have Bartolomé San Juan killed, to acquire the defunct man's mine, and to take possession of his daughter Susana, the woman of Pedro's dreams. The history of Pedro's dealings with Comala, then, consists in a chain of sexually, economically, and politically aggressive acts against the other inhabitants. Their interaction is invariably antagonistic, except for his treatment of Susana San Juan. Only she quells his hostility.

The first view of Pedro shows that, in spite of his son Abundio's judgment that he is "just pure hate" (4), he is capable of tender sentiment. During his childhood, when his mother scolds him for dallying in the bathroom, Pedro meditates lyrically:

I was thinking of you, Susana. In the green hills. When we flew kites in the windy season. We heard the sounds of the village down below

7. This summary of the novel's *sujet* admittedly distorts the novel because the deeds never did "happen" in any order other than that constituted by the narrative. To reproduce the *fabula* in its original order, however, would make the commentary upon it every bit as opaque as the original.

us while we were up there upon the hill, and the wind was tugging the string away from me. "Help me, Susana." And gentle hands grasped my hands. "Let out more string." . . . Your lips were moist, as if they had been kissing the dew. [9–10]

This inconsistency in Pedro's character (of which the reader is aware but the other characters are not) is what Carlos Blanco Aguinaga has called the "dual nature, the tension that two planes of life (external violence, dream-like internal slowness) create in him, what makes Pedro Páramo a character of tragic dimension."[8] The disparity also works simultaneously to elevate the novel from a mere denunciation of *caciquismo* (the feudal tyranny of rural landlords) to a statement about the essentially solitary plight of contemporary humanity.

Pedro Páramo is not only a split character along the internal/external line drawn by Blanco Aguinaga. Like Artemio Cruz, Pedro is also distanced from himself in a temporal sense. Even as an adult he remains obsessed with the image of Susana San Juan ("I've waited thirty years for you to come back, Susana," Pedro Páramo said. "I hoped to have everything. Not just something; everything. Everything we could possibly want . . . and all of it for you" [80]). After many failures, he succeeds in convincing her father to bring her to the Media Luna (their safety is threatened by the incipient Revolution), seemingly fulfilling Pedro's fondest desire. But Comala is not a place for wish fulfillment. Susana suffers from childhood traumas inflicted on her by her father, Bartolomé, who in search of riches lowered her into a dark pit and forced her to handle human skeletal remains (94–95). She is also distraught over her dead lover, Florencio. The combined effect of these factors leaves her hopelessly crazy ("Are you insane?"/"Of course I am, Bartolomé. Didn't you know?" [83]). A clinician might classify her schizophrenic or possibly catatonic. In the terminology of this formal literary analysis, however, she constitutes an extreme illustration of intra-elemental irony. She spends all her time in bed, pining deliriously over Florencio and convulsing in a pool of sweat. So Pedro's victory is a hollow one; he possesses her body (not sexually

8. Carlos Blanco Aguinaga, "Realidad y estilo de Juan Rulfo," *Nueva Novela Latinoamericana*, ed. Jorge Lafforgue (Buenos Aires: Pardos, 1969), p. 111 (my translation).

but by its sheer physical proximity), but her mind is "elsewhere." Pedro's one attempt at a nonantagonistic relationship, what he admits to be the cause of all his other conflicts (80), is a failure. He asks for the moon (power and love), but has to settle for the Media Luna (power alone). He is definitively isolated from all of Comala.

Pedro's failed love for Susana thus has a net result of amplifying the hostility it might have mollified. In spite of Susana's insanity, he never abandons his childhood love for her. When she dies, as a final token of his adoration, Pedro arranges to give her a magnificent funeral, with three consecutive days of bell tolling. In a scene whose general contours bear a resemblance to those of Gabriel García Márquez's short story "Big Mama's Wake" ["Los funerales de la Mamá Grande"],[9] the townspeople mistake the incessant chimes of mourning for a call to celebrate. For once, Pedro loses control; death becomes a grotesque motive for joyous festivity. The angry *cacique* sees no humor in the irony and takes his revenge by annihilating the village. It is from this point that Comala becomes the ghost town Juan Preciado discovers when sent there by his mother.

This maternal figure, Dolores Preciado, is another character obsessed with the past. Her memories of Comala come to the reader via Juan, as he converses with Dorotea in what is eventually revealed to be their tomb. Since he can repeat verbatim such long descriptions of Comala as "Green fields. You can see the horizon rise and fall when the wind moves in the wheat, or when the rain ruffles it in the afternoon. The color of the earth, the smell of alfalfa and bread. A village that smells of new honey" (16), we can infer that she repeated this litany often to her son. The intoxicating imagery goes beyond evoking the past, denoting rather an attempt to relive it. The contrast between the nostalgic illusion of Comala imparted to Juan by his mother, and the utter lack of sensation, other than empty echoes, he finds when he arrives there, leads Rodríguez Alcalá to see Comala as a paradise lost (see n. 5). Dolores' role in the novel is small but nonetheless constitutes a key link in perpetuating the tradition of death. It is in fulfillment of her dying wish that her son journeys to Comala and comes to recount

9. Gabriel García Márquez, *Los funerales de la Mamá Grande* (Xalapa, Mexico: Universidad Veracruzana, 1962).

its present state. Like Susana and Pedro, Dolores is a troubled, doubled character whose internal irony is temporally motivated.

The last major character who is internally distanced is Father Rentería, the village priest. After his brother is killed and his niece, Ana, is raped by Pedro's son, Miguel, and after hearing every week in the confessional about the deaths and the illegitimate children Pedro engenders, Father Rentería understandably refuses to administer the last sacraments to Miguel. When Pedro donates "alms" to the church, however, the priest does grant the petition; this leads ultimately to his being denied absolution by his ecclesiastical colleague in Contla. Father Rentería's terrible guilt for having sold absolution brings him to the brink of an ethical abyss. He repeatedly thinks of himself in deprecatory terms ("I died. I'm the corpse" [68]) and tells his niece that he is "not sick, Ana. I'm bad, I'm an evil man" (71). Father Rentería is unique in being the only Comalan whose death is neither shown nor recounted, as he leaves town in order to join the *cristeros* (militant religious) movement. This actualizing of his ideals constitutes a reduction of his inner space to zero. It also marks his conversion to a morally superior stance and makes him the most appealing character in the novel. At the same time, however, it makes imperative his expulsion from Comala, assuring the homogeneous negativism of the work.

A measure of the failure of intersubjective communion in the novel can be found in Pedro's legitimate son, Juan Preciado. Juan becomes neither a friend nor a foe of Pedro Páramo; the two characters never meet. They come into contact only indirectly, through Juan's deceased mother (Pedro's wife), through his half-brother Abundio (Pedro's son and assassin, who takes Juan into Comala), and through Susana, whom Juan hears moan and lament in her grave. Along with his tenuous relation to Pedro, moreover, his posture with respect to Dorotea, *la Cuarraca*, is important in terms of narrative irony. Juan and Dorotea share a unique intimacy. In the novel's present time, they occupy the same coffin; their spatial proximity will continue throughout eternity. Despite her muteness while she was alive, Dorotea informs Juan of details of his burial, in which she participated. Juan in return uses his superior sense of hearing (he died while still young) to relate to Dorotea what the other voices in the cemetery are saying. These data may seem trifling until one considers that Dorotea appears to fill the void in Juan's life-death left by Pedro, threatening thereby the novel's demonic tone.

But the dreary resonance reasserts itself when the neat sepulchral arrangement is considered in its total context. As with the paradoxical unity of the psyche, coincident with the cessation of its existence at the end of *The Death of Artemio Cruz*, the intimacy of Juan and Dorotea is subverted and devalued. It occurs, after all, between two phantasms, two no-bodies who might have benefited from the relationship when alive, but who are no longer in a realm where it matters. The meaning of their closeness is not only neutralized; it is ironically reversed and, in the process, magnified negatively. If Comala is indeed Hell, it may be the damnation of these inhabitants to realize that they overcame solitude too late, and to remember it forever.

Juan plays a crucial role on another front too, for he is the reader's chief aide through approximately the first half of the book. It is his voice that initiates the reader into the structure of life in Comala, or so it seems. Only at the novel's midpoint is it revealed that the indoctrination reveals instead the structure of death. The initial impression the reader receives is that *Pedro Páramo* has two narrators. There is a first-person narrator of limited perspective, the aforementioned Juan, who dominates the first half of the novel. A third-person omniscient narrator also occasionally speaks in the first half and then carries the novel to its close. I have stated that Juan "tells" Dorotea of his experiences upon arriving in Comala and, now that he is dead and buried, that he "relates" to her the murmurings of the other tomb-dwellers. I have purposely avoided the verb "to narrate" because—we are still working within Booth's model—a narrator addresses the reader directly and solely. Juan never does address the reader; what appears to be a monologue is actually a truncated dialogue that the reader inadvertently overhears. Juan's misprision as narrator is guaranteed by the shape of the narrative, and the belated removal of his disguise is the most prominent peripety in *Pedro Páramo*. Juan begins his relation with "I came to Comala because I was told that my father, a certain Pedro Páramo, was living here" (1), and he continues his saga haltingly until p. 56. There it is revealed that he is engaged in a dialogue with the taciturn Dorotea. Dead and buried like himself, she finally answers him. From the moment she breaks silence it is clear that Juan is not a narrator, but merely a *relator,* a character with a relatively long yarn to spin, as Carlos Blanco Aguinaga and Luis Leal have observed in their essays on the novel.[10]

He is presented to the reader by the one omniscient, third-person narrator, who has chosen to remain invisible and to let the characters speak for themselves. A similar technique is used in the dialogue chapters of Manuel Puig's *Betrayed by Rita Hayworth* (see chapter 3), where no indication is given of who delivers which lines. Both novels leave the reader to gather identities and circumstances from the unintroduced voice's own words. What appears to be the *narration* (the act of telling) of the novel *Pedro Páramo* is revealed to be part of the *narrated* (what is told or presented by the narrator). Juan Preciado's protracted relation is then just another means of recalling the past within the narrative framework (to a lesser extent Fulgor, Susana, Damiana, and Pedro serve the same purpose). It is a means designed to keep the reader in the dark with respect to his own temporal and spatial coordinates.

In spite of the inevitable confusion with regard to Juan's function in the novel, he is a nonironic relator. He does not purposely mislead his listener—he is unaware of the reader's presence and knows nothing of the machinations of the author or the omniscient narrator. He is quite forthright, in fact, in admitting on several occasions that he is either baffled by or ignorant of the nature of his circumstance. The Juan-of-the-past whom he describes, just like the reader, is discovering for the first time the characteristics of death-life in Comala. Together they wander in fear through the town's dark streets, learn of Pedro Páramo's ruthless conduct, and realize that Lola Preciados, dead for a week, has warned Damiana Cisneros of Juan's arrival. When Juan confesses, "I didn't know what to think" (7), the reader is equally mystified as to this communication between living and dead beings. Later, of course, it is revealed that Damiana is also dead, and one is then uncertain whether this makes Lola's communication any more or less astonishing. As neophytes in Comala, undergoing the same initiation ritual, Juan-of-the-past and the reader are confrères.

---

10. Blanco Aguinaga, "Realidad y estilo," p. 89; Luis Leal, "La estructura de Pedro Páramo," *Anuario de Letras* 4 (1964): 288.

Static Irony

In the present, however, as Juan relates his experience to Dorotea, he is better informed than both his listener and the eavesdropping reader. He enjoys the advantage of hindsight. Consistent with his sincerity, however, one can discern on his part a desire to reproduce faithfully for his listener the way things "happened." Consider the following passage:

Noises. Voices. Murmurs. Faraway songs.

My love gave me a handkerchief
with a border of tears. . . .

In falsetto, as if those who sang them were women. [44]

In an effort to communicate effectively, Juan uses a telegraphic style, presenting the object nouns alone and omitting subjects and verbs (thereby partially removing himself as a barrier between the experience and the listener). He then gives a line of the song he heard (he avoids paraphrase) and finishes with the vague construction "as if," which underlines the distance from which the voices arrived ("Faraway songs") and the uncertainty he felt because he had to depend solely on his auditory sense. One cannot exaggerate the importance to the reader of Juan's disconcertion in the past and candid portrayal of it in the present, for they serve as the only guide to Comala's unfamiliar reality.

The stance taken by the third-person omniscient narrator, as revealed in the form of his narrative, is antithetical to the candor of Juan Preciado. Despite his ability to know all that transpires in Comala, this narrator frequently either feigns ignorance of certain details or claims he cannot remember them all or their order of occurrence. He thus creates new mysteries and deprives the reader of information necessary for the clarification of those already existing. The narrator can, for instance, penetrate the mind of the characters to present the many short streams of consciousness (2, 6, 10, etc.), or, less often, reveal their thoughts through the indirect free style, as when Fulgor reflects upon the young Pedro's audacity: "Who was this boy to speak to him like that? His father, Don Lucas Páramo, had never insulted him like that, and here was this Pedro, who hardly knew anything about the Media Luna or how to run it, treating him like a farm hand" (33). The knowledge of the narrator extends in all temporal directions as well. Since his narrative includes both the present and the past, these times are obviously within his domain. One can even find instances of his referring to the eternal future, such as, "But which world was Susana San Juan living in? That was one of the things that Pedro Páramo never found out" (93). Never is a long time indeed, one which only an omniscient narrator could span with certainty.

In spite of this evidence of his capacity to convey all the information necessary to the most precise understanding of the plot, the narrator repeatedly balks at providing such a service. At times he ironically claims to be unaware of certain events (see, for instance, where in the original version he says of Miguel Páramo, "And who knows what kind of proposition he made her" [67]).[11] We have already seen this strategy, in Narrator III of *The Death of Artemio Cruz*. And like that narrator, this one goes from scene to scene without providing transitions. After the first four narrative fragments of the novel are related from the present perspective of Juan Preciado, the fifth jumps into the past to show a little boy talking to his mother and dreaming of his girlfriend. There is no way for the reader to know, or reason for him to suspect, that the boy in the fifth fragment is Pedro Páramo, and not Juan Preciado. Since the mother does not address the boy by name, there is nothing but the pattern established by the previous chapters by which to identify him. Like a modern Lazarillo, the narrator has calculated the omission of the transition to lead the blind reader into making an incorrect assumption.[12]

More evidence of the narrator's duplicity is found in his tendency to withhold information from the reader until the end of a passage, scene, or chapter, and then finally to reveal it, giving the section

11. In this sole instance, because of the absence of an important textual element in the published translation, the English version is my own.
12. It may be argued that throughout this section I unjustly favor the reader, when he has no more *right* to expect clarity from a work of fiction than he has to expect the cosmos to reveal its secrets to him personally. Without faulting such reasoning I must counter that the majority of contemporary readers, probably raised on nineteenth-century fiction, popular detective and science fiction, television series, and commercial movies, are conditioned to expect clarity, whether they deserve it or not. See María Luisa Bastos, "Clichés lingüísticos y ambigüedad en *Pedro Páramo*," *Revista Iberoamericana* 44, no. 102 (1978): 31–44.

new significance. This was noted in episodes IIIb and IIIc of *The Death of Artemio Cruz*. (I am unaware of an existing term for the technique,[13] but it is used in *Pedro Páramo* so frequently as to justify repeating and even labeling it: it can be called simply *deferred illumination,* for the postponed sense it provides.) Typical of the way it appears on a small scale is the following passage: " 'I, Fulgor Sedano, age 54, single, profession manager, empowered to initiate and settle lawsuits, charge and assert the following . . .' This is what he said when he presented the claim against Toribio Aldrete" (31). The first sentence, set off in quotation marks, is presented in a vacuum (it is the opening sentence of a fragment). Isolated as it is, the line could easily be taken to represent the thoughts or dreams of a character as well as a statement uttered out loud. Only after this initial perplexing experience is the context of the legalistic formulation disclosed, for the second sentence is actually a scene-setting introduction to the first. A less ironical narrator might have reversed the sentences, avoiding the misapprehension this form invites.

The deferred-illumination technique is applied elsewhere to much larger narrative units in order to achieve analogous effects. Until Juan Preciado's death and the nature of his dialogue with Dorotea in their grave are revealed, the ubiquity of death in Comala is unclear, since the village seems to maintain some of the characteristics of a living community (Eduviges appears at first to be alive, as does Juan). Once the reader is apprised of the status of the relator, however, he is able to understand how Juan could have met and spoken with Adundio, even though "Abundio's dead" (14). A dead man who walks and talks is baffling, but a tale about such

13. Its preponderant use has been observed by Didier T. Joén, who attributes to it the lyrical quality of the novel, for "the essential structure of the lyric consists in a progression of images toward a climax of greater intensity in which the total meaning of the poem, illuminated with new light, is revealed to us" ("La estructura lírica de *Pedro Páramo,*" *Revista Hispánica Moderna* 33, no. 3–4 [1967]: 224–32; my translation). For other structural studies, broadly defined, see Gerald L. Head, "El castigo de Toribio Aldrete y la estructura de *Pedro Páramo,*" in *Otros mundos, otros fuegos: Fantasía y realismo mágico en Iberoamérica* (East Lansing: Latin American Studies Center, Michigan State University, 1976), 379–82; Lucila Inés Mena, "Estructura narrativa y significado social de *Pedro Páramo,*" *Cuadernos Americanos* 37, no. 217 (1978): 165–88; and Nicolás Emilio Alvarez, "Agonía y muerte de Juan Preciado," *Revista de Estudios Hispánicos* 13 (1979): 209–26.

apparitions, told by a spirit, is less incongruous. The reader's difficulty stems from the narrator's refusal to declare his frame of reference: the rules become apparent only after the game is well under way.

Along with these challenges to conventional narration, the narrator cultivates an accompanying descriptive vagueness. First, the text is liberally sprinkled with demonstrative pronouns with unspecified antecedents, as in the quote above, "This is what he said when he presented the claim against Toribio Aldrete" (31), and in "That is what Damiana Cisneros was telling me" (39). These demonstratives may allude to a word, a complete dissertation, an isolated action, or a concatenation of events. Another way of blurring descriptive outlines is through subject pronouns that are placed before their referent, really another example of deferred illumination. In "They pounded at the door, but he didn't answer" (64), for example, "they" and "he" evoke many potential images that are superimposed on the one that eventually proves to be correct. Indefiniteness in characterization, moreover, is effected through an almost total lack of physical description (exceptions are Damiana [14] and Pedro, whose body is said to constitute a "huge form" [104]). Because a greater portion of the novel consists in dialogue and narration of action than in description, the characters tend to be bodyless voices that echo in the void. A similar trait can be found in Guillermo Cabrera Infante's *Three Trapped Tigers* (see chapter 4), but with a different motive. Cabrera Infante's characters and narrators often chatter in order to hear themselves talk, out of the pure joy of articulation. The characters in *Pedro Páramo* are never so playful. Their purpose in speaking is as undefined as their physiques, but perhaps one reason they vocalize is to recuperate an infernal past and thereby explain a meaningless eternal present.[14]

In general, then, thanks to ironical narrative strategies, Comala's conflictive political situation carries over into the arena occupied by the narrator and the reader. Through a lack of information (Who is dead? Who alive?) and a scarcity of signs (When do changes in time

14. Whatever their motives, as Lanin A. Gyurko has seen in "Rulfo's Aesthetic Nihilism: Narrative Antecedents of 'Pedro Páramo,'" *Hispanic Review* 40, no. 4 (1972), their efforts are thwarted, for "the monologues of the author's characters never lead to insight, resolution, or purgation" (466).

and place occur?), the reader is forced to recreate the work by reordering its parts, treating the novel like a verbal jigsaw puzzle.[15] The typical cause-and-effect relation among events is here converted to effect-and-cause, or sometimes to effect-and-effect, with no access to any cause. Indeed, some mysteries are never cleared up, even by the end of the novel. Who, for instance, is the man rejected by Chona on pp. 43–44, and what has he, or his rejection, to do with Pedro Páramo?[16] Of course, to ask that question is to leap from the narration to the narrated and to imply that irony may be created by *what* is said or done as well as *how*. That, in effect, is very much the case. The biggest irony-inciting issue is that of death, about which the reader must overcome his expectations and prejudices.[17] He must learn to accept the supernatural as casually as the inhabitants of Comala. But the resulting peace in reading must be purchased at the cost of his most cherished assumptions.

In the first chapter the reader is introduced to the death theme when it is revealed that Juan's mother has just died ("I promised her I would come to see him as soon as she died" [1]), a passage that also provides the motive for his pilgrimage. At the end of the chapter Abundio tells Juan, "Pedro Páramo died a long time ago" (5), but there is still no indication of anything supernatural. It is not until Juan arrives at the house of Eduviges that the line between life and death begins to blur.

She initially apologizes for the clutter in her house by explaining that Juan's mother "didn't let me know [of his arrival] till just today" (8). When he informs her that his mother is already dead, he

15. Joseph Sommers, in "Through the Window of the Grave: Juan Rulfo," *New Mexico Quarterly* 38, no. 1 (1968): 99, interprets this to mean that Rulfo "requires the reader to suffer with him, to participate in the superhuman attempt to render chaos orderly."

16. One can only conjecture about this loose thread in the fabric of the plot. Chona's refusal to elope might be a sign that she has found steady "employment" with Pedro, whose nefarious influence in the vicinity has expanded. The chronological disarray of the chapters makes it impossible to be certain of the role this scene plays in the destruction of Comala, and bespeaks eloquently the novel's insistent indeterminacy.

17. John A. Crow, "*Pedro Páramo:* A Twentieth-Century Dance of Death," in *Homage to Irving A. Leonard: Essays on Hispanic Art, History, and Literature*, ed. Raquel Chang-Rodríguez and Donald A. Yates (East Lansing: Latin American Studies Center, Michigan State University, 1973), pp. 219–27.

is disconcerted by her reasoning: "Oh, then that's why her voice sounded so weak. As if she were a long way away" (8). At first Eduviges seems to suggest that the dead live on in their own way, apparently able to communicate with the living, but not without being subject to certain physical limitations, such as distance. But then her comments cast a dubious shadow on even that idea. Later, for instance, Juan and the reader learn that Abundio, who gave Juan a ride into Comala, is also dead; although they cannot be sure that there are not two men known by the same name. According to Eduviges, Abundio is deaf, but the man whom Juan encountered heard perfectly well (14). Thus it now appears that in death individuals may recover faculties that were impaired during life—Abundio can hear, just as Dorotea speaks. To add to the mystery, Eduviges applies the logic of the natural world when she says, "Then it couldn't be the same one. Besides, Abundio's dead. I'm sure he must be dead. Didn't he tell you? It couldn't be the same one" (14). The reader, who is less versed in the nature of the Comalan cosmos than Eduviges, must bow to her reasoning. At this point he must reassess his assumptions about the supernatural and reinstate the physical laws associated with the extraliterary world.

The presence of the supernatural is further suggested when Eduviges enters a trance and claims to hear the deceased Miguel Páramo's horse galloping along the roads of the Media Luna. When Juan declares that he has heard nothing, she explains, "Then it must have been my sixth sense" (19). As she tells Juan of Miguel's death, she offers a unique perspective on the experience of death as seen from the Other Side, a small-scale model of what the novel as a whole represents. Repeating Miguel's words, she says, " 'We jumped [the stone wall] and kept on going' " (20). Death's omnipresence in Comala, insinuated in this scene, is later manifested unequivocally through a series of successive approximations, a chain of revelations about the demise of certain characters—Abundio, Eduviges, Damiana, the incestuous couple—who were previously considered to be alive. It is a chain that eventually leads back to the relator Juan Preciado himself. The closing of the circular chain of death is signaled by the words, "I told you at the beginning. They said that Pedro Páramo was my father, and I came to look for him" (58). At this moment, when death is seen to encompass all Comala, the past and present are fused: the time of Juan's historical *related* (what he tells to Dorotea), which has gradually progressed toward the present, now coincides with the time of his *relation* (the act of telling). Meanwhile, the words by which this connection is effected recapitulate the beginning of the process by alluding to the novel's opening line. From this point on, Juan's relation deals only with the present, and the importance of his role diminishes relative to that of the central figure, Pedro Páramo.

From this point on, also, as the reader moves away from Juan, he draws correspondingly closer to the narrator. The first shift occurs because Juan, the reader learns, was not addressing him directly, but was talking to Dorotea, Juan's nonironical gravemate. The new rapport with the narrator comes about for two reasons: in addition to the narrator's method no longer seeming so strange, the plot in what is roughly the second half of the novel becomes more linear. It traces the events that eventually lead to the death of Pedro Páramo, with only occasional flashes forward to Juan and Dorotea, who listen to and comment on the ravings of Susana San Juan in the cemetery. The dilution of Juan's role in the second half of the novel is easily explained, but to do so one must examine the role of the implied author.

The nature of the author of *Pedro Páramo* is such that he is not distinguishable from the omniscient narrator; they are mutually noncritical. The narrator says nothing to distance himself from the author along either a moral, cognitive, temporal, or spatial axis, as does, for instance, the narrator Toto in *Betrayed by Rita Hayworth*. And unlike Narrator III of *The Death of Artemio Cruz*, who is omniscient while Cruz lives but nonexistent when he dies, this narrator remains with the author outside the time and space of Comala. He is not, however, the "same" as the author, for they have different textual functions. This difference can be understood as being akin to that between the mind and the voice. The author makes the decisions as to form, order of presentation, length of parts, subject matter treated in each part, and so forth, decisions that are realized through the articulation (or silence) of the narrator. What has been referred to, then, as an ironical narrator is more precisely the ironical voice through which the author has chosen to speak, for he must speak through some kind of mediating voice. For him to communicate "directly" to the reader is an impossibility, since it would be to bypass the text entirely, and such a shortcut can lead only to meaningless silence.[18]

These are some examples of the author's presence behind the text: it is his decision to dedicate many chapters to Juan Preciado's half-dialogue in the first half of the novel (recreating in the reader the uncertainty of the character) and to pay him considerably less heed in the second half. The wisdom of this decision lies in the suspense created initially by the combination of the reader's disorientation and Juan's fear of dying. Once Juan has related his death, bracketing the possibility of fear (since the "worst" has happened), he is left with only the infinite present to talk about. Just as it is less horrible, Juan's present is also less interesting. The reader's attention therefore veers to how Pedro destroyed Comala and was eventually destroyed himself, a change of focus that is encouraged further by the holes built into the first half of the novel. The filling of the lacunae—and the consequent near-satisfaction of the reader's curiosity—is the function of the second half. This is but one more step in executing the strategy observed earlier in which the novel evinces the inverted, ironical form of effect-and-cause.

The author obviously also determines the manner in which the novel ends, not with the most chronologically posterior moment, but with the death of Pedro, which occurs years before the opening scene. That description takes the following unceremonious form: "He leaned against Damiana and tried to walk. After a few steps he fell down, pleading within but not speaking a single word. He struck a feeble blow against the ground and then crumbled to pieces as if he were a heap of stones" (123). In this concluding paragraph there is a progression from uprightness and movement to stasis and silence. In contrast to the constant rain in Comala and to the sweat bath in which Susana lay while alive, death is shown as a process of drying and disintegration, followed by a gradual reconversion to inorganic matter. The transition portrayed from a vital to a mortal condition reduces life to nothing more than a moist, ambulatory version of death. It is consistent with the indiscriminate devaluation of existence represented throughout the novel, for Pedro's death

18. The problem of the author who unsuccessfully attempts to eschew the text's mediation is treated felicitously by Jorge Luis Borges in "Borges y yo," in *El hacedor* (Madrid: Alianza/Emecé, 1975 [1960]), pp. 69–70.

makes no difference. Life in Comala is a slow process of dying. Pedro disseminates death throughout his life, and it finally takes root in him, not as a poetically just resolution but as one of limitless random occurrences in a senseless world. Indeed, a strong case can be made for Abundio's murder of Pedro as a mercy killing, an unearned early parole from a life sentence.

Another terminus in the novel, the temporal end point of the narrated, is "buried" inconspicuously thirteen chapters from the conclusion. In it Juan and Dorotea conjecture about Susana's lamentations. Dorotea's last line is, "I think her coffin must have broken. I can hear the boards squeaking," to which Juan responds, "Yes, I can hear them too" (99). Chronologically, then, the novel ends with the possible breaking open of a casket, which makes a sound, causing in turn more sounds in the form of the voices of the characters. Comala's endless present consists in the gradual degeneration of everything material (the boards), the breakdown of all limitations of space (the dimensions of the casket), and an eternally self-generating resounding: an "I hear it" that is heard and causes another "I hear it" ad infinitum, but that never quite conveys the "it" that is heard.

Pedro Páramo is thus eschatologically doubled. It has a male terminus, located at one of the novel's extremities, which closes the narration and brings it back to its deathly, petrified origin. And it has a female terminus, an ethereal aperture that is recessed within the corpus and promises perpetual representation. These several ends precipitate a curious double recognition and put into question the triumph of nothingness that threatens to impose itself. On the one hand, the plurality is the readily recognizable gesture of an ironist at work, for multiple articulations are a hallmark of verbal irony. On the other hand, the two conclusions represent a recognition of failure on the author's part to achieve the sort of blanket negation of values the work so often approaches. That is, the male ending, nihilistic and solipsistic, is already negated by the act of symbolizing through which it exists. This fruitful act is itself symbolized in the female ending. The metaphor of death into which the novel develops is embodied in the man. But it can exist as a metaphor only in life, incarnate in the woman. The matrix that circumscribes and bonds these contraries is irony, nihilism's frustration.

The potentially absolute mutual antipathy between author and reader is therefore attenuated considerably by the exquisite form the still sobering vision takes. In spite of the inevitable negation of radical negation, the ironical author creates anyway—perhaps for no other reason than to convince himself of the vanity of what ordinarily might be called his enterprise but in the context of *Pedro Páramo* is more appropriately termed an "undertaking." One of contemporary art's chief functions, after all, is to proclaim the death of Truth, and then to fill the resulting void with Beauty (the Truth-of-no-Truth). That substitution is articulated in *Pedro Páramo* through Juan Preciado, the man who searches for his origin, hoping to find the plenitude of life in the knowledge of his identity, only to be swept away by the larger structure, the alluring, all-pervasive Death of Comala. This same movement is simultaneously mirrored verbally in Juan's ingenuous attempt to recount his life, only to have his relation subsumed under the greater totality of the omniscient narrator, whose voice stands as the truth within a novel that denies the possibility of just such a voice. He is, lastly, like the skeptical artist who tries to exorcise his estrangement by objectifying it in a unique and irreducible work, only to have it appropriated in order to illustrate a theory of inevitable contradiction. Perhaps Rulfo is right after all. His unhappy work has assumed the role of pretextual pawn for the discourse of literary criticism—and has undergone a death of still another sort.

CHAPTER 3

Betrayed by Rita Hayworth:
The Androgynous Text

Like Rulfo's *Pedro Páramo*, *Betrayed by Rita Hayworth*[1] is an extraordinarily mature first novel. In contrast to the laconic Rulfo, though, Manuel Puig has shown himself to be a fecund author by publishing six more excellent novels to date: *Heartbreak Tango: A Serial* (1973), *The Buenos Aires Affair: A Detective Novel* (1976), *Kiss of the Spider Woman* (1979), *Angelic Pubis* (*Pubis angelical*, 1979), *Eternal Malediction unto the Reader of These Pages* (1982), and *Requited Love's Blood* (*Sangre de amor correspondido*, 1982). What Ronald Christ has said of Puig's first two novels applies as well to all except possibly *Eternal Malediction*: "[They] present characters who suck the thumb of popular culture to avoid chewing the gristle of reality."[2] If Puig's novels are "pop," that term is applicable only if distilled of the derogatory sense scholars tend to lend it. Puig's writing should not be equated with the commercially exploitative reading matter that can be consumed while standing on a subway platform. His popular strain, rather, invariably appears

1. The novel was originally published in 1968. The first English edition, translated by Suzanne Jill Levine, is dated 1971. Page references in this chapter are to the New York: Vintage Books, 1981 edition and will appear parenthetically within the text. The novel is mentioned briefly by Severo Sarduy in "Notas a las notas a las notas . . . A propósito de Manuel Puig," *Revista Iberoamericana* 37, no. 76–77 (1971): 555–68, and is reviewed in general terms by José María Carranza in "Sobre Manuel Puig," *Revista Iberoamericana* 38, no. 78 (1972): 152. See also Armando Maldonado, "Manuel Puig: The Aesthetics of Cinematic and Psychological Fiction," (unpublished Ph.D. dissertation, University of Oklahoma, 1977).
2. Ronald Christ, "Fact and Fiction," *Review* 73 (Fall 1973): 49.

in a problematic context. He incorporates into his fiction elements of mass culture—radionovelas, comic books, glamour magazines, and in *Betrayed by Rita Hayworth,* commercial movies—in order to unveil their delightfully insidious role in shaping contemporary life.[3]

Another thread that runs through all Puig's novels can be called the politics of sexuality. Acts of aggression and submission—the intersubjective equivalent of war—are committed repeatedly in different forms and degrees between members of opposite sexes or of the same sex. These power games in turn interact with the cultural artifacts cited above, informing the stereotypes projected on a mass scale even as they are derived from them. From the incongruous interplay of some of the most superficial objects produced by the Western culture industry, on the one hand, and the most profound and mysterious drives of the human animal, on the other, there emerges a pervasive languorous melancholy. It is the sad lassitude of loss, although no one in Puig's novelistic world can identify what he or she has lost. An irony in this case, of course, is that Puig's characters feel the lack of that which they have never possessed. On the contrary, it is they who have been possessed, by an expectation of wholeness which they have unreflectively gleaned from the media. In this imposed expectation resides also the most basic difference between Rulfo and Puig as authors: the inhabitants of Comala have long since abandoned any presupposition of plenty. Whereas Rulfo posits in *Pedro Páramo* a nothingness valid for all eternity, Puig's expanding opus exemplifies the ironist's need to reiterate a tentative conviction: the tantalizing plenitude of life is always, in the words of Paul Simon's popular ditty, "slip-slidin' away."[4]

That the wholeness promised in commercial artifacts translates imperfectly into life explains how, in *Betrayed by Rita Hayworth,*

3. On the role of film in the novel, see Andrew Sarris, "Re-running Puig and Cabrera Infante," *Review* 73 (Spring 1973): 46–48. This article is treated more fully in chapter 4. The use of nostalgia in Puig's first two novels is examined in David William Foster, "Manuel Puig and the Uses of Nostalgia," *Latin American Literary Review* 1, no. 1 (1972): 79–82.

4. The pertinent refrain goes, "The nearer your destination, / The more it's slip-slidin' away."

the movies can be construed to betray the spectator.[5] In that the novel stubbornly resists facile closure and operates instead according to a principle of insufficiency, it offers itself as an antidote for the sugary venom served up daily by the entertainment industry. This insufficiency is conveyed through a prose that has been described as, among other things, "alienated." Marta Morello Frosch sees at work "language that has been betrayed, replaced, inverted, and finally reduced to what it should not be: a means for non-communication."[6] Similarly, Emir Rodríguez Monegal notes:

> The language spoken by the characters is a combination of the basic language of the region and of the period, finely embroidered and embellished with other types of language or writing. The language of film scripts . . . the language of radio and television soap-opera. . . . Many of these types are not really spoken languages but rather literary ones, and for that reason produce even more alienating results by being incorporated with no transcription [transition?] whatsoever into the spoken patterns of the characters.[7]

The linguistic alienation and the thematic estrangement implied in the sense of missing plenitude infiltrate the novel's structure on still another, symbolic level. The largest narrative units—the two parts into which the original version of the novel is divided—enact an erotic struggle that places them at a magnified intratextual distance from each other. But in order to understand the sense in which this

5. The plight of the viewer is simple in comparison to that of the star herself, who sees or imagines her own image on the screen and may be tempted to try to act out that idealized role off the screen as well. The inevitable confrontation with the insuperable distance between Rita's selves leads to a second betrayal, which is lost in translating the title figuratively. The title in Spanish, which reads *La traición de Rita Hayworth* (*The Betrayal of Rita Hayworth*), allows Hayworth to be the object as well as the agent of infidelity.

6. Marta Morello Frosch, "The New Art of Narrating Films," *Review 72* (Winter–Spring 1972): 52.

7. Emir Rodríguez Monegal, "A Literary Myth Exploded," *Review 72* (Winter–Spring 1972): 63. Wolfgang A. Luchting offers an interesting although ultimately unconvincing hypothesis as to the cause of the characters' disillusionment in "Betrayed by Education: Manuel Puig's *La traición de Rita Hayworth*," *Proceedings of the Pacific Northwest Conference on Foreign Languages* 28, no. 1 (1977): 134–37. See also Jorge Rodríguez Padrón, "Manuel Puig y la capacidad expresiva de la lengua popular," *Cuadernos Hispanoamericanos* 82, no. 245 (1970): 490–97.

is so, we must first examine the novel's narrative order and establish systematically the many forms of irony that arise in the text.

The following diagram illustrates pertinent aspects of the novel's narrational scheme: D = dialogue; S = stream of consciousness; W = writing.

Part I

Ch.	I	II	III	IV	V	VI	VII	VIII
Date	1933	1933	1939	1941	1942	1942	1943	1943
Mode	D	D	S	D	S	S	S	S
Narr.	M's family	B's maids	Toto	Choli	Toto	Teté	Delia	Mita

Part II

Ch.	IX	X	XI	XII	XIII	XIV	XV	XVI
Date	1944	1945	1946	1947	1947	1947	1948	1933
Mode	S	S	S	W	W	W	W	W
Narr.	Héctor	Paqui	Cobito	Esther	Toto	Anon.	Herminia	Berto

Each chapter is preceded by a heading that includes four bits of information: the chapter number, the place, the date, and the narrator (if any) to figure in it. These indications do not appear in *Pedro Páramo*, where missing orienting data become the object of the reader's speculation. The "action" of the novel takes place in Buenos Aires and the fictitious town of Coronel Vallejos during the period spanning 1933 through 1948. Within this interval the "protagonist," José "Toto" Casals, grows from babyhood to puberty, when his troublesome identity is largely forged. "Action" is put into quotation marks because the present time of each of the sixteen chapters is singularly devoid of action as that term is normally understood. Rather than incur a sort of novelistic epiphany contrary to its nature on other planes, *Betrayed by Rita Hayworth* consists mainly in idle talk, mental meanderings, and various forms of writing: in sum, it inscribes a concerted circumvention of action. The three types of activity (perhaps this word is more apt) that the novel does represent correspond to the three narrational modes designated in the diagram: dialogue (chapters I, II, and IV), interior monologue (III, V–XI), and assorted forms of writing (XII–XVI).

"Protagonist" is likewise in quotes because the novel, in a strict sense, has none; no character maintains a position of central interest to the reader or importance to the development of the novel. (Indeed, "development" too might be put into question, but it would be premature for us to follow that line of argument.) Nonetheless, Toto approximates the role of protagonist more closely than any other character and for ease of reference he will be considered as such until the need to refine the term arises.

Section #1: Dialogues

I	II		IV

In all three of the chapters that take the form of a dialogue, the primary characters are set apart both from the secondary ones and from each other. The principal figures are Toto, his mother Mita, and his father Berto. They are the characters whose presence dominates the work, while those considered secondary appear and disappear intermittently, forming an almost indistinguishable mass.

Chapter I takes place at "Mita's Parents' Place" (7), but in the absence of Mita. She is in Coronel Vallejos, having moved there with Berto after their wedding, slightly over a year earlier. In view of the fact that Mita's is the first name mentioned and that she is frequently the topic of conversation in the household (during the chapter they stray from and return to her approximately twelve times), we may consider her a central character. In spite of her absence she is still prominent in her family's mind. Most of their sentiment toward her takes the form of worry, both over her husband's nerves (12) and her wasted years of study (10). But the geographic distance that separates them, allowing her to visit only once a year, overrides the family's attempts to compensate with their concern. In the end they decide to deceive her in a letter in order to create the illusion of intimacy ("Tell her you met Sofía Cabalús [an old friend of Mita's], lie to her" [14]), perhaps realizing that they now have little in common with her. Whereas they apparently spend their time working or chatting, she has a college education and enjoys reading in her spare time. Even though the family does not say directly that they disapprove of Mita's "habit," they do assert that Sofia's "father went crazy, he hardly ever makes it to class. And all they do at home is read" (10). Mita is thus guilty by association. She lives not only in another town but on a different plane from that of her family. Their good intentions and hope for her happiness cannot bridge the cultural gap between them. Her status as an active member of the family expired in the past, and she is now just another recurring topic of conversation, along with the embroidery, the movies, and the dirty laundry.

In the second chapter Mita is once again elsewhere, this time at work in the hospital while the scene takes place, according to the chapter title, "At Berto's" (17). The conversation is principally between the nursemaid, Amparo, and another family servant, Felisa. There are, however, occasional comments by Amparo to the infant Toto and sporadic interruptions by Berto, who is composing a letter in the next room. Berto's manner with Amparo tends to be brusque. He does not speak to her at all during the chapter, in fact, except to shout a command through the wall ("Come here, Amparo!" [18], etc.). One of these imperatives ("Never tell Mita we have a secret" [21]) could be taken as the sign of an illicit bond. But the secret in question concerns her seeing Berto's eavesdropping on a conversation between Mita and her sister Adela (21). This scene of double dramatic irony is one indication that Berto lacks a frank relation with his wife. Their mutual duplicity is reinforced later when Felisa gossips to Amparo, "Don't say that in front of Mister Berto, the missis cries when he's not looking" (23). One of the issues between Mita and Berto, we deduce, is that he favors repression over expression.

A glance at Berto's dealings with his son Toto adds to the family portrait. Although the father undoubtedly has affection for the boy ("How's my little fella?" [21]), he leaves all the feeding, grooming, and diaper changing to the nursemaid. Mita too delegates such chores to others ("Mita has a maid who cooks and cleans the house and a girl who takes care of the baby while she works in the hospital" [9]), but clearly she has little choice in the matter. She spends long hours at the hospital and pharmacy trying to keep pace with Berto's speculative business fiascos. In spite of her laboring out of love for her family, the working mother is apart from her child a considerable portion of the time, a mitigating factor in their relationship.

The fourth chapter is called "Choli's Conversation with Mita, 1941" (37), but it is more precisely a truncated dialogue, since the only voice heard is Choli's. Mita is once again somewhere else; the signal for her replies (which remain undisclosed) is a dash followed by an empty space in the text. This ostensibly amicable telephone conversation is also earmarked by a distance, both spatial and intellectual, between the interlocutors. It seems strange, for instance, that they talk by means of a technological device when they could meet in person. Choli is in the same village, but for some reason (conjecture: Berto's opposition) does not visit Mita's house ("I'm only passing through Vallejos this time" [39]). The traveling saleswoman for Hollywood cosmetics, potentially as pathetic as Arthur Miller's Willy Loman, stays instead at one more hotel along her route.

As the colloquy develops, Choli reveals herself to be quite different from the Mita who has emerged in the previous chapters. Mita holds a job that requires technical training and enjoys reading in her spare time. Choli, in contrast, has no formal training, thinks of nothing but fads and fashions, and insecurely tries to cover her vacuousness with a cosmetic stream of words ("And I know how to carry on a conversation too, don't I? Even if I didn't go to college, right?" [40]). Her questions seek reassuring answers from Mita, who cannot avoid seeing the superficiality and ignorance in some of Choli's admissions ("I almost died when I saw how far the United States was from England. I thought London was the chic part, but closer" [47]). Even though her exact responses are unknown, it is obvious that Mita does not accept Choli's Hollywood ethic of glamorous façades. As the chapter—and the first modal category— closes, the space between the characters remains wide open. It should be noted for future reference that most of the characters who appear in these dialogue chapters are female.

Section #2, Subsection A: Toto's Interior Monologues

		III		V	

It is necessary to have hindsight to be certain of Toto's capital importance to the novel. As the only one to have two full chapters

(III and V) narrated from his perspective, Toto is, first of all, the most completely portrayed character in the novel. He is, moreover, the novel's principal vehicle for developing the cinematic motif, and he thus activates the interplay of cultural objects and social practices alluded to earlier. Crucial, too, is his symbolic value. These three factors, inaccessible to the reader in a first reading, explain why Toto's interior monologues are dealt with separately from those of the other characters.

From the start it is evident that Toto is an exceptionally bright child with an inquisitive, active mind. His monologue abounds in interrogatives and verbatim recollection. He remembers details and jumps from thought to thought as well as from real facts to imagined ones without apparent provocation (see especially pp. 24–25). In the following passage, for example, the topic of his thought changes three times within the confines of one sentence:

[1] Uncle Perico, always in the bar with the country people, after the cattle fair they go to play billiards, they never go to the movies and [2] it's a pity the bushes on the bottom of the sea eat the pretty fishies in many colors, they should eat the bad fishes that look like octopuses and sharks but [3] in the picture cards mommy says the movie that's going to turn out the fanciest is *The Great Ziegfeld* which they're finally showing this Thursday. [33, my numeration]

The narrative evokes a mind that releases energy in multiple directions at once and demands great attention and energy from the others in its proximity. An adult who lives with Toto summarizes the experience, not without affection: "He's driving us out of our minds every minute of the day" (33).

Two incidents illustrate how Berto relates to the demands of his son. The first occurs when Toto asks to be accompanied to the toilet at a school benefit show. Berto is unmoved by the child's plight (" 'Daddy, have to go weewee!' 'You can go by yourself,' 'I can't reach the light!' " [25]), and eventually finds a girl to take the little boy to the ladies' room. In the second incident he calls his nursemaid "¡Felisa fuckface!," an obscenity of whose meaning he is ignorant. Predictably enough, Berto's solution to the problem is through an intermediary: " 'This child is very naughty, I'm going to put him down for Baby-Soccer so he can play with the other boys' "

(33). Berto's answers continue to be stereotypically *machista,* and his stance vis-à-vis Toto, relatively aloof.

Mita, on the other hand, makes a point of doing things with Toto when she is free. Even though her frequent and prolonged absences still trouble him, the preference he shows for Mita is obvious ("I hide my head between Daddy's pantlegs, but much better for hiding are your [Mita's] petticoats because I hide my head and if Daddy opens your legs you see me" [34 in original version; omitted in published translation]). She was the last person to see him before their respective naps (27) and will be the first to see him when he awakes (36). She is unmistakably his prime human interest, second only in importance perhaps to his obsession with the movies. He internalizes movies and "lives" them, and when he is not seeing a film he either recreates them in his imagination or fantasizes in anticipation of the next one. If he were so involved with a person, it would be a case of complete disirony, antagonistic to our thesis concerning insufficiency and the lack of resolution on many levels of the novel. But Toto directs his unmitigated attention toward an image on a screen, a phenomenon that qualifies as a "thing" only with certain major reservations. To be sure, Toto is at many removes from communing analogously with other persons. It is in fact because he is left alone so often that he turns to fantasies, films fill the affective vacuum in his life. As he grows so accustomed to dealing with them that people take only secondary importance, the movies become a barrier, an ironizing element.

The distant relations continue into the fifth chapter, the site of Toto's second interior monologue. Mita continues to be affectionate but is still absent from the scene (and, we must assume, from many like it). Berto's lack of demonstrativeness is so much the norm that by now Toto uses it as a point of reference for father-son relations ("Alicita's father touched me the same way, he is a father of girls. The Gonaźlez girl's father is the Gonaźlez girl's father but he also has two boys and he mustn't touch like that" [53]). There are, however, several basic changes in the nine-year-old narrator-character, principal among which is his desire to go beyond the family circle to seek affection. He is infatuated with Alicita and dreams of sharing with her the thoughts he reveals to no one else (56–57). But the child's hopes are shattered apparently without cause when his former playmate utters the fateful words, "Toto, you can't come to play" (67). In the second part of the chapter he tries to flee from the party and the sting of his defeat but, crest-fallen, he must finally accept losing her to his rival ("But it was Alicita. Playing dominoes, sitting next to Luisito Castro" [69]).

The tendency to escape to a fantasy world rather than deal with his troubles becomes increasingly characteristic of Toto as he grows up. Whereas in chapter III he is content to describe the fantasies presented on the screen (see, for instance, his description of a Fred Astaire film on pp. 28–29), his ability to create illusions and to participate actively in them develops in chapter V. He incorporates himself and his personal acquaintances, like the he-man Raúl Gar-cía, into the movies he has seen or heard about: "How nice it would be to live in a cabin, because with all his strength he [Raúl] can kill the bears and if I faint on the sled in the snow he can come and save me and have a glass of beer ready for me in the cabin with white bread sandwiches that we brought from town" (66). As Toto pre-fers the company of his mother to that of his father, so does he project himself into the cliché role of the helpless ingenue. His affair with films has "dramatic" consequences: they imprint rigid, though inverted from the norm, behavioral archetypes on his impressiona-ble psyche.

His withdrawal into fantasy reaches its apotheosis in the Alicita incident. Perhaps in emulation of his father, Toto does not turn to his parents for comfort; he takes pains to avoid having them know of the incident (68). He predictably turns inward and imagines the demise of his rival (73) and his own success in winning Alicita's affection. This will be accomplished by his entering the body of her uncle and becoming infused with his being ("I'm going to be inside of him like the soul is inside the body, I'm going to be next to his soul, wrapped up in his soul" [74]). Then, when Alicita thinks she is kissing her uncle, she will "actually" be kissing Toto. This conclud-ing scene creates two seeming disironies: the union with the uncle, and the joy of Alicita's tender kisses. But the vision is again under-cut by its context. It is, first, the result of the child's spiritual di-vorce from his parents. The merger with the soul of the uncle, moreover, is not out of any affection for the man, but is only a vehicle for winning the girl. And even this end, which is based on all the feeling Toto is capable of mustering, is devalued by the fact that Alicita would be the victim of his deceit. The hypothetical scene thus amounts to a prepubescent symbolic rape. Although the chapter concludes with Toto's fantasy still in progress, his eventual disillusionment is already prefigured in his amorous failure at the birthday party. Celluloid-inspired notions of romantic love and happy endings conspire to ensure his deflation upon reencountering mundane existence.

Section #2, Subsection B: Other Interior Monologues

Part I				Part II			
	VI	VII	VIII	IX	X	XI	

Chapters VI–XI are discussed as a unit because they all make use of the interior monologue, a technique that promotes a particular sort of interaction between narrator and reader. The reader, eavesdropping on the narrator's thoughts, is privy to information meant to be shared with no one. The narrator is exposed to the reader without any possibility of dissimulation, permitting the reader to compare a given narrator's limited vision with that of other narrators, and placing the reader in some cases in a superior, judgmental position.

These chapters disclose respectively the mental activity of Teté, Delia, Mita, Héctor, Paquita, and Cobito. Mita has been termed a primary character; two other narrators, Delia and Cobito, appear for the first time. Teté, Héctor, and Paquita fall in between, each having appeared briefly or been mentioned tangentially previous to the chapter he or she narrates. At this point, however, the distinction between primary and secondary characters becomes problematical (another departure from stock commercial cinematic practice). In each chapter, the protagonist of the interior monologue is the narrator himself, to whom all other matters are peripheral. To scrutinize the interaction of only the Casals family in these introverted chapters leads to indeterminate data based on insufficient evidence and creates the impression that the novel enters into a kind of narrative-irony entropy. That is, if we focus only on the "protagonists," nothing seems to be happening. A more fruitful approach is to pay little attention to this zone where things drift in a gray limbo and heed instead the voice through which the ambiguity is conveyed.

The voices in chapters VI and VII belong to marginal members of the Casals household. Teté, who speaks first, is a frightened little girl whose mother is gravely ill and whom Mita has agreed to care for. The second narrator, Delia, is an impoverished and lovesick maid. The chapters inscribe analogous trajectories with respect to the reader's response to the narrators' plight. In each case the first impression is sympathetic (Teté, raised by nuns and acutely aware of her own impurity, is beleaguered by a sense of guilt and by visions of death; Delia has lost López, her true love, and is left with a life she terms "a glorious pail of shit" [103]). At some point in their monologues, however, both Teté and Delia contradict themselves, by word or deed, and reveal the self-deception that underlies their initial poses. In the novel's first (minimal) instance of present action, Teté accepts an orange from Mita after having firmly resolved not to. The lines, "yes, an orange, oh yes Mita . . . this one's good, I'll suck it, make a little hole in it and I'll suck it" (79), convey a sensual reveling that disperses the aura of spirituality Teté attempts to evoke. In a similar vein, shortly after swearing that her spiritual union with López is "all that matters to me" (102), Delia confesses that "with a full stomach I don't think about a thing because I'm already out, sleeping like a log till the next day" (103). Having been almost touched by Teté and Delia, only to find that they have no need of pity, the reader retreats and leaves them to their respective self-delusion.

The reader approaches Mita's chapter with great expectations, almost as if waiting in line with ticket in hand. Since the opening pages she has been alluded to, described, and used as a point of reference. Indeed, the entire first half of the novel can be regarded as a gradual approach to this character, starting with Mita's parents, her servants, her friend, her son, and so on. The process eventually leads to her own interior monologue in chapter VIII. Since she is the character who receives the least ironical treatment (she displays such admirable traits as generosity, compassion, and faithfulness), perhaps she will evade the pattern of despondency and ennui.

One of the biggest surprises in meeting Mita "in person" is that she is not the person others see her to be. True, she does embody the positive qualities previously attributed to her. But what no one else knows about Mita, and what makes all the external descriptions of her partial—and therefore inaccurate—is the pain she experiences as a woman. Her second child has died in infancy, and she fears she may never recover from the loss ("A wound hurts till it heals, when will it heal?, a wound that doesn't heal is probably infected" [111]). Rather than comfort her, Berto remains as unyielding as ever ("The worst part is that Berto forbids us to cry each time we remember" [109]). This prohibition leads her to ask bitterly of men: "They hold [their fears] back because they feel less, or is it because they feel nothing at all?" (112). Even amidst her family, Mita clearly feels isolated.

The actual encounter with Mita may also come as something of a disappointment. The self-inflicted nature of her woes (by submitting to her husband she perpetuates the inequitable order) is bound to tarnish her image to some extent. Yet the reader must realize that he, too, submits willingly to a given order, an order that has created certain illusions about Mita. The disillusionment we experience upon confronting her parallels her discontent with the prosaic shape of her own life. It is not because she is perfect but quite the contrary—because she has frailties and does not meet our expectations—that we can identify with Mita. And in a similarly paradoxical fashion, the chief source of her problems—her acceptance of a consecrated female role, which leads to her subjugation by Berto—also offers a possible solution to those problems: maternity. Mita's maternal drive leads her to act as proxy mother for Teté, Héctor, and Paquita, and to look forward to having another child of her own (113). Her commitment to healing and to the continuation of life, in spite of all its frustrations and disappointments, marks her as the novel's embodiment of hope, of affirmation.

Mita's is the last chapter in part I of the novel (the division into two parts is inexplicably and lamentably missing from the English translation). All the narrators in this part of the novel—except Toto, whose sexuality may be considered problematical[8]—are female; the majority of those in part II are male.

The narrators of the remaining three "introverted" chapters, the first chapters of part II, follow the pattern inscribed by Teté and Delia. Their monologues reveal a feeling of estrangement from the

8. In an interview with Ronald Christ, Puig has described Toto as a "latent homosexual," certainly a determination which the novel permits, but not a conclusion one is forced to draw. See "An Interview with Manuel Puig," *Partisan Review* 44, no. 1 (1977): 52–61.

rest of humanity, usually a sympathy-evoking situation, yet the form of the narratives distances the reader from the narrators. Héctor (chapter IX), for instance, whose sad gaze is confirmed by both Delia and Mita, thinks of himself as an intruder in his Aunt Mita's house, no matter how often she tells him otherwise ("Mita isn't like an aunt, she's more than an aunt and she doesn't want to fuck me up, does she love me more than an aunt?" [122]). He tries to compensate for the feeling of motherlessness ("I don't . . . trust anybody, only your mother, he who has one" [131]) by fornicating with as many girls as possible while remaining emotionally indifferent. His foul language augments his gruff exterior, which, even as it seems to protect him, also deepens his loneliness. At the end of his monologue he lapses into one of his customary athletic fantasies by which he bolsters his deflated ego and taps his main source of gratification.

The reader already knows of Paquita, the narrator of chapter X, from Toto's description of her in chapter V, where she was promiscuously involved with Raúl García during the González girl's birthday party. This time the reader finds her waiting to confess her mortal sins, which have apparently continued to amass. As the chapter unfolds, and Paquita shows she is fond of eavesdropping on private conversations (between Toto and Ñata, 137–38) and possesses a hyperbolic sensuality (witness the delight with which she fondles the book earlier read by the swimming instructor, 140), it becomes apparent that she, like Teté, relishes her pecadillos. It is also clear, when her father catches her with a man in a hotel room and her thoughts are not about the immorality of the act but that "God made him [her father] forgive me and not hit me, he didn't even shout at me or tell Mom" (145), that she confesses not out of conviction but rather out of fear of the consequences. Her final, eagerly pious incantation ("I'm going to say a whole rosary to the Virgin, no, to God our Almighty Father, for Celia's soul to rest in peace" [146]), therefore, is put into question by its impious motivation. Her cynical approach to religion ensures that her resolution will soon be forgotten and that the sin-and-repent cycle will begin anew.

Cobito (chapter XI), too, even though he is poor and fatherless, sabotages any possibility of reader sympathy. In spite of his sense of disenfranchisement ("And who am I going to learn from now?

Who's behind the counter? Nobody!" [161]), Cobito bombards the reader with negative stimuli. Among them are his chapter-opening fantasies as a gangland hood which, along with their humorous appropriation of commonplace criminal jargon, show the hostility he bears toward society. He later actualizes his aggressions by attempting a homosexual assault on Toto, using chloroform to knock his victim out. When the attempt fails, he and Colombo conspire to cast the blame on another friend of theirs, thus invalidating that nominal alliance ("We'll say it was this lily-livered Paraguayan's idea, eh, Colombo?" [160]). Cobito's thoughts and deeds of betrayal, both of himself and others, inspire in all Cobito's acquaintances, and in the reader, only repugnance.

With the exception of Mita, all these narrator-characters participate in the gradual process of estranging the reader, despite the pathetic insufficiency of their existence. In Mita, the reader finds an impressive array of what Western civilization considers virtuous characteristics. Even in her failings she reflects the reader's own tendencies. Only the context in which her monologue appears inhibits her total alliance with the reader. The absence of a unifying voice in these six interior-monologue chapters pulverizes the text. The discontinuous narrative surface spawns an epistemological relativity (Who is telling the truth? How do we know?) that fosters ambivalence and estrangement in the reader.[9]

Section 3: Represented Writings

XII	XIII	XIV	XV	XVI	END

The third and final section of the novel consists in various written texts: Esther's diary, José "Toto" Casals' prizewinning essay, the anonymous letter to the Dean of Students, the entry in Herminia's commonplace book, and Berto's letter to his brother Jaime. Except the final chapter, which like the first two is dated 1933, the chapters move chronologically from 1947 to 1948.

9. The possible sexual connotations of the absent narratorial voice are discussed in Alicia Borinsky, "Castración y lujos: La escritura de Manuel Puig," *Revista Iberoamericana* 41, no. 90 (1975): 29–46; see also Augusto C. Sarrocchi, "Sobre el narrador de *La traición de Rita Hayworth*," *Signos* 9–10 (1973–74): 95–104.

As with the "introverted" chapters, the character who narrates the text commands more attention than do his subjects. But since these chapters represent not only thoughts, but thoughts rendered in writing, there is an additional mediating factor to consider: the writer's relation to his text. While the novel dwells within the minds of the various characters (chapters III, V–XI), there is at least an assurance of spontaneity in what appears on the printed page. The narrator has no power to manipulate the reader—of whom the narrator is oblivious. In these "extroverted" chapters, however, each narrator has had the opportunity to formulate a textual strategy. The reader must therefore proceed with heightened alertness to the possible rhetorical tactics being deployed. What is suppressed, for example, becomes as significant as what is mentioned. And the disposition of elements within the text can no longer be taken for granted as a feature incidental to the "contents." In short, the reader, in his traditional search for what "really happens" in the novel, runs squarely into the presence of a fictional author. As authors are known to invent, select, or edit data, the reader must confront the inevitability of a degree of falsification in writing.[10]

Written texts represented in the novel also bring to bear the writer's style as a factor in creating narrative irony. Now that the character has chosen to write, how does he do it? Are his metaphors apt or do they undermine his professed purposes in writing? Does he have control of his pen, or does it run away from him? Along with the character's attitude the reader can now judge his competency. More than ever, then, "form" is a major factor in the "theme" of any given passage. The introduction of writing as a mediating factor in the final five chapters implies a potentially greater distance between the reader and the text. The thematic alienation established in chapters I–XI is set within a newly tenuous context, and this greater complexity lends additional dimension to the novel's narrative irony.

Esther, the narrator in chapter XII, is more appealing than many of the other young characters. She displays generosity (albeit theoretical, since the bicycle she would like to buy for her nephew is contingent upon her becoming a doctor), gratefulness (toward the principal of the school that has offered her a scholarship), and love

---

10. For a more thorough explanation of the falsification inherent in writing, see chapter 4, especially pp. 122–23.

for her parents. As the bright and ambitious daughter of a lower-class family, she knows that school represents her only chance to better herself and others ("How beautiful it is to be useful to humanity" [180]).

But as with so many other characters in the novel, Esther says too much, and in so doing, nullifies the good will she initially inspires. The first thing that might put the reader off is her wholesale acceptance of the Peronist-populist party line, not because of her political leanings as such (the implied reader is apolitical or polypolitical while reading), but because of her indiscriminate and ingenuous parroting of someone else's terminology and reasoning. One cannot read "Work is holy, and thus the worker is sanctified, his sweat bathes him in divine grace" (181) without being struck by the melodramatic naiveté of the statement.

In contrast to Esther's ingenuous grasp of politics, however, her style shows her to be a cautious, even guarded author. When she tells of the one wish she would cherish above all others, she writes: "Four letters rose to my throat, intoxicated me like a sip of the strongest grappa, and one more foolish teenager . . . asked for Love" (170). By using the self-deprecatory expression "foolish teenager" she shows her awareness of the innocent idealism in her wish for Love (raised by its capital L to its most sublime essence). This gesture, of course, makes her not quite so innocent as the expression might indicate, but it still allows her to hold onto that romantic sentiment. Later Esther's self-critical tendency grows to the point where she can hardly state anything without simultaneously commenting on it: "If in days past I have seen myself emaciatingly thin (egoism devours), or dishevelledly ridiculous (dreams mess up my hair), today I would like to see myself not pretty (isn't that already progress?) but with an immaculately white apron (no plaits, nor vain adornments, just snowy white)" (179). Because she is insufficiently critical in life and perhaps too coy in matters of art, no communion obtains between Esther and the reader.

The narrator of chapter XIII, José L. Casals, takes a less ironical stance before his writing. The essay he submits to the annual literary competition demonstrates none of the sophisticated hedging of Esther's diary entries, and even contains open admissions of puzzlement and wonder ("There is something that escapes my understanding" [188]). There are, in addition, examples of awkward constructions ("Carla . . . retires to do her toilet" [187]), too obvious symbolic interpretations ("Carla is white like snow, the symbol of purity" [189]), and occasional prolixity ("And then comes the yellow of the daisies, which blossom without anybody planting them and appear without having to look for them, like good news when you least expect it, and the color of the oranges, which are already ripe by summer, is very appropriately called orange" [188]), all of which contribute to the impression of an amateur writer at work. The reader can lower his defenses and absorb freely what Toto has to say about "The Movie I Liked Best."

But like every seemingly nonironic situation in the novel, this one is subverted by its context. The subversion consists in, among other things, statements made by other characters about the essay's author, Toto. Esther reports that "Casals says that the best thing for overnight students is to study so that time goes by more easily" (168). And Cobito, when he asks, "Why the fuck do you study so much, Casals?" gets the response, "Time goes by faster that way" (151). Even if we were to distrust these narrators (suspicion has been raised as to their reliability), Toto's own unspoken words elsewhere are certainly worthy of greater confidence. In chapter V he says to himself, "What can I draw until three o'clock? Naptime is the biggest bore" (53), and later, "Now I'm going to draw the posters of a detective movie and naptime never ends" (67). These passages point to one thing: Toto's creative pursuits are in large measure an escape, a flight from boredom. There is reason to believe, therefore, that the prizewinning essay, too, is nothing more than an attempt to find diversion from the monotony of his existence. Most telling of Toto's objectionable motives is his later confession to Herminia that he dislikes Romantic music, when Strauss, the hero of the movie he describes, is the quintessential Romantic composer. What appears to be a novitiate's sincere attempt at expression thus manifests itself indirectly as the work of a prematurely jaded pragmatist, one who cares little what he puts on paper, as long as it covers the page and fills the time.

Chapter XIV, the shortest of the novel, represents an anonymous letter from an irate student to the Dean of Students of George Washington High School. The letter is so vitriolic that an assessment as to the veracity of its allegations is impossible. This indeterminacy tends again to displace the reader's focus onto the writer of the letter. And while the writer's identity is uncertain, the reader is not bereft of clues leading to the outraged and outrageous author's name. The tone of the letter is, to put it mildly, offensive. It calls the Dean "big shot," ridicules his judgment of Toto as the best student ("getting back to Casals the brat, that little louse also happens to be addicted to strange habits" [198]), and is inappropriately and insultingly familiar ("It looks like you put your foot in it this time," "Let me open your eyes," etc. [197]). It also makes free use of obscenities and finishes with the facetious phrase "spiritual father." All these clues point to one suspect: Cobito Umansky.

The letter is consistent with Cobito's fondness for pranks. He himself relates in chapter XI the unsuccessful coup he attempted with Colombo on Toto (159–60). The reader also knows, through Esther, that Cobito has been expelled from school for insulting a supervisor (176). The abusive language of the letter, moreover, corresponds to the general linguistic register of Cobito's interior monologue, and the expression "spiritual father" appears in his chapter three times in reference to the Dean (154, 156, 160). The case against him is substantial.

And yet, none of the above proves anything. It can be argued convincingly that the letter was contrived to appear as if Cobito had written it in order—in the criminal jargon of the character and the cinematic terminology of the novel—to "frame" him. Assuming the chronological order of the chapters to be intact, has he not established an alibi in his absence from school when this letter appears? The sinister scribe could be any number of students known to the reader (the Paraguayan, Esther, Toto himself), or even someone completely unknown (new characters often appear unceremoniously). The reader is free to suspect whomever he wishes, but he must ultimately admit that he will never be positive about the letter-writer's identity. In more than one sense the note inscribes an insurrection against "authority" and, in so doing, provides the reader with a sample of the insufficiency that plagues so many of the novel's characters.

Herminia's book of thoughts, reproduced in chapter XV, is the most recently written document in the novel. It provides a final glimpse of the characters who appear throughout, although, once again, their portrait is tinted by the very personal colors of the narrator. In this case, the predominant shade is a gray that corresponds to the bleak outlook of the asthmatic and aging spinster (as she sees herself). Her chapter marks a nadir in the spiral of disenchantment in which all the characters are to some extent caught.

Herminia's "philosophy" of life is that "strength consists in living without thinking" (210). This appears to be more than empty rhetoric, for her meandering text indicates that she writes automatically, without thinking about where she is going or where she has come from. Then, periodically, when she realizes how she has rambled, as in "Unintentionally, I have gone off on a tangent" (201), she corrects herself, only to lapse shortly thereafter into another digression. Not thinking is Herminia's way of escaping her misery, which she attributes to her poverty. She recognizes that she has hardly experienced life, but in her state of ill health she wishes only to be submerged in permanent forgetfulness. She dismisses suicide because "I don't want to go on to the next life to keep on suffering" (209). Where the lives of others are concerned, however, she sees only the positive aspects. She describes Toto as "a boy who has everything in life" (206) and focuses on all the Casals' shiny, luxurious possessions. In spite of her effort to confront life unflinchingly, she does maintain that the middle-class ethic is the way to happiness ("I would change places with any housewife, and have my own house, radio, bathroom, and a husband who's not too common, who's tolerable, that's all" [204]). And despite her pessimism she does have experiences which she herself admits are positive ("I don't know if it was for the anger or what but I sat down to play Beethoven's 'L'Aurore' and it came out better than ever" [213]). Whether it is through her envious assessment of the lives of others, her unreflective attachment to a questionable ideal, or her refusal to tally the positive aspects in her present life, Herminia explodes every proposition she posits. If there is a point where this novel makes contact with Rulfo's *Pedro Páramo,* it is here in Herminia's desperate negativism.

Nonetheless, the reader has no choice but to depend on her for a parting (albeit partial) view of the characters. Mita and Berto are shown to be affluent and outwardly harmonious. Héctor still fornicates as much as possible, lately with Delia. Paquita announces her engagement at the age of seventeen to a bank teller, and Toto develops into an atheistic pedant whom Herminia judges to be somewhat effeminate. No one dies; no one triumphs. At the chronological end point of the novel, in fact, nothing of consequence is resolved. No indication is given as to what the future of the characters will be like, unless Herminia herself is to be the embodiment of that dismal future. Since her physical ailments qualify her as a special case, however, that inference need not be drawn. Irony, which chiefly takes the shape of contradiction in *The Death of Artemio Cruz* and of nihilism in *Pedro Páramo*, manifests itself here as inconclusiveness.[11] The novel's irony is an aimless drifting that gives rise to both parody and satire, for as *Betrayed by Rita Hayworth* offers implicit commentary on formulaic celluloid texts it also questions a broad spectrum of sociopsychic norms.[12]

The one frequently mentioned character whose voice is not heard until the very last chapter is Berto. And even then, typically, he does not fully avail himself of the chance. Consistent with his belief that expressing one's feelings is a sign of weakness, he indicates in the letter to his brother Jaime that he will tear the letter up after writing it (222). The reader, then, knows what Jaime will never know, that Berto is full of rancor, not just over Jaime's not writing but also because of his interference years before with Berto's education. The characters in this scene are thus triply distanced: in their geographic locales (Jaime is in Spain, Berto in Argentina), in Berto's resentment toward his older brother, and in his inability to communicate his acrid sentiments.

Consistent with other reports, too, one can observe a similar impasse between Berto and Mita. He eavesdrops on Mita's conversation with her sister Adela, becomes enraged with her for not defending him against Adela's allegations ("Mita should have stopped her short and told her to go to hell, and she didn't say anything, she almost seemed to agree" [221]), and then lets his anger well up within him. He shunts onto others the obligation to guess his emotional state, in spite of his every effort to keep that state masked. Berto's repressed anger could have been shown in an

11. This insufficiency is explored in David R. Southard, "Betrayed by Manuel Puig: Reader Deception and Anti-Climax in His Novels," *Latin American Literary Review* 4, no. 9 (1976): 22–28.

12. For the sense in which one can view the work as a satire but not as a parody see Alfred J. MacAdam, *The Dreams of Reason: Modern Latin American Narratives* (Chicago: University of Chicago Press, 1977), pp. 91–101.

interior monologue, but the unsent letter, which dramatizes the act of *not* communicating, is a more effective manner of presenting the barrier that insulates him from the other characters and from the reader: the unspoken word.

As in chapters IX–XI, a majority of the narrators in this third section of the novel is male.

What emerges from a chapter-by-chapter analysis is that each character in *Betrayed by Rita Hayworth* muddles through a solitary, boring, drab existence. Even Mita, the one character given a kind of treatment that could endear her to the reader, is engulfed by the relentless despair conveyed in the second half of the novel and by the bitter last glimpse of her in Berto's letter. In order to grasp the extent of Puig's artistry by capturing the manner in which the structure itself reflects these thematic concerns, it is necessary to resurrect my periodic cryptic references to sexuality. In the process, I hope to show how the three sections of the novel (according to their narrative mode) elide into the two parts designated by the author (in the original Spanish version) and to demonstrate in what sense these remaining two parts finally fuse into one.

Part I of the novel and Mita are analogous in so many ways that their relation comes to be metaphorical. Mita is, first of all, the character who appears or is mentioned most often in part I, and her chapter occupies the important position at its conclusion. In addition, she displays the indomitable hope inherent in youth (even after tragedy strikes she can think only of creating more life), a stage of life that coincides with the time period spanned in part I (the first ten years of the novel). Moreover, and most significant, she is a woman (Mita = *mito femenino*). All the narrators in part I (except Toto, a prepubescent, latently homosexual male) are female, as are most of the characters in the chapters without narrators. And beyond that thematic presence, part I bears structural characteristics that make it emblematic of the female sex in physiological terms. That is, the narrational mode of the chapters moves from dialogues (I, II, and IV) to streams of consciousness (III, V–VIII), thus inscribing an introversion, a textual invagination.

Part II, in contrast, is older (it spans the last five years of the novel) and more cynical (the trend toward increasing disillusionment and despair has already been traced). It is to be identified metaphorically with Berto, whose chapter stands at its conclusion, in opposition to Mita's. In addition to Berto's presence, the masculinity of part II is derived from its predominantly male narrators and the movement of its narrative perspective from the stream of consciousness (chapters IX–XI) to various forms of written expression (XII–XVI), a turning outward that corresponds to the phallus.

We can observe further that the second part, associated with the man, functions in accordance with the stereotypical male social role. It pricks the balloon of illusions set afloat in part I, the novel's female analogue. Berto's conjugal role is characterized not so much by *penetración* (penetration) as by *pene-traición* (penis betrayal). His marriage is fraught with friction, a friction caused by the antagonistic fusion of parts. And, naturally, conceived in the disharmonious union of the female and male halves is the offspring Toto, the *todo* (whole), the new totality that is more than the sum of its parent components and embodies the contradictions and insufficiency of their intercourse.

Betrayed by Rita Hayworth effaces the distinction between primary and secondary characters. In spite of appearing in every chapter (by denotation or allusion), Toto cannot be deemed the novel's principal character. The text is so imbued with his presence that he is associated instead with the sum of its parts: the novel itself. The resulting androgynous text is ironic in its lack of a unifying narrative voice, in the estrangement of its mediocre characters and its beleaguered reader, and in its ambivalent appropriation of consumer-oriented artifacts. It is also ironic in the self-conscious and polysemous senses of the word, for as it portrays humdrum small-town Argentine life, it also unveils itself as its own protagonist.

CHAPTER 4

Three Trapped Tigers:
The Absent Voice in the Gallery

Three Trapped Tigers,[1] by the Cuban exile Guillermo Cabrera
Infante, and Manuel Puig's *Betrayed by Rita Hayworth*, with their
many references to the film world, reflect the strong influence of
Hollywood culture on Latin America in the 1930s to 1950s. Like
Puig's characters in *Rita Hayworth*, those of Cabrera Infante favor
the cinematic universe over the prosaic details of daily life, fully
aware that they prefer, as one critic has put it, the "reel" to the
"real."[2] But the motif is treated differently in *Three Trapped Tigers*. The film critic Andrew Sarris points out: "Puig, who was born
in 1932, has managed to will himself into the time of his own
infancy and childhood up to the time of his adolescence whereas
Cabrera Infante has limited himself to that point in history at which
he came of age and class consciousness."[3] Cabrera Infante also uses
a "shotgun" method of presentation, mentioning myriad titles of
films and stars almost in series, creating a glossy surface beneath

1. Page references, included parenthetically in the text, are to the first U.S.
edition, translated by Donald Gardner and Suzanne Jill Levine in collaboration with
the author (New York: Harper & Row, 1971). The Spanish version of the novel was
first published by Seix Barral in its definitive form and under the present title of *Tres
tristes tigres* in 1967.
2. Phyllis Mitchell, "The Reel against the Real: Cinema in the Novels of Guillermo Cabrera Infante and Manuel Puig," *Latin American Literary Review* 6, no. 11
(1979): 22–29. Mitchell's argument, in short, is that "the immediacy projected by
the film deceives [the characters] into thinking that what is in front of their eyes must
be the reality for which they are searching, especially since it is so much more
appealing than the reality which actually surrounds them" (28).
3. Andrew Sarris, "Rerunning Puig and Cabrera Infante," *Review* 73 (Fall
1973): 47–48.

which he rarely probes. Along with nightclubs, gambling casinos, fast cars, and strong rum, film fits into a general pattern of escapes available to the inhabitants of pre-Castro Havana. Within such a richly varied scheme, no single movie appears to merit detailed attention.

One may speculate on the factors that could account for the distinctions: the temporal setting of *Rita Hayworth*, approximately fifteen years earlier than that of *Three Trapped Tigers;* its author's greater distance from North America's driving pace; the fewer numbers of movies and other diversions from which to choose in the provincial town of Coronel Vallejos; and, not least, Puig's introspective temperament. These forces coalesce somehow to allow Puig to deal with each film in a more extended and complex manner. Whole scenes and plots of films are evoked and examined in *Rita Hayworth,* as if there were nothing better to do. The baroque superfluity of stimulus in *TTT,* however (an ingredient which displeases Sarris[4]), need not be considered a flaw in the work. It is, among other things, an accurate linguistic mirroring of a basic quality of mid-twentieth-century urban existence.

Beyond the obvious mediating element of the movies, Cabrera Infante's work shares many narrative devices with *Betrayed by Rita Hayworth,* producing difficulties for the reader similar to those discussed in chapter 3. Both authors use effectively the technique of placing before the reader's eyes, with little introduction or explanation, a series of fragmented and discontinuous texts (Cabrera Infante is even less helpful, in this respect, than Puig). The significance of a passage is allowed to emerge through its context, a context that it in turn enhances. As in Puig's novel, in *Three Trapped Tigers* the reader is often victimized by a playful author, who conceals the identity of the narrator and the eventual outcome (if any) of the episodes.

Another common feature of the two works is the predominance (in *TTT* the omnipresence) of the first-person point of view. Cabrera Infante's much-mentioned "gallery of voices,"[5] as it recap-

4. Sarris, "Rerunning," "I feel that Puig has been more successful in distilling his sensibility for the task at hand whereas Cabrera Infante's sensibility spills all over his characters" (p. 48).
5. See Rita Guibert, "The Tongue-Twisted Tiger," *Review* 72 (Winter–Spring 1972): 14.

tures the speech of prerevolutionary nocturnal Havana, creates a network of limited perspectives, causing instances of cancellation or reinforcement of one version of an incident by another. The value of the therapy administered in the continuing saga of the woman who talks to her psychiatrist (ultimately identified as Laura), for instance, is severely undermined by Cué's casual remark, "Psychiatry leads to disaster" (434). (The extent of the subversion depends on Cué's credibility, admittedly not overwhelming.) The good looks of Vivian Smith-Corona, on the other hand, are attested to by both Eribó and Cué, establishing that fact as the truth within the confines of the novel.

Both works, moreover, constitute what appears to be a rambling, amorphous narrative mass. *Three Trapped Tigers* consists of a "Prologue," followed by eight chapters of unpredictable length ("Mirrormaze," narrated by Arsenio, is 38 pages long; Silvestre's "Bachata" is 157), and a 1-page "Epilogue." Within the chapters are several serialized narratives (the psychiatric sessions; Códac's story about Estrella Rodríguez, "I Heard Her Sing"), as well as some more traditionally continuous narratives (Eribó's seven-part history in "Seseribó"; the stories in "Vae Visitors"; the major part of "Bachata"; Códac's homage to Bustrófedon in "Brainteaser," etc.). The surface irregularity of the text, coupled with the absence of conventional plot and character development, contribute to the reader's sense of chaos and anarchy within the novel. It is a sense not dissimilar to that experienced by the reader of *Pedro Páramo,* but note the different manners of causation: instead of a relator who gradually conditions the reader to lose himself in a structure of death (see chapter 2), here we have a chorus of narrators who cannot agree on the key in which they sing. The cacophonous narration is termed by Códac as a "caos concéntrico": a confusing game that is ruled by a principle whose main characteristic is absence.

By discussing only the similarities between Puig's and Cabrera Infante's two novels, one risks making them appear more nearly identical than they really are. The two offer unique reading experiences. In addition to its relative linguistic and formal moderation, *Betrayed by Rita Hayworth* is distinguished by what might be termed "psychological realism." Puig gives each of his characters a microphone and, faithful to the mimetic principle, allows each to show how he or she arrives at personal disillusionment. Cabrera Infante, in contrast, is not concerned with creating a lifelike portrait of how people act or think, though he does take pains to reproduce their manner of speech. He practices, in fact, a self-conscious artificiality that never allows the reader to forget that he is dealing with personae, not persons.

One way Cabrera Infante avoids psychological realism is to suspend cause-and-effect relationships, allowing the characters to act inconsistently or without apparent motivation, as Códac does in the following passage:

> *I don't know what I said to him* about his missing molar of a boss because now I was drinking not coffee but a rum on the rocks not the beach rocks as you might imagine but bar rocks and *I thought I would phone* Magalena and when I got into the phone booth *I remembered I didn't have her number* but then I saw a whole telephone directory written over the walls and I selected a number because in any case *I had already inserted a coin* and I dialed it and waited while the phone rang and rang and rang and finally I heard a man's voice very weak and tired say Hello? and I said, Is that you, Hellen? and the man replied in his voice that wasn't a voice, No, señor and I asked him Who then, her sister? and he said, Hello hello and I said Ah so you're a double Hellen, and he said, almost screaming, What's the idea, waking people up at this time of the night! and *I told him to go fuck his missing molar* and hung up and picked up my fork and began cutting up my steak very carefully. [296–97, italics mine]

The sudden impulse to call Magalena, whose number he does not know, reveals Códac's capriciousness. He is no less capricious in his narrating. His reason for dialing a stranger's number is obviously false, for he could easily hang up and repossess his coin. Choosing a number at random, he asks for an imaginary woman whose name is likely to be confused with the greeting "hello," then acts as if it were the other party's fault for not being the one he wanted. He closes with an obscenity that only he himself could decipher, as the missing molar refers to the barkeeper's boss, who has no connection at all with the scene in the phone booth. The incident ends with his return to his steak, as if none of the preceding action had even occurred. Character, narrator, and author are obviously playing whimsically, doing as they please despite social and literary conventions. Nowhere does such an alignment of gratuitous elements occur in Puig's novel, which along several axes belongs to a different mode of narrative fiction.

The gratuitously playful character and largely semantic interest of the novel has not always won accolades. Shortly after *TTT* first appeared, Julio E. Miranda wrote:

> What pure and simple foolishness, what amusement for Cabrera Infante, who claims—perhaps he doesn't even claim—to justify blank pages, little sketches, pages written backwards or filled with a single word repeated over and over, very long pedantic-humoristic dialogues, with the development of a supposed narration. Because there is no such thing, there is no narration, there are no characters—if we make an exception of Estrella and some others—; Arsenio Cué, Silvestre and Ribot are one and the same, uniform without personal substance. Each one recounts his parts of the novel, and they think alike, they say the same banalities, they play the same word games. They are, when all is said and done, Cabrera Infante speaking and speaking of himself.[6]

Miranda's summary evaluation should not be allowed to stand as the last word. His ill-founded premise that literature can make a statement only through positing, and not through negating, is a narrow critical view that eliminates the possibility of appreciating a work like *Tristram Shandy*, whose presence can be felt throughout Cabrera Infante's novel. Moreover, the obviously hurried and inaccurate manner of Miranda's reading not only prevents him from perceiving differences between the characters, but also leads him to refer confusedly to "the photographer Ribot"[7]: the photographer is, appropriately, named Códac, while Ribot, also punningly called Vincent Bon Gogh by his friends, is a commercial artist and bongo player. Confusions aside, the characters in *Three Trapped Tigers* are precisely and consistently delineated. Mapping the distinctions between them, in effect, is the necessary first step toward understanding the immense linguistic game constituted by *Three Trapped Tigers*.

6. Julio E. Miranda, *Cuadernos hispanoamericanos* 74, no. 220 (1968): 204. The translation is mine.
7. Miranda, *Cuadernos*, p. 203.

Static Irony

Arsenio Cué is an actor with a mania for speed. As Silvestre describes him, "Cué had this obsession with time. What I mean is that he would search for time in space, and they were nothing but a search, our continual, interminable journeys along the Malecón" (320). He wants to move through space so swiftly that time cannot catch him, to live in an eternal present, unbothered either by memories or by thoughts of the future. Arsenio's escapism, Silvestre tells us, manifests itself in a taste for the artificial:

> We took a turn to the left, and rode parallel to the sea, like the canals of this rich man's Venice whose happy owners could keep their automobiles in the carport and their motor launches in the yacht port and feel hemmed in by all you need for the flight. I knew this was the paradise of the Cués. The project (or its realization) was false, or fictitious, but like everything in this country nature lent it its true beauty. [345–46]

Another distinctive characteristic of Cué is his belief in the truth of numbers, of which he says, "It's almost the only thing I do believe in. Two and two will always be four and the day they make five, start running" (338). Silvestre concurs, saying, "Arsenio Cué was as much enamored of numbers as he was of himself" (354). Significantly, Cué's favorite number, which he considers to be El Número, is 3, the number that appears in the title and also the number of letters in his name. An important characteristic of Cué's, his affinity for violence, is demonstrated three times: when he crushes Tony's fingers at the country club swimming pool (99–100), when he threatens to join Fidel Castro's revolutionary forces as a guerrilla (374–75), and when he assaults the Frenchman in the nightclub urinal (465–66).

Silvestre, who shares many experiences with Cué certainly perceives these experiences differently. Of Cué he says, "While we were going over space he succeeded in evading what he always avoided, I think, which was to go over another space outside of time. Or to be precise—remembering. The opposite of me, because I like remembering things better than living them or living things knowing they can never be lost because I can always evoke them again" (321). Silvestre's job as film critic with the magazine *Carteles* allows him, like Proust, to evoke the past in his writing (the totally present nature of acting, it might be added, is remarkably well suited to Cué's temporal obsession as well). But Silvestre's cinemania goes beyond his job. He frequently reduces his experiences to the two-dimensionality of a movie screen: "I saw the canals, the roadsteads and the sea filing slowly past and finally I saw that the bar and the swamp and the vegetation all merged in one dimension and although there was a variety of color and I remembered everything as I had seen it just before, in depth, the light vibrated over the landscape and I felt I was in a movie" (346). At other times he couches his descriptions in film terminology: "There are times when I think it could be the beginning of a fadeout and that someday a black light will be projected on my screen. A thing that will happen sooner or later, but I'm talking about blindness not death. This total blackout will be the worst possible fate for my movie eyes—but not for the eyes of memory" (328). As he narrates, Silvestre reveals his belief that life is nothing more than a full-length technicolor extravaganza with a cast of millions. In addition, Silvestre is less of a pedantic punster than Cué (Magalena tells him so on p. 428), and, as a member of the same profession as the deceased Bustrófedon, sees himself as the latter's disciple in the world of words.

The mulatto drummer Ribot does not share the sensibilities of Cué and Silvestre. He is more interested in playing his drums ("When I start playing I forget everything else" [94]), or having sex with Cuba Vanegas or Vivian Smith-Corona, than in the interminable and desultory word play that enchants the others. Although his character receives less exposure than the other "tigers," there is sufficient evidence for a sexual rivalry between him and Cué. At one point Ribot says, "I saw plenty of Arsenio Cué and my friend Silvestre" (96), implying that Cué is not the friend that his old high-school classmate is. Elsewhere Ribot comments that Cué "was confronting the world, petulant, pedantic, and pathetic" (94). Cué, in turn, refers condescendingly to the drummer as "a poor fellow" (468), who could not take Vivian to bed "because he's a mulatto, and, what's worse, because he's poor" (469). Cué and Ribot are not only distinct characters but, in several respects, opposed to each other; their mutual antipathy is overt.

The fourth member of the circle (there are five in all) is Códac, who earns his living by going from nightclub to nightclub taking pictures. His special passion is for the singer Estrella Rodríguez, whom he calls "The Black Whale," a parodical reference to Melville's seagoing leviathan. The explanation for his obsession with the gargantuan woman could reside in what Silvestre observes as "Códac's temptation wanting all the women to have a single vagina" (343), the need to search for the biggest, most absolute, and total center of life, of which La Estrella is the incarnation. Códac, moreover, is the coiner of the phrase "in every actor there is an acress struggling to get out" (329), an apparent swipe at Cué (does anyone in the novel like Cué?), who is distinguished from the photographer by his constant running away from, rather than seeking, the authentic and the vital.

Miranda's charge that all the characters are the same is simply not true. Though all of them are artists of one sort or another (Ribot is a drummer; Cué, an actor; Códac, a photographer; and Silvestre, a writer), their differences are ineradicable. Sarris' objection that Cabrera Infante's characters "dissolve into a series of stylistic options"[8] can actually be taken as unintentional praise: *Three Trapped Tigers* shows that characterization is nothing more than different arrangements of words, each "personality" depending upon a distinct linguistic subsystem.

It is possible, in fact, to find passages in which the characters define themselves merely through the stylistic options that they exercise. The following passage is typical of Ribot, for example:

> I played and played and I saw Arsenio Cué call the waiter and ask for the check and I went on and on and on and I saw him wake up Silvestre and playing I saw the swarthy, skinflint writer get up and begin to go out with Vivian and Sibila supporting his arms and I went on playing as Cué was paying all that money by himself and playing the waiter came back and Cué gave him a tip which must have been a good one judging by the waiter's satisfied face playing and I saw him go away as well and all of them meet up at the door and the doorman opening the crimson curtains and playing they crossed the classy well-lighted gambling saloon and the curtain closed on, behind them playing. They didn't even say so much as bye-bye. But I didn't care because I was playing and I went on playing and I continued to go on playing for a good while longer. [95–96]

8. Sarris, "Rerunning," p. 47.

The repetition of "playing" shows how much Ribot becomes involved with the ongoing action (the present participle appears unusually often throughout his narration). In addition, the sense of the repeated verb provides a graphic example of a tenet of the novel: one can tell a tale and never stop playing. The "playing" simultaneously marks the rhythm which flows through his Afro-Cuban blood, that rhythm being also the cause for his solitude ("They didn't even say so much as bye-bye"), which he ultimately accepts.

Here is a passage typical of Cué:

> Livia turns her shortsighted look on him [Silvestre] first and then her arrogant look and then her look of a femme fatale and then her look of acknowledgment and then her enchanting look and then her charmed look: Livia, as you can see, has quite an arsenal of looks, which, if they could be traded for hand grenades, would turn her eyes into the magazine of one of Batista's barracks. *You* she said, removing the pin of the look she keeps for the assault on well-known strangers and at the count of seven throwing it at Silvestre. The fused stare blows right in his face: *You must be one of Arsen's intellectual friends, aren't you?* [140, italics in original]

As a professional actor he is aware of how facial expressions can be changed to suit the occasion (Arsenio could detect no less than an arsenal of expressions), revealing nothing of what lies beneath the surface. Aside from his use of italics instead of quotation marks (a sign of petulant pedantry?), his narrations are characterized by the discontinuous spoken line ("You. . . . You must be . . .") by which (always the egotist) he draws attention to himself as narrator and underlines the split personality of the actor who forgets what he was before he began playing roles.

Códac's singularity is revealed to a large extent in his descriptions, like the following:

> La Estrella kept sliding off my body and climbing back onto it again making unbelievably weird noises, as if she were singing and snoring at the same time and in between her groans she was speaking to me, whispering, gasping in her rasping baritone *mi amor* please kiss me *mi negro* please kill me *mi chino* come come come, things which would have made me die laughing if I'd been able to breathe and I pushed her

with what strength I had left, using a half-crushed leg as a fulcrum and making a springboard not of the bed but of the wall (because I'd been driven back against the wall by that expansion wave of fat, flattened, almost obliterated by that black universe that was expanding in my direction at the speed of love), I managed to give her a final big push and succeeded in putting her off balance and out of bed, *my* bed. She fell on the floor and there she stayed puffing and panting and sobbing but I leaped out of bed and switched on the light and then I *saw* her. She was stark naked and her breasts were as fat as her arms and twice as large as my head, and one of them fell over on one side and touched the floor and the other jutted out over the central breaker of the three great rollers that separated her legs from what would have been her neck if she had had one. [162–63]

The object of his narration, the bigger-than-life singer Estrella Rodríguez, with whom he has become obsessed, does not pose quietly, but leaps from the picture into the reality of the photographer, overwhelming him with her mass. Códac cannot maintain esthetic distance in the first half of the passage, and so he can give only the sound impressions (noises, singing, snoring, groans) he receives. Too much is happening at once for him to set off her words with appropriate punctuation, and he is too close, too involved with the matter to laugh (laughter being a basic distancing mechanism). It is not until he musters all his strength and throws her back that he can gain the perspective that allows a visual description, which then is as graphic and detailed as we would expect of one with a trained eye. Códac is a searcher, passionate and sensual, who is attracted by the repulsive, which he then must reject in order to integrate it into his art.

The most self-conscious and prolific narrator is Silvestre. Although all the "tigers" are able craftsmen, only Silvestre is a writer by profession. His narrative personality is encapsuled in this passage:

I was teaching my brother to ride a bike one day and I pushed him very hard and he went off at full speed and crashed into a bench and the handlebars hit him in the chest and he fainted and vomited blood, he was like dead for half an hour or maybe ten minutes, I don't know. But what I did know was that it was I who had done it and a year or two later when my brother got TB I continued to think that it was all my fault. I told Cué about it, then. I mean now. [327]

The story he tells of his brother's injury shows the development of his literary values through time. What once brought him sadness and guilt feelings is now merely the "content" of an anecdote; as he says elsewhere, "It wasn't a moral tale," but "an exercise in nostalgia" (472). The telling of the story is now the object ("I told Cué about it") because it allows him to regain the past and play with it ("then. I mean now."). The jump from ethics to esthetics is underlined by the fact that "now," the present of the narration, is the moment of writing, when he is seated at his typewriter. Since Silvestre is describing a time other than that present (when, in the past, he was riding with Cué), "then" would be the more accurate adverb. By including both terms, however, he lays bare the temporal duplicity inherent in his narration and admits he is writing for the nostalgic joy he derives from the very act.

Perhaps what makes both Sarris and Miranda uneasy is Cabrera Infante's willingness to see his characters as nothing more than "stylistic options," as mere pretexts to use one kind of language and not another. It seems to diminish their ontological importance and, in Ortegan terms, to dehumanize them. Rather than argue that the characters are believable—a stance that would be possible to maintain but hardly worth the trouble with respect to a work not concerned with conventional mimesis—let us take a completely different tack. An appreciation of the novel's artistry and a comprehension of its system are possible only if one accepts this premise: if the characters were not so blatantly "flat," they would not be nearly so sharp a reflector upon the linguistic vehicle by which they exist. Consequently, the work would not be so impressive an affirmation of the primacy of language. Let us consider what that primacy entails.

We have noted that the characters are not always in accord. The way they interact, even those who like each other, is often discordant. One of their favorite games, for instance, involves purposely misunderstanding their interlocutor by choosing the wrong antecedent to a referent. The following passages are typical:

1. (talking about Havana's "walking center which moves")
   (Silvestre): Batista's trying to move it across the bay.
   　(Cué): No future in that. You wait and see.
   (Silvestre): What, Batista's regime? [326]

2. (talking about translators from English to Cuban Spanish)
   (S.): And Alejo? I said, carried away by the literary game and
   gossip.
   (C.): Carpentier?
   (S.): Is there another Alejo?
   (C.): Yes, Antonio Alejo, a painter who is also a friend. (369)
3. (talking about joining the revolutionary forces)
   (C.): I'll be right back. I'm going to the can first.
   (S.): Are you crazy? It's like the Foreign Legion.
   (C.): What? The john?
   (S.): Not the john, dammit. Going to the Sierra, going off to fight.
   [376]

On other occasions the rule is to talk about a theme of which one
companion is ignorant, and to keep him in the dark as long as
possible (Ribot narrates, with Silvestre playing the role of the
scapegoat):

—Come on, what you mean? Silvestre said.
—We don't *mean* anything, I said. I don't know if I said it rudely.—
Just words.
—Quite the reverse, Cué said.—We do mean, words don't.
—Reverse of what? said Silvestre, ritardando.
—Of everything, Cué said.
—What everything? said Silvestre.
I said nothing.
—Silvestre, Cué said,—this fellah (pointing to me) wants to know if
it's true or not.
It was a game of cat and mouse. Of mice and cat.
—Is *what* true? said Silvestre. I continued to say nothing. I kept my
arms folded mentally and physically.
—If it's true that Vivian is an easy lay or bedable. Or if she isn't. [105]

The friendship among the "tigers" is more of an agreement to
allow each to abuse the others verbally (to be the butt of word
games, to permit the speaker to indulge in self-gratifying pronouncements) than to convey thoughts or express feelings. Their
use of language, then, though it requires several participants, is
curiously asocial. Every word uttered turns inward upon the speaker, illustrating his isolation from the others. Their conversations
become verbal chess matches and contests of getting in the last

112

word. Near the end of "Bachata," Silvestre writes determinedly, "I wasn't going to let Arsenio make the last phrase. . . . —You're going to listen to me. It's me who's doing the talking now. *I* am going to have the last word" (469). The relationship among the main characters, in view of the frequency with which they verbalize and the infrequency with which they communicate, could hardly be less intimate.

One member of the clan is obviously missing from the above description of the characters. Despite the fact that this character does not narrate a section of his own, his presence permeates the fabric of the novel. I refer, of course, to the unique Bustrófedon, whose life and life-after-death exist purely at the level of language. In addition to bequeathing his memoirs (four pages of blank paper, pp. 280–83) and a series of parodical tape recordings of celebrated Cuban writers (pp. 237–77), he leaves as a heritage to his friends his incredible punning and word-transforming ability. All the main characters come from the *interior,* the provincial part of Cuba which is not Havana (see, for example, a rare admission of this on p. 327). Their natural manner of speaking, which occasionally erupts through the surface, was not always the trilingual jargon they presently affect. Bustrófedon is their mentor, their guru in the enterprise to erase the last traces of their origin. Sometimes they acknowledge his influence explicitly, as with Códac ("and if I talk like Bustrófedon from now on till the end of time I'm not sorry except that I do it consciously & conscientiously and the only thing I regret is that I can't talk normally and naturally and all the time [by all the time I mean time past as well as time future] like this" [227]) and Silvestre ("We began with a Bu[stro]ffoonery, of course, preposthumous but never too late for this master, the Maestro-phodon, my Maelstromedon, the Ground Maestro" [419]). At other times they simply mimic his method, as when Silvestre plays with the title of a photographic mural: "He, Eve's novelty, Fall. Vale of all Vanity. The valley of Viñales" (371). In either case, by merely opening their mouths, the remaining "tigers" pay homage to Him, the formerly ambulatory lexicon, the generator of their discourse. As occurs at the conclusion of *The Death of Artemio Cruz,* we note here a disirony that reverts at once to an irony on another level: the plenitude implicit in the disciples' loyalty to their master's memory can be inscribed only within a horizon of insuffi-

Static Irony

ciency. Their intimacy is based, paradoxically, on the removal occasioned by Buströfedon's death.

When the main characters assume the role of narrator, they are torn between the nostalgic desire to recreate the past (that which is narrated) and the pleasure of hearing their own voices in the present (the narration). The narrated consists principally of conversations the narrator has overheard or in which he has participated. To a much lesser extent, the narrated also includes some events (rainstorms, Buström's death, Magalena's entrapment with Beba, a waiter's anger, etc.) which serve as stimulus for the numerous conversations. Relating the events presents little difficulty, for it calls upon nothing more than language's traditionally referential function. But the novel's major undertaking—freezing spoken language in its flow—is as impossible as seeing the candle flame after it is extinguished (see the quotation taken from Lewis Carroll in the novel's epigraph).

The inadequacy of the tools with which the narrators must work forces each one to excuse his narrating in the same way: Códac says, "A beauty, ain't it? But you'd have to hear him say it to get the full flavor" (78); Ribot says, "You got to hear Innasio himself singing it" (87); Cué says, "I know I'm making it sound complicated but you would have had to have seen it, seen and heard" (146); and even Silvestre, the professional writer, must admit, "You'd have to hear Arsenio Cué and see the face of the ladies in waiting" (406). The reader, of course, cannot hear the characters' voices and cannot hope to grasp the essence of all the palaver. The status of the dialogue represented in the narration is consequently diminished before the majesty of the narration itself. We thus encounter a justification for the numerous parenthetical interruptions that characterize much of the text. What is lost on the narrated level is compensated for by the narrator's enthusiasm at the discovery of his own voice, an attainable, false, Buström-influenced voice that competes with the past as the reason for writing. Like a person pulling himself up by his own bootstraps, the narration discards its foundation (the past represented in the anecdote). It then becomes its own object of interest, reinforcing itself with each successfully uttered word and generating new words through each reinforcement. The attitude of the narrators toward their anecdote and toward the characters therein is one of indifference, and their relationship is therefore distant.

114

In addition to the high degree of self-consciousness in the narrators, they also show keen awareness of the reader's presence. The narrators address the reader(s) directly ("You who live on the other side of the page" [373]), showing consideration for his or her feelings ("I had remembered all the afternoons of my life [don't bother, I'm not going to list them for you, dear reader]" [329]), or making excuses for the quality of what is narrated ("I could hear the water beating against her breath, an image that has no logic to it, but what do you expect? Nothing had any logic at that moment" [430]). The inclusion of an "explicit reader" within the work underlines the fictional status of the discourse (the narrating voice knows that it exists only in print) and constitutes an attempt to establish a nexus between the textual and extratextual worlds. Much like an amoeba feeding by virtue of its pseudopodia, however, the literary work engulfs the external object (the reader), assimilating it into the novel as another character within the fiction. The explicit reader, then, along with the narrators' verbal self-gratification, stands as an additional barrier between the implied reader and the narrator.

The implied reader, let us recall, is created by the interaction of the text and the social milieu into which the text is launched. Certain of the implied reader's aspects may coincide with the explicitly mentioned reader, depending on the circumstances of the latter's appearance. If the explicit reader is created with values different from those of the community or is attributed with less knowledge of the fictional universe than one could possibly gain from the reading, it is possible for the implied reader to deal ironically with his explicit counterpart. The female reader whom Tristram Shandy addresses as "Madame," who tends to become distracted from her reading and to overlook significant passages, exemplifies such a situation.[9] In the case of *Three Trapped Tigers*, however, the references to the explicit reader are too infrequent and too fleeting for his character to be sufficiently developed in order to permit an evaluation of his competency. The distance between the implied reader and narrator is not dependent on any perceptible difference between the explicit and implied readers. It is rather due to the explicit reader's presence, which introduces an additional fictional layer whose opacity threatens to screen out the central fictions.

9. Lawrence Sterne, *Tristram Shandy* (New York: Signet, 1962), p. 174.

The playful, punning narrators demand a great deal of the implied reader. As in the novels of Fuentes, Rulfo, and Puig, the narrators in *TTT* withhold information that would help the reader. Arsenio, for example, does not reveal his identity in his first narrative (47–54) until the last page. Silvestre, for another, does not reveal what is of capital importance to him, his plans to marry Laura Díaz, until 153 pages have elapsed in "Bachata," although he alludes to her cryptically along the way ("Should I speak to him now or wait till later?" [379, etc.]). What is unique in *Three Trapped Tigers*, however, is how the reader is distanced by a device that does not exploit his relative ignorance of the fictional world.

The reader is frequently subjected to passages that call attention to the possible variants of a word, as illustrated to the extreme in the following:

> I remember one day we'd gone out to eat together, he and Bustrofedonte (which was Rine's name that week, because his name wasn't just Man's Best Friend but also: Rinecerous, Rinaidecamp, Rinaissance, leading to general Rinformation and Rineffulgence followed by a Rinegation and back to Rinessentials and Rinephemera, Rinetcetera, Rineffervescent, Bonofarniente, Bonosirviente, Busnofedante, Bustopedant: rineing ringing the changes on his name to show the ring and range and changes in their friendship. [213–14]

Each of the words that constitute a series of variants on a single neologism represents a stutter in the progress of the spoken sentence, an inability to quit a syntactical category and move on to the next.[10] If this lack of normal progression were represented graphically, the same passage would appear as follows:

> I remember one day we'd gone out to eat together, he and Bustrofedonte (which was Rine's name that week, because his name wasn't just Man's Best Friend but also: Rinecerous,
> Rinaidecamp,
> Rinaissance,

10. Stephanie Merrim, in her excellent study, "A Secret Idiom: The Grammar and Role of Language in *Tres Tristes tigres*," *Latin American Literary Review* 8, no. 16 (1980): 96–117, identifies this tendency in Bustro and in the entire novelistic structure as "aphasia: a contiguity disorder that impedes the metonymic organization of discourse" (105).

leading to general Rinformation and
Rineffulgence followed by a
Rinegation and back to
Rinessentials and
Rinephemera,
Rinetcetera,
Rineffervescent,
Bonofarniente,
Bonosirviente,
Busnofedante,
Bustopedant: rineing ringing the changes
on his name to show the ring and range and changes in their friend-
ship.

In this sort of pasage, the [Bustro]hedonistic narrator conditions the
reader gradually to change his thought pattern from "horizontal" to
"vertical." This means that the normally sequential reading of a
sentence is interrupted by a nonsequential, associative, paradigmatic
reading. The natural conclusion to the process of verticalizing the
text is for it to degenerate into upright columns of self-contained
linguistic units, which is precisely what occurs on pp. 287–89; lists
of names with plural meanings vie with the sentence as the elemental
unit of thought to constitute the text.

Repeated exposure to this phenomenon makes the reader hyper-
conscious of the many senses of any given word and encourages
him to dwell upon the possible rhymes, homonyms, antonyms, one-
letter permutations, and so forth he can conjure up even after the
narrator has stopped punning. The reader's eye

aye

I no longer scans the

page at a regular pace, for the interruption in his reading routine
forces him to be as conscious of the act he performs as the narrator
is of his own. As the referential value of the words becomes ob-
scured behind their emerging wordness, a distinction arises that is
analogous to the one I have drawn between the narration and the
narrated. What is *read* (the normal associations the reader makes
between the language on the page and what that language denotes)
is separated from the reading (the associations and variants he is
encouraged to imagine beyond the text, and his consciousness of

117

being engaged in that imaginative activity). Both the read and the reading may be present in any encounter with written language, but rarely does a text mold the reader to go beyond the text itself and direct him to be so conscious of his role as does *Three Trapped Tigers*. In order for the reader to contemplate his own activity as directed he must divide himself into subject and object, a phenomenon I have termed intra-elemental irony.

The term *vertical reading* is not gratuitously chosen. The narrators call attention to the vertical and horizontal as such when they playfully invert the axes in their descriptions. Silvestre, for example, calls the bathroom mirror in which Cué admires himself "his vertical river" (377), referring of course to Narcissus' mythical pond. Later he relates that Cué "continued to hurtle at full tilt down his horizontal precipice" (384), suggesting that Cué is constantly in some type of lateral free-fall. One of the "tigers'" favorite forms of humor, in fact, is to take a situation and invert the axes in order to come up with something ludicrous. In "Bachata" Cué and Silvestre try desperately to make the girls laugh by attributing imaginary inventions to their friend Rine Leal, two of which are: "—Another invention of this epic epoch is the rubber road for cars with wheels made of concrete or asphalt, according to taste. An accidental discovery to end all accidents" (416); and "—There's also his invention of rolling cities. Instead of you traveling to them it's they that come to the traveler" (416). The motif of switching axes stresses the conventionality of reading and writing lines of prose horizontally. Rather than verticalize the entire text (which would be just as singleminded as an all-horizontal text), the author suggests verticality as an alternative and thereby raises the possibility without falling into an equally confining mode.

As a consequence of the vertical reading, tension builds gradually between the narrator and the reader. Andrew Sarris registers its presence when he says: "It is difficult to imagine a reader whose sensibility could stay afloat through every wave of Cabrera Infante's turbulent ironies."[11] Since the sentence continuity is often broken and the anecdote is diminished in importance, the reader's interest is largely dependent on the local (word-, phrase-, or sentence-length) activity of the narrator. Every successful pun threat-

11. Sarris, "Rerunning," p. 46.

ens to be the last; each new sentence confronts the challenge of being a complete joke, with no support from what precedes or follows, as would be the case in a well-wrought, continuous plot. The jokes in "Bachata" cited above based on axis inverting are met with stony silence (see pp. 411–36), a foreboding prefiguration of the reader's reaction at any given juncture. Besieged by language run amok, the reader, like Magalena and Beba, feels at times that he is being relegated to the back seat while the narrator joyrides orgiastically.

Like Puig in *Betrayed by Rita Hayworth,* Cabrera Infante disappears behind the voices, thoughts, and writings of his characters, refraining from expressing his ideas directly or discursively. But Puig's character Toto at times elaborates artistic theories which are outmoded or ingenuous. Cabrera Infante's characters' pronouncements on esthetics, in contrast, tend more to coincide with the views of the author. Bustrófedon's comments that "the only possible literature was written on walls" and "the other literature should be written on the air, in other words you make it simply by talking" (277–78), and Silvestre's explanation that his tale "wasn't a moral tale, . . . I'd told it for its own sake . . . it was an exercise in nostalgia" (472), are summary explanations of why the novel consists mainly of word play and dialogue, and why it lacks any ostensible ethical or political message. At such a privileged moment of coincidence, the author (who maintains the values), the narrator or character (the vehicle by which the values are posited), and the reader (who is finally fully apprised of the operant creative systems) exist in a direct, nonironic relationship.

But these moments are infrequent and short-lived. They are, moreover, undercut by the written nature of the text in which they appear, for the text can never be "the spoken." And these moments of alignment are further devalued by the author when he intentionally blurs the line between himself and the text. As the signatory of the unprintable letter to Silvestre (474), "GCI" becomes a character in the novel. He is the "explicit author," supposedly responsible for everything that appears in the work, the mirror image of the explicit reader. To confuse further the issue as to who is inside the novel and who is outside, Silvestre shows that he is aware of the novelistic context in which he appears. Referring to Cué's story, which is interrupted before it ends, he says, "His story is on page forty-seven" (458). By including himself as a character in his novel, and then endowing his other creations with knowledge that is ordinarily only the province of the author, Cabrera Infante explodes each apparent disirony at the moment of its genesis.

The presence of the implied author, as that term has been understood so far (the idealized entity that can be inferred from everything that is read; "He is the sum of his choices"[12]), is felt most strongly at the beginning and end of things. At the beginning of every chapter, for instance, are the chapter titles, which indicate both his activity as a denominator and his inclination for puns ("Rompecabezas," for one, translated as "Brainteaser," is both a puzzle and the chapter in which Bustro's cranium is literally broken open by a surgeon). The implied author is also responsible for the unconventional editing that allows Arsenio's story to end with the impression that he is shot to death, only to be continued 404 pages later with the explanation that the shots missed and Cué fainted. We can also credit the author with interrupting Códac's narrative about Bustro's illness (one of the few passages where the narrated is of genuine interest for the ideas it conveys) and inserting Laura Díaz's sixth session with her analyst (173). The reader must hang on through the entire section "Vae Visitors" before returning to Bustro and learning he dies on the operating table. By beginning, ending, and juxtaposing narratives in an unpredictable manner, by withholding information and misleading the reader, the author abuses him in much the same way as in the novels studied previously.

Despite the rambling appearance of the narrative, however, one finds a definite symmetry in the ordering of the parts. A balance is struck, for example, between "Mirrormaze" and "Bachata." The former, whose title promises a reflection, does turn out to be the mirror image of the latter. Both begin with Cué and Silvestre touring Havana in their eternal convertible (or is it their convertible eternity?), but the first is narrated from Cué's point of view ("Silvestre and I were driving my car down O Street" [135]), and the second from Silvestre's ("It will be a pity Bustrófedon didn't come with us because we were going along El Malecón at forty, fifty,

12. Wayne C. Booth, *The Rhetoric of Fiction* (Chicago: University of Chicago Press, 1961), p. 75.

eighty miles an hour" [317]). Similarly, the opening section of "Beginners," in which Laura as a little girl explains how she used to hint at an incident that may never have occurred (and which she never elucidates fully), is mirrored in the epilogue by the crazy woman whose narrative degenerates into silence (no one will listen to an insane person, and without a listener one "cant go no further" [487]). These examples of symmetry exist around a common (absent) center, Bustrófedon, whose ingenious verbal effluvium borders on the insane (he dies of a cerebral malfunction), yet captures listeners and imitators. In all three cases the words become meaningless, or rather find their meaning not in what they refer to, but in their own articulation. This uniformity of ends and center is what leads Cabrera Infante to discard the "Meta-End" he planned to attach to the text, in which the "correct" history of Estrella Rodríguez's death is recounted.[13] Although the comments of the author (whom we may consider a well-informed but certainly not an omniscient reader) are not binding on an understanding of the text, it is reassuring that he claims to have intended what is observable in the work.

The other measure of the author's incomplete detachment is the consistency that can be observed by tracing a single notion and finding its presence at several levels of the work. The number 3, for example, which appears with remarkable frequency and in a wide variety of roles, first catches the reader's eye in the title. Later we find that Cué, in his fascination with numbers, considers 3 *El Número*, not as a symbol of the Trinity but because it is the smallest prime number. An examination of the narrators' styles shows also that whenever a word is repeated, it is repeated twice, as in "come come come" in the passage quoted from Códac (162) and "rang and rang and rang" (297). The number is also assimilated into the characters' word games ("Everything happens in trees, Tarzan would say" [460]). And finally, the characters' relationships form an intricate network of triangles that could serve as the object of a

---

13. The author prefaces the separate publication of his "Meta-End" with these words: "The novelistic fragment that I am sending you is the end of *Tres tristes tigres*. I never included it in the book because there was already too much symmetry to add this parody" (*Alacrán Azul* 1, no. 1 [1970]: 18). The English translation of the "Meta-End" appears in *Latin American Literary Review* 8, no. 16 (1980): 88–95.

study not within the purview of this one: the Cué-Silvestre-Laura triangle (both men fall in love with her); the Cué-Ribot-Vivian triangle (Cué sleeps with her; Ribot would like to); the Cué-Tony-Vivian triangle (Cué tromps on Tony's hand for sleeping with Vivian); and the Cué-Sibila-Tony triangle (Cué and Sibila are sweethearts; Sibila and Tony are sister and brother).

Further consistency is seen in the fact that the author has woven his fabric with false thread throughout. Falseness and artifice characterize the novel, from its smallest unit to its largest. While the "tigers" do differ from one another, and are not "the same as the author," it would be pointless to deny their caricaturesque nature. These obviously artificial creations also relate to each other in a patently false way. As Emir Rodríguez Monegal has observed of Silvestre and Cué, "They speak, they quote, they invent, so as not to talk about what really interests them."[14] Their strained merriment, we might add, is motivated by the fear of confronting the emptiness beneath the surface of their linguistic shield.

All the central characters are artists, that is, creators of illusions, dealers in unreality. Their falsity [falsedad] gains additional relief with the inclusion of the adolescent Vivian Smith-Corona, who precociously assumes an adult role and, therefore, a false age [falsa edad]. She is, however, only one of the many secondary female characters, most of whom are described in terms of their physical appearance (Cuba Vanegas, Magalena, Livia, Irenita) and are devout users of masking cosmetics. And when the central characters assume the role of first-person narrator, they continue their false ways by attempting to cloak their provincial origins in a Bustrófedon-inspired, ahistorical, cosmopolitan voice.

The novel's setting, nocturnal Havana, consists of scores of vinyl-and-formica, air-conditioned nightclubs like the Tropicana. It is representative of the many escapes available to participants in Havana's night life. Some others that appear with some frequency are the sundry Hollywood productions, which portray an existence that never existed, as well as alcohol and harder drugs, which tend to repress unpleasant reflections on quotidian life.

The false narrators and characters are joined by a false reader

14. "Structure and Meanings of *Three Trapped Tigers*," *Latin American Literary Review* 1, no. 2 (Spring 1973): 32.

and author, who turn out to be just two more characters in the novel. With the characters, plot, and setting so overtly contrived, the focus naturally shifts to the contrivance, to the art object and what it has to say about other such objects. "Vae Visitors," with its multilingual footnotes and its intentionally awkward and nongrammatical constructions, and the prologue, which both mistranslates itself and misrepresents Cuba to its foreign visitors, are statements on translation, which portrays itself as equal to the original, and yet never fails to violate and betray that original.[15] And beyond that, it talks about all literature as betrayal, because writing seeks to represent a reality, when that reality cannot be rendered in other terms than its own.[16] The culprit is language itself. If the world suggests to us what terms are necessary for its linguistic representation, it is also true that language is an opaque mechanism and that any reality must be made to conform to the constraints of the linguistic system. The writer, then, must always create fiction, even when he purports to write factual history. As we know since Plato's *Cratylus,* the word is not the same as the thing. And the word *word* is not the Word itself, but a symbolic reflection thereof. Constituted by language and principally concerned with language, everything in the novel must show itself to be as deforming as its medium. In effect, *Three Trapped Tigers* practices a Brechtian kind of alienating realism, for it evokes no illusions without also reminding the reader of the illusion's imaginary nature. The characters, for instance, may be momentarily affected by the death of Bustrófedon (indeed, Códac's bitterness toward the surgeon is uniquely moving), but by the end of the scene he is sure to mock its feigned reality ("A nice sentence, ain't it? Too bad it's not mine" [233]). The characters and their situation are only part of a simulacrum. It is a false character, related to a false reader by a false narrator in a false scene created by a false author that cast language into the limelight as the only truth, then expose its essential falsity as well.

15. Rodríguez Monegal, "Structure and Meanings," pp. 26ff. Octavio Paz, in *Traducción: Literatura y literalidad* (Barcelona: Tusquets Editor, 1970?), p. 9, puts it this way: "Each text is unique and, simultaneously, is the translation of another text. No text is entirely original because language itself, in its essence, is already a translation: the translation of some other sign and of some other sentence." "Translation" mine.
16. José Schraibman, "Cabrera Infante, tras la búsqueda del lenguaje," *Insula 25,* no. 286 (1970): 1.

So even though the author avoids openly embracing the values of one character or one narrator's point of view, instead donning confusing masks to conceal his real face, his obvious commitment to his art limits the distance from which he deals with it. To the extent that his undertaking is foreordained to fail—in that pre-revolutionary Havana cannot be recreated in the Europe of the mid-1960s—he cannot reduce the distance completely. But by recognizing the imperfection of the work within the very work, by having all the principal narrators state frankly that "This you had to hear," the author can soften the sting of failure in his attempt to achieve the absolute. In fact, it is he who decides what the absolute will be in his work, and he need only attend constantly to that standard. In the process he achieves an appealing level of honesty. The author's open confession, however, is offset again by the number of times the reader is intentionally misled, left uninformed, or made the brunt of jokes. The reader cannot help but be envious of one who not only makes play of his work, but also unilaterally decides the rules of the game.

The game, seemingly amorphous because of its surface complexity, may finally be summarized in the Spanish words *palabra hablada*, "spoken word."[17] This formulation not only provides a key to the linguistic mode most esteemed in the novel, but also constitutes a structural analogue for the text. Like these exemplary constructs, the novel consists of unrelated, artificial units that are arranged linearly. Within this seemingly random contiguity, however, there is order. There are recurrent elements (the vowel "a" in every syllable of the words; the serialized narratives and insistent word play and artifice in the novel) that occur amidst nonrepeating elements (most of the consonants; Bustro's memoirs, Cué's complete works, Silvestre's narrative, etc.). These elements have referential value (the sounds represented by the letters considered individually and jointly; the humorous and descriptive aspect of many sections of the novel) as well as acquired value from their context (the second "a" in each word receives a pronounced stress, the words rhyme assonantly; the anecdote of one narrative is rein-

---

17. Merrim concurs: "By substituting the oral for the written and emphasizing sound over meaning, *Tres tristes tigres* defines itself as a large-scale tongue-twister" (101).

forced, developed, limited, or subverted by that of another). And, ultimately, both the words and the novel in question, when considered as totalities, serve the same ironic function, that of simultaneously referring to themselves, to the world, and to preexisting linguistic entities—other words and other texts. What makes the "tigers" feel so trapped amidst all these dazzling reflections is the realization that the transcendental value signaled by the whole complex intellectual pastime, like Bustrófedon who governs the novelistic discourse, is a void.

PART II

KINETIC IRONY

CHAPTER *5*

Aunt Julia and the Scriptwriter:
An Affair with Irony

Mario Vargas Llosa's literary production over the past two dec-
ades etches the demythification of Peru, at least as that country was
evoked nostalgically in works like Ciro Alegría's *Broad and Alien Is
the World* (*El mundo es ancho y ajeno*) and José María Arguedas'
Deep Rivers (*Los ríos profundos*). Vargas Llosa envisages contemporary man as relatively small and weak, and shackled by a structure not of his own making, much like a fly caught in a web. In his
works, man is doomed no matter what: either to the decadence of
his capitulation to external pressures or to severe social sanctions
for his nonconformity. Some early prose works like *The Time of the
Hero* (*La ciudad y los perros*)[1] and "The Cubs" ("Los cachorros")[2]
focus on youth. They portray the experiences of boys in a military
academy in Lima, but where we might expect reveries of innocence
we find instead an institution that proves to be a miniature reflection of and training ground for the military bureaucracy at large.
The narratives allege that stagnation and hypocrisy must be learned
early in order to perpetuate such a system. Vargas' celebrated *The
Green House* (*La casa verde*)[3]—set in Peru's three principal regions,
the coastal desert, the central highland, and the eastern jungle—
provides a more panoramic view of egoism, betrayal, and exploita-

1. Mario Vargas Llosa, *The Time of the Hero,* tr. Lysander Kemp (New York:
Grove Press, 1966). The original version is Barcelona: Seix Barral, 1962.
2. Mario Vargas Llosa, "The Cubs," in *The Cubs and Other Stories,* tr. Gregory
Kolovakos and Ronald Christ (New York: Harper & Row, 1979). The original
version is Barcelona: Seix Barral, 1967.
3. Mario Vargas Llosa, *The Green House,* tr. Gregory Rabassa (New York:
Harper & Row, 1968). The original version is Barcelona: Seix Barral, 1965.

Kinetic Irony

tion. The ambitious *Conversation in the Cathedral* (*Conversación en la catedral*),[4] set significantly in a bar rather than a house of worship, is an epic study of private and public depravity in a universe of Byzantine relationships and bizarre turns of fate. Switching gears slightly during the seventies, Vargas Llosa continued producing at an almost industrial rate, with *Captain Pantoja and the Special Service* (*Pantaleón y las visitadoras*),[5] whose farcical treatment of an obsessively conscientious army officer does not lessen its impact as a scathing indictment of the military mentality. Returning to the motif of prostitution so basic to *The Green House*, Vargas Llosa traces in *Captain Pantoja* the process by which the armed forces attempt to regiment the soldiers' fornication in order to reduce the frequency of rapes and to increase personnel efficiency in the torrid Amazon region. It is the overwhelming success of the project, and its consequent publicity, that brings about its failure. Whereas *Captain Pantoja* is Vargas Llosa's first novel to employ comic effects as a basic textual component, all his novels are replete with a strong sense of irony, both verbal and cosmic. In the tradition of the Romantics, Vargas Llosa's fiction projects a composite image of a world that is either godless or attended by forces characterized by perversity and sadism. In general, these narratives, all written at least partly outside Peru, exhibit the readable traits of suspense and action. Their linguistic and technical opacity (which may displace the author's sense of estrangement onto the reader) is limited to jumps in time and space (save *Captain Pantoja*, which is chronologically linear), unannounced changes in narrative perspective, and a highly personal writing style.

It was not until 1977, the same year Vargas Llosa was honored by election to the presidency of the PEN (poets, essayists, novelists) Club, that he returned to his native land and altered his focus. With *Aunt Julia and the Scriptwriter* (*La tía Julia y el escribidor*),[6] the

4. Mario Vargas Llosa, *Conversation in the Cathedral*, tr. Gregory Rabassa (New York: Harper & Row, 1975). The original version is Barcelona: Seix Barral, 1969.

5. Mario Vargas Llosa, *Captain Pantoja and the Special Service*, tr. Gregory Kolovakos and Ronald Christ (New York: Harper & Row, 1978). The original version is Barcelona: Seix Barral, 1973.

6. Mario Vargas Llosa, *Aunt Julia and the Scriptwriter* (Barcelona: Seix Barral, 1977). Page references are to the English translation by Helen R. Lane (New York: Farrar, Straus & Giroux, 1982) and appear parenthetically in the text.

author has offered a work that forgoes explicit social commentary and turns inward instead to present the demythification of Mario Vargas Llosa. (Though no causal relationship between the place of writing and the narrative's subject matter is implied, the structural analogue is striking: within Peru the author gives an internal view, while from afar he describes what lies outside him).[7] As its title indicates, *Aunt Julia and the Scriptwriter* is a bipartite novel. The odd-numbered chapters (plus the epilogue, chapter XX) recount the events leading up to the author's first marriage, at the age of eighteen, to his aunt (by marriage and then divorce), Julia. The author bares his intimacy to a surprising degree, using family names and historical places and incidents.[8] The male protagonist of the sections dealing with Julia, for example, is alternately known affectionately as either Marito or Varguitas. These chapters portray a boy impatiently yearning to be two things just beyond his grasp: a man and a writer. With some twenty-three years' distance on the incident, Vargas Llosa, clearly the man and writer Marito wanted to become back then, has composed an early autobiography, the memoirs of his own ritualistic passage. Slightly self-mocking, but still perceptibly admiring, he has managed in his present voice to cast his past self as a plausible hero.

The other half of the novel, that of the scriptwriter Pedro Camacho, is situated in the even-numbered chapters (except chapter XX). There we find Camacho's radio serials, the consumer-aimed goods of a self-taught scribbler who cranks out scripts almost as fast as they can be read over the airwaves. These texts are of a radically different mode of writing. They bear the marks of typical assembly-line mass entertainment: formula and cliché. They are positioned in such a way, moreover, as to reveal themselves as symbolic ex-

7. Mario Vargas Llosa, *La guerra del fin del mundo* (Barcelona: Seix Barral, 1981), written in Peru and set in northeastern Brazil, breaks with the pattern set by Vargas' previous novels with respect to these two factors. Nonetheless, the novel bears many marks of the author's fiction: a straightforward prose style (*The Time of the Hero*), unrelenting imaginative power (*The Green House*), an epic scope outlined in mammoth proportions (*Conversation in the Cathedral*), and an incongruous meeting of religious and political fanaticism (*Captain Pantoja and the Special Service*).

8. This is revealed in a conversation between the author and José Miguel Oviedo that appears in *Mario Vargas Llosa: A Collection of Critical Essays*, ed. Charles Rossman and Alan Warren Friedman (Austin: University of Texas Press, 1978), pp. 152–65.

pressions of the obsessions of Camacho's precarious mental configuration (Camacho appears as a character in Mario's memoirs
where he acts out the pathologies he expresses in his writing). Given
the tenuous relationship the scriptwriter has with external reality
and the restrictions imposed by the rigid radio format (uniform
length, wide audience appeal, etc.), these stories constitute the extreme opposite literary pole from that of the autobiographical sections. Camacho eventually loses his mind, moving characters ca-
priciously from one series of soap operas into those of another
series and resuscitating some he has already killed off. His plots
become catastrophic, apocalyptic, demonic. He loses his position
with Radio Panamericana, is institutionalized, and is reduced finally to an errand boy for a moribund scandal sheet. But until his
forced demotion, his voice assures the presence of an interplay in
alternating chapters between history and fiction, autobiography
and fantasy, and serious and popular narrative. Although all these
categories, too, are eventually exploded, the internal dialogue they
maintain constitutes the basic tension that generates the novelistic
discourse.

As Booth emphasizes, irony can be curiously unstable.[9] It may
not only signal a paradoxical situation but also embody a paradox
and mean the opposite of itself. Previously in this study, for instance, irony (distance) has been synonymous with alienation, deceit,
repression, or conflict; and disirony (proximity, coalescence) has
carried the positive valence connected with intimacy, honesty,
openness, or understanding. As regards the literary production of
Pedro Camacho, however, the scales are refreshingly reversed.
Camacho lacks that irony which is the sine qua non of post-Romantic artistic expression: what we commonly call *esthetic distance.*

The mature narrating voice of Mario Vargas, in contrast, con-
trols with consummate skill the reader's attitude toward Camacho,
Aunt Julia, and her impetuous suitor, Marito. Not an end in themselves, the affective rankings prepare the reader to be disposed
toward a particular verbal style and view of the world. The options

9. Wayne C. Booth, *A Rhetoric of Irony* (Chicago: University of Chicago Press,
1974). Booth's third and final section is titled "Instabilities" (see pp. 233–77).

apparently offered by *Aunt Julia and the Scriptwriter* are to be or
not to be ironic. But given the example set by the author's manip-
ulative persona, only the ironic mode is ever really taken seriously.

Before coming upon Pedro Camacho's writing or even meeting
the scriptwriter in person, the reader hears about him through an
intermediary. The owner of Radio Panamericana, Genaro Jr., informs Marito that Camacho has been hired and will come to Lima.
The warning is: "He's not a man—he's an industry! . . . He writes
all the stage plays put on in Bolivia and acts in all of them. And he
also writes all the radio serials, directs them, and plays the male
lead in every one of them" (9). When Marito has the opportunity to
observe Pedro in action he testifies to the veracity of his legend: "I
watched and couldn't believe my eyes: he never stopped to search
for a word or ponder an idea, not the slightest shadow of a doubt
ever appeared in his fanatic, bulging little eyes. He gave the impression that he was writing out a fair copy of a text that he knew by
heart, typing something that was being dictated to him" (129). Like
a contemporary Lope de Vega, Camacho is a "monster of nature,"
a prodigiously fecund writing machine.

But as occurred occasionally with the great *comediante,* such
productivity is not without its cost. Within an industrial rhetoric,
Camacho's merchandise suffers from a lack of quality control. According to Varguitas, "Once a chapter was finished, he never made
corrections in it or even read it over; he handed it to the secretary to
have copies run off and immediately started in on the next one"
(129). It is clear, besides, that even if he decreased the rate at which
he wrote, Pedro's notions about art would not allow for significant
improvement in his product. His views are an unlikely combination
of naiveté and pretentiousness. We see his ingenuousness in his
choice of a place of work: a pigeonhole office located practically in
the street. Pedro's explanation is, "I write about life and the impact
of reality is crucial to my work" (43), as if one could not create
literary realism in isolation. But what are "life" and "reality" for
Pedro? Not the ambiguous flux, the undifferentiated continuum of
modernity, but rather "a straightforward yes or no, masculine men
and feminine women, night or day. In my works," he pontificates,
"there are always blue bloods or the hoi polloi, prostitutes or
madonnas. The bourgeoisie doesn't inspire or interest me—or my

public, either" (50). While such clear-cut divisions may account for Camacho's popularity, their correspondence to the reality he claims to be reflecting is dubious.

The distortion in his vision is compounded further by another factor of which he is ignorant: the immanent otherness of writing. Writing is translation, the rendering of raw phenomena into language; its own internal exigencies force the rendering to be always imperfect, always different from the object evoked. Because it purports sameness and delivers difference, writing is necessarily betrayal. That betrayal eludes Pedro Camacho, but nonetheless characterizes his text. His penchant for polar opposites in life guarantees a double distortion. Camacho's works are stereotypes of stereotypes, a sort of quadratic melodrama, at least twice removed from "the impact of reality."

To make matters worse, he is not content to be an artist of whatever caliber he may be; he has the obnoxious habit of perorating imperiously on Art. Marito remarks on several occasions that Camacho "was one of those men who have no need of conversational partners: all they require is listeners" (42) and that "his need to theorize, to turn everything into an impersonal truth, an eternal axiom, was as compulsive as his need to write" (130). The reader is thus subjected to such edicts as "Clock time means nothing where art is concerned" (41), or "In every vagina an artist is buried" (159). But what ultimately determines the ironic stance of the reader vis-à-vis Pedro touches the reader more intimately than the disapproval outlined here.

During one of their ritualistic coffee breaks (for Pedro, verbena-and-mint herb tea breaks), Marito notices in Pedro's study a thick book entitled *Ten Thousand Literary Quotations Drawn from the Hundred Best Writers in the World* and subtitled "What Cervantes, Shakespeare, Molière, etc., Have Had to Say about God, Life, Death, Love, Suffering, etc." Pedro calls the book "an old traveling companion who's been through thick and thin with me. . . . A faithful friend and an invaluable help in my work" (51). This manual constitutes Pedro's "intellectual" formation and is a major generator of his ephemeral text. Later Varguitas comments to Julia: "Pedro Camacho is an 'intellectual' in quotation marks. Did you notice that there wasn't a single book in his room? He has explained to me that he doesn't read, because other writers might influence his style" (135). In those three short words, "he doesn't read," the reader's discontent finally finds its seat. Pedro's lack of esthetic distance stems simply from inexperience with the literary medium. Unlike Julia—who, as we shall see, is another nonreader, but who makes no pretense of belonging to the world of letters— Pedro has the temerity to make others listen to his prattle. His combination of bombast and ignorance makes him the reader's antagonist, a member of an irreconcilably different band. Nothing else about Pedro—his ascetic devotion to his craft, the sparkle of his beady eyes, or the costumes he dons to inspire himself on Sundays—can efface that breach. When Pedro is pathetically reduced to a post as errand boy for a newspaper about to go out of business, there is a sense of poetic justice, not because he is evil but, in the plain words of his employer, "because he doesn't know how to write" (372).

The foil for Camacho-as-author is Marito, the potential short-story writer who feels his vocation strongly but has not yet managed to gain a toehold in the guild. In nonliterary (but still linguistic) matters, however, the character who provides the clearest contrast to Camacho is Aunt Julia. This winsome woman in her early thirties comes to Lima after her divorce to live with her sister and other members of her extended family. There she meets Mario, some fourteen years her junior, falls in love with him without realizing it, later becomes fully aware of the magnitude of her feelings, and eventually marries him against all odds and family wishes. Her strength and optimism amidst adversity attract the reader as greatly as Camacho's pompousness puts him off. In his verbalizations, Camacho deflects individual sememes (the basic unit of signification) and converts every phenomenon he encounters into a general category or a stereotype ("Clocktime means nothing where art is concerned," etc.). Julia is on a different wavelength. She receives life's assaults in their given specificity, adroitly parrying the blows one at a time by her gift of the intuitive ironic twist. We find, in fact, in the autobiographical sections of *Aunt Julia and the Scriptwriter* not only a history of the author's love affair with his ex-aunt; in addition, Julia, by virtue of her customary verbal dance, carries on an affair with her secret admirer the reader.

The reader, in fact, starts ahead of Mario, whose first reaction to Julia is: "I hated her instantly" (8). Detecting his unjustified air of self-importance, she teases him where it hurts most: "To tell you the truth, you look like a babe in arms, Marito, Aunt Julia said, giving me the *coup de grâce*" (8). This initial view of Julia is emblematic of both the sense of humor I mentioned and her rare ability to assess a situation accurately. Unlike the insulated reader, Mario cannot yet appreciate these qualities; he is too preoccupied with maintaining his inflated self-image as "a full-grown man of eighteen" (8). When he makes a principled but sweeping statement against the institution of marriage, in favor of free sex, Julia lets him have it again, with "What an obscene thing love has become among kids today, Marito" (13). Not only does she stand up for her sentimental views of an earlier day but, in her use of "kids" and "Marito," she reminds him of the scanty experience from which his theory springs. Fortunately for Mario, along with the uncomplicated clarity of youth, he also has its resiliency; these encounters do nothing to diminish his ardor. They seem rather to serve as a springboard for the unlikely pair's amorous adventure.

Further evidence of Julia's indomitably positive attitude is to be found in her responses to the numerous unattractive suitors who besiege her. One Senator Salcedo, reputedly impotent since he was held up at knife point in medias res with a cabaret girl, comes to call on Julia. She turns him down flat, citing candidly not the desire for a virile and vigorous husband, but the very opposite: "If I were certain he'd stay that way, I'd marry him for his dough . . . but what if I cured him? Can't you see that old gaffer trying to make up for lost time with me?" (47). Even Marito, feeling twinges of jealousy regarding his "competitors," can appreciate her inverted approach to awkward situations. At one point, for instance, she tells him the story of her divorce, which came about mainly because of her inability to conceive. When Mario assures her that if he got married he would never want to have children, she asks him flirtatiously, "Does that mean that I can present myself as a candidate and line up with the others?" (88). The adult Mario who acts as narrator bestows upon her this praise: "She was very good at clever repartee [and] told risqué stories charmingly" (88). Her rebelliousness and impish wit charm the reader as they do her aspiring lover.

In all her locutions, Julia conveys honest and reasonable assessments of people and situations. When Mario goes into fits of jealousy or appears to be taking things too seriously, she has the good sense to remind him: "That little game of holding hands, of kissing at the movies isn't really serious, and above all, it doesn't give you any hold over me. You have to get that through your head, my boy" (161). Such barbed diminutives cause Mario to complain, "The truth of the matter is that you're talking to me as though you were my mama," to which she promptly replies, "The fact is, I *could* be your mama" (161). Even when Marito proposes marriage to her, she shows an intuitive understanding of his motives. Rather than answer yes or no, she presents him with a question in return: "Are you asking me to marry you to show your family you're grown up now?" Confronted with the truth, he must answer, "There's that, too" (242). She keeps the relationship chaste and within proportion, often in spite of herself.

Julia is in love with the impetuous youth and would like nothing better than to cast off the straitjacket of her good sense. Her customary decisiveness cedes to a new vacillation. First she obeys the impulse of one polar force, then finds herself on a collision course with its opposite. She buys a plane ticket to La Paz in order to avoid the explosion sure to occur when Mario's parents arrive in Lima, asserting: "what's happening between us is stupid. You know very well we can't get married" (271). But then her speech bucks arhythmically as she breaks form and jumps from her usual level of specificity. From her flat refusal she generalizes her circumstance in the articulation of a fractured proverb: "Anyone who sleeps with little kids always wakes up soaking wet" (271). The introduction of humor into a truly grave situation is characteristic of Julia, but something more is going on here. The weighty scene and the buoyant language constitute an incongruity, tantamount to a splitting of Julia herself. Reason or feelings? She confesses that her motive for refusing his proposal is not lack of love but rather fear of failure: "Do you think it's fair that in two or three years you'll leave me and I'll have to start all over again?" (271). But finally, impressed by Mario's resoluteness, her resistance worn thin, she accepts: "If you'll swear to put up with me for five years, without losing your heart to anyone else, loving only me, okay. . . . For five years of happiness I'll do this utterly mad thing" (272).

Mad, she says, because it can't possibly succeed and is opposed by everyone who cares for either of them. But the significance of her folly is not clear unless considered within its total context. That is,

Julia's craziness flowers almost at once with Pedro Camacho's "nervous breakdown" and commitment to a mental institution. Again the titular characters appear as dichotomous. But if Pedro is pathetic in his insanity, how can we say that the former is admirable?

The answer lies in the employment of the spoken word. Camacho loses his mind, confuses his characters in the mire of his myriad soap operas, yields to his obsessions with the catastrophic, and that is all. He is never capable of labeling what happens to him, of commenting reflexively and thereby mitigating through words the collapse of his world. Julia, on the other hand, can and does articulate "I'll do this utterly mad thing." Insanity is not a taboo subject with Julia, as it is with Camacho. This linguistic formulation implies a clear vision of the distinction between the sane and the insane and ensures that her use of "craziness" is limited only to the figurative sense of that word. If she then chooses to follow her emotions instead of her intellect, she is still acting within a rational framework. She is doing, in fact, what many a humorist does with language: voluntarily mislabeling or distorting reality (sight gags do the same thing but with visual rather than linguistic images), but not without showing evidence of controlling that distortion. Humor and irony, though not identical,[10] share that space circumscribed by the voluntary misnaming of perceptions. It is largely Julia's ability to be crazy by her own volition, to press the wrong-label button, and, in this case, to misname her own nonexistent insanity, that accounts for her beguiling the reader. Correspondingly, Camacho's neurotic silence discourages readerly intimacy.

The reader is in league with Julia, he competes gamely for her

10. Henri Bergson, in *Laughter: An Essay on the Meaning of the Comic,* tr. Cloudesley Brereton and Fred Rothwell (London: Macmillan, 1911), describes the two concepts as follows: "Sometimes we state what ought to be done, and pretend to believe that this is just what is actually being done; then we have irony. Sometimes, on the contrary, we describe with scrupulous minuteness what is being done, and pretend to believe that this is just what ought to be done; such is often the method of *humour.* Humour, thus defined, is the counterpart of irony. Both are forms of satire, but irony is oratorical in its nature, whilst humour partakes of the scientific" (p. 127, italics in original). This is not the place to enter into a detailed critique of Bergson's account, but it would be negligent not to mention that he compares what he considers *all* of irony with *part* of humor, and, as is clear from the last sentence quoted, he is treating irony only in its "oratorical" (herein called "rhetorical") sense.

affections with Varguitas; he looks upon Camacho with a mixture of irritation and pathos. There are two characters in the extreme ranges of the reader's reactions—admiration and scorn—and one in a gray middle zone. The novel's basic scheme is complete but for the narrator's locus in the fictional universe. More particularly, we can now appreciate the delicacy of the synapse between the mature Mario, the voice of the authorial present, and Marito Varguitas, an image of the past. Our analysis of these elements will, at the same time, lead us to consider the unique properties that define the genre of autobiography.[11]

There is a common-sense notion that Mario Vargas Llosa is Mario Vargas Llosa and that if at one stage in his life he was known as Marito Varguitas those diminutives do nothing to alter his essential identity. One is tempted to look right through the narrator, then, to see what he has to tell us and get at the "history" of his life, which is what we have been doing in our treatment of the other lives in the text so far.[12] We should be aware, however, that the "facts" in his tale are selected according to a system of value—literary, philosophical, psychological, political, and so on—that is not only highly personal but also specific to a given point in time. *Aunt Julia and the Scriptwriter,* as an autobiographical narrative, invites an additional reading, a running commentary on the attitudes the narrator (Mario of the present) expresses as he tells his anecdote, an archeological delving into its underpinnings. A scrutiny of his ground rules, the space opened by Vargas Llosa's current taboos, obsessions, and affections, probes at motivations of which he himself may be unaware. Such a basic dismantling of Vargas Llosa's writ-

11. Philippe Lejeune, in *Le pacte autobiographique* (Paris: Seuil, 1975), defines autobiography as a "retrospective prose account that a real person makes of his own existence, with emphasis placed on his individual life, in particular on the history of his personality" (p. 14, my translation). Structurally, *Aunt Julia and the Scriptwriter* conforms to the generic requirement of an identity among the character, the narrator, and the flesh-and-blood person named as author on the title page (this description of course excludes the chapters devoted to Camacho's fantasmagorical scribblings). What is lacking—what determines its status as an autobiographical novel—is the "pact" between author and reader that the events reported in the account be historically verifiable.

12. I treat this aspect of the novel in greater depth in "*La tía Julia* (historia) *y el escribidor* (ficción)," in *Actas del Simposio sobre la Historia en la Ficción Hispanoamericana,* ed. Roberto González Echevarría (Caracas: Monte Avila, forthcoming).

ing is possible only if we apprehend the author's difference from himself, the intratextual distance between young Mario, the doer, the hero of the romantic saga, and the mature Mario, the speaker, and the standard by which the hero is measured.

The space between them is, in general, not great. The narrator admires much of what he did as a young man, and he is proud of the way he behaved throughout most of the affair with Aunt Julia. Although they are years apart, the basic mode of the narration positions the two Marios as proximately as a face and its formfitting mask. Just as the major contours of the mask and the face coincide, the primary values of the character are in accord with those of the narrator. This affinity is evident from the beginning of Marito's relationship with Julia. It is an act of bravado that starts the whole affair, an impulsive kiss Marito gives Aunt Julia on a nightclub dance floor: "Just as the orchestra stopped playing and Aunt Julia started to step away from me, I held her back and planted a kiss on her cheek, very close to her lips. She looked at me in astonishment, as though she'd witnessed a miracle" (58). In spite of the imprudence of his action, it is a decisive, strong move, and self-initiated action is a basic ingredient in the mature Mario's view of manliness. So, for that matter, is jealousy. When Doctor Guillermo Osores, "rich, responsible, good-looking, and with only two sons, who are already almost grown up" (155), begins to call on Aunt Julia, Mario admits: "I felt such pangs of jealousy that I lost my appetite, and sat there in a bitter, foul mood" (155), and "I felt restless and upset, full of unusual impulses such as wanting to get drunk or punch somebody in the nose" (156). Not even Aunt Julia, the object of Marito's desire, is exempt from his possessive masculine rage. Incensed at her continued condescension, he rebukes her: "'I've forbidden you to call me Marito,' I reminded her. I could feel that my anger was getting the better of me, that my voice was trembling and I no longer had any idea what I was saying. 'And I now forbid you to call me a kid'" (160). It is easy to burlesque such an attitude, but Mario's precious manhood is at stake, and he is not about to admit defeat. In fact, it is his faith in his wholeness as a man that enables him to win Aunt Julia over and woo her into matrimony.

Wholeness as a man implies, among other things, aggressively seductive behavior, as the following account demonstrates: "I made no effort to hide the desire she aroused in me; as we danced, my lips nuzzled her neck, my tongue stole into her mouth and sipped her saliva, I held her very close so as to feel her breasts, her belly, and her thighs, and then, back at the table, under the cover of darkness, I fondled her legs and breasts" (198). Yet despite their strong mutual physical attraction, the pair remain chaste almost until the day they are married. When, prior to that consummate moment, their embraces are interrupted in order (supposedly) to pronounce their wedding vows, there is unmitigated joy in Mario's reporting: "We leapt up from the bed, dazed and happy, and Aunt Julia, beet-red with embarrassment, straightened her clothes, as meantime, like a little boy, I closed my eyes and thought about abstract, respectable things—numbers, triangles, circles, my granny, my mama—to make my erection go away" (302).

They are "happy" because they are passionately enamoured and Mario, though presumably not fond of coitus interruptus, can think of no more felicitous motive for such a break than to participate in the wedding he has struggled so determinedly to bring about. Later, Marito shows how to fulfill his manly obligations of supporting the family by maintaining his job at Radio Central and taking on enough outside work to treble his salary. And finally, he confronts his father, the man whose model, in rebellion, he has emulated all along. Marito convinces the elder Vargas of the seriousness of his intentions: "Stammering, I promised to get my university degree, and he nodded approvingly. As we said goodbye, after a second's hesitation we put our arms around each other" (356). His ritualistic passage into manhood, begun with a precocious kiss and ended with a fatherly embrace, is complete. The adolescent has shown varying degrees of daring, willfulness, passion, tenderness, and responsibility, all qualities his mature self recalls with pride. In short, Marito was all he could be at the time; the Julia interlude provided an indispensable link between the narrator's childhood and his present, with which he is now eminently content. Human passages and transitions are notoriously rough around the edges. Mario's account indicates he feels that Marito underwent his not only satisfactorily, but with a rare and admirable flair.

The narrator's face differs from its glovelike mask in some noteworthy ways, however. For one thing, the face has weathered the passage of time and has witnessed the increased pronouncement

141

and separation of its constituent features, the lost tautness of its skin, and the inevitable accompanying wrinkles. In places the text shows diminutive hollows where the mask has stretched out, and distortion where the fit is tight. And even more basic to the narrative, the mask knows nothing of the face behind it. The narrator's greater wisdom and experience are always present, and occasionally, to make the distinction manifest, the narrator steps back and peeks out from behind his disguise.[13] He makes fun of Marito's immature impatience, opening an ironic space that is indispensable to the readability of secular autobiography. Only in the memoirs of a god can this past-present distance be lacking, for self-effacement is no virtue in a deity.

The main thrust of the narrator's portrayal of his passage from boyhood to manhood is that his desire far outreached his ability to satisfy that desire. He wanted to be a writer and an autonomous adult with such intensity that he came to believe his wishes to be fact. From the narrator's present vantage point, Marito's feeling obliged to prove those things is ample proof of the very opposite: he was obviously uncertain of his ability on either score. His blindness to the way others saw him was as constant a source of conflict then as it is of jocularity now. The twofold pretentiousness of the adolescent personality explains why, from time to time, Mario takes delight in ridiculing his earlier self.

One of the youth's traits in his headlong rush into manhood is to try to impress others with his razor-sharp intellect. Early in the novel, when Aunt Julia asserts the superiority of falling in love over today's banal "messing around" [hacer cosas], Marito attempts to lay waste such sentimental pap: "I explained to her that love didn't exist, that it was the invention of an Italian named Petrarch and the Provençal troubadours. That what people thought was a crystal-clear outpouring of emotion, a pure effusion of sentiment, was merely the instinctive desire of cats in heat hidden beneath the poetic words and myths of literature" (13). It is clear to Mario in the present how pretentious Marito sounds, but just to be sure he

13. Mario's "real face" is of course another mask, a literary persona the flesh-and-blood author adopts for the duration of the text. No attempt is made here to establish a continuum between the text and the world to which it purportedly refers. Even in orthodox autobiography (of which Aunt Julia is emphatically not an example) that connection is by no means unequivocal.

tags on an extra barb: "I didn't really believe a word of what I was saying and was simply trying to impress her" (13). "Trying to impress" and "impressing" are certainly not identical notions. The narrator knows this, and, thanks to this explanation, the reader also knows that the narrator knows it.

Another ability Marito displays in his youth is to perceive inconsistencies in everyone else's words and deeds while remaining blind to his own. The same budding intellect that explodes popular amorous myths shortly thereafter falls crashingly in love and takes itself so seriously as to propose marriage to Aunt Julia. What he will do for a living, where they will live, how they will survive do not occur to him in his haste. Fortunately, he enlists the aid of his cousin Nancy, who solves one of these problems by arranging to rent a one-room apartment from a friend. As narrator, Mario cannot forgo the opportunity to expose his former shortcomings: "I was amazed at my cousin's practicality; while I wandered about in the romantic stratosphere of the problems before me, she was capable of turning her mind to the down-to-earth problem of where the two of us would live" (263). If growing up is the gradual process of aligning what one says with what one does then the narrator underscores that Marito at the age of eighteen still has a long way to grow.

Marito's "certainty" of having arrived at the plenitude of manhood depends principally on his virility, his sexual development and experience. His immediate association of these two notions surfaces in the declaration: "I am a full-grown, experienced man. . . . I'm eighteen years old. And I lost my virginity five years ago" (88). The present Mario ridicules the above statement by two principal means, one practically immediate and one deferred. The short-term measure is to have Aunt Julia, the other participant in the dialogue, come back with a customarily rapid retort: "Well, what does that make me then, if I'm thirty-two and lost mine fifteen years ago? . . . A decrepit old lady!" (88). She summarily relativizes his ambitious claim by locating it within a broader context. The second tactic in the self-belittling strategy is to attack young Mario on his own terrain, to signal those aspects of his physique that remain embarrassingly boyish. In a later narration describing the couple's preparations to elope, Mario seizes the opportunity to pounce on Marito through the judicious use of parentheses: "I had put my toothbrush, a comb, and a razor (which, *to tell the truth,* I didn't often need as yet) in my pockets" (298, my italics). Marito is an impetuous lover, not the man Mario Vargas is today; today he is in touch with "the truth" and can fix the norms to which everything in the novel may be compared.

So much for social maturity. He portrays his artistic development as even more retarded than his physical and emotional growth. The most accurate adjective to describe his writing in those days is "unedited." For one reason or another, no one will publish his stories, though the chain of rejections does not discourage him from writing more of them. The problem appears to reside in Marito's literary voice; he is not yet sure enough of who he is in order to project himself convincingly, and he is likely to be swayed unduly by other, already established writers. In one instance he reports that "I was going to entitle my story the 'The Qualitative Leap,' and I wanted it to be as coldly objective, intellectual, tense, and ironic as one of Borges's—an author whom I had just discovered at that time" (44). Not only is he impressed by the Borgesian style, but he swallows whole some of Borges' literary notions: "I was thoroughly convinced that a slip of my pen or a mistake in spelling was never a mere happenstance but rather a reminder, a warning (from my subconscious, God, or some other being) that the sentence simply wouldn't do at all and had to be rewritten" (44). Such a line could have been lifted from a number of stories in *Ficciones*.[14] Its incorporation in the narration, which is otherwise consistent and balanced in tone, is both parodic of Borges and critical of his emulator. As long as Marito imitates any artist so closely in word or in concept, he will never be a writer.

Imbued with a sense of what might be called "textual destiny," the young artist begins to find omens at every turn. When the

14. Jorge Luis Borges, *Ficciones,* ed. and tr. Anthony Kerrigan (New York: Grove Press, 1962). First published under that title in 1956, the collection is comprised of two books of stories which appeared initially in 1941 and 1944. Gabriel García Márquez, too, in his interview with Plinio Apuleyo Mendoza, *El olor de la guayaba* (Bogotá: Oveja Negra, 1982), has expressed an adherence to that view: "When I make a mistake, or I don't like the written word, or simply when I make a typographical error, because of some sort of vice, mania, or scruple, I put the sheet of paper aside and pick up a new one. I can use up as many as five hundred sheets to write a twelve-page story. That is, I have not been able to get over the obsession that a typing error seems to be an error of creation" (p. 29, my translation).

cleaning woman accidentally throws a draft of another potential story in the trash, he confesses, "Instead of being upset, I felt as though I'd been freed of a weight and took the whole thing as having been a warning from the gods" (86). "God" is now "gods": as with Borges, reference to a deity with Marito has become just a trope, a literary device. In regard to still another story, one that ends impiously with Christ falling off the cross cursing, Mario relates: "I wanted it to be a funny story, and to learn the techniques of writing humor, I read—on jitneys, express buses, and in bed before falling asleep—all the witty authors I could get my hands on, from Mark Twain and Bernard Shaw to Jardiel Poncela and Fernández Flórez. But *as usual I couldn't get the story to turn out right,* and Pascual and Big Pablito kept count of the number of sheets of paper I consigned to the wastebasket" (97, my italics). While providing us with valuable insights into his sources and the types of humor Mario esteems, this passage enacts a curious dance in its final sentence. It contains a categorical statement of inability ("as usual," etc.) but does not dwell on that negative note. Fleeing the tragic mode, the narration jumps to the sympathetic characters Pascual and Big Pablito, who in counting the abortive attempts, make their friend's failure a spectator sport. It is clear that Marito has not arrived at writing's Sacred Portals. By his own admission the most innovative play he has ever seen at that time is Arthur Miller's *Death of a Salesman,* and the closest thing to a writer he has personally known is Pedro Camacho. Such inexperience unequivocally separates the man from the boy.

The writer Vargas Llosa is today at times a humorist, although as *Captain Pantoja and the Special Service* attests, the comic effects need not always be at the expense of his own adolescence. In both novels, one of his most reliable techniques for creating humor is to portray a character hyperbolically, exaggerating grotesquely some of its negative qualities. No one should confuse such caricatures with a mimetic rendering of extraliterary experience; they are rather testimony to the pleasure one can derive from the eccentric use of language. A ready example is the description of Uncle Pancracio, one of Aunt Julia's early suitors, "absolutely ridiculous in his hopelessly old-fashioned suit. . . . He'd been a widower for ages, he walked with his feet spread apart, like the hands of a clock at ten past ten, and in the family his visits set tongues to wagging maliciously because he brazenly pinched the maidservants in full view of everybody" (11). Nothing about this character is even remotely attractive. First, his clothes are labeled out of style, then his age is stated in inflated terms. Chronometric language evokes the physical form of a duck, an image likely to repel the opposite sex. To have him then ignore his own image and assault women makes him ridiculous; to have him do it where all can witness his impropriety shows his incivility and moves the description into the realm of the grotesque.

A similar comic procedure functions in the description of a bullfighter whom Marito interviews. Here, however, the narrator depends on an accretion of hyperbolic pejoratives:

> I was dumbfounded when I realized that he was less intelligent than the bulls he fought and almost as incapable as they were of expressing himself in words. He was unable to put a coherent sentence together, his verb tenses were all wrong, his manner of coordinating his ideas made one think of tumors, aphasia, monkey men. And the form in which they were uttered was no less extraordinary than the content: his speech habits were most unfortunate, an intonation full of diminutives and apocopes and shading off, during his frequent mental vacuums, into zoological grunts. [225]

The figuration runs to absolutes ("He was unable," "all wrong") and appropriates the lexicons of illness ("tumors," "aphasia") and bestiality ("monkey men," "zoological grunts"). More dimension is achieved through the inarticulateness of the *torero*, already a stereotype in Hispanic literature. The destruction is further enhanced by the inclusion of the term "diminutives," of which the descriptee is doubtless wholly ignorant. The finishing touch comes through the Greek "apocope," the omission of the last sound or syllable in a word. Its use signals a cultural formation in Mario that is ironically incongruous with the baseness of his subject matter. The ludicrous suitor and tongue-tied bullfighter do not provide the only hilarity in the novel, nor are the means listed here for portraying them the only techniques employed, but they do suggest the line along which the novel's lighter moments run. These passages bolster the contention of a humorous narrative presence distinct from the younger, singleminded self that presence evokes verbally.

This distinction is essential if Mario is to avoid the saccharine aftertaste of a nostalgic identification with one's own youth. To adhere excessively to the past would be to advocate escapism. Our narrative archeology, then, reveals a primary guideline that is negative: the past is remembered not through a sentimental fog but through a critical lens of accomplishment in the near-present. Another caveat his narration heeds is this: a narrator may either report history as it occurs or invent imaginary events; if he reports history, he may either maintain or invert the order in which things "occurred" (the second choice in each case being a sort of rebellion fiction allows against the oppression of historical actuality). But what a narrator may not do within his rebelliousness is lose track of what is real and what isn't; of what the norm is, even when it is being violated. Disorientation regarding the line between the real and the imaginary is what traps Pedro Camacho, with whom Mario wants at all costs not to be confused. In resurrecting deceased characters and moving others from one serial to another—in losing control over his medium—Camacho goes beyond the bounds of competent authorship. He betrays his social function as the tireless and vigilant chronicler, a role Mario relishes. Even when joking, Mario is the dedicated fictionalizer, serving the community by helping integrate its collective experience in making sense of apparently disjointed phenomena. Camacho, in contrast, fails as a role model, staining his own image and that of writers in general. He must thus wear the label of "scriptwriter," a warning to would-be Camachos everywhere.

Of the two principles reigning in Mario's narration, the insistence on lucidity in writing would appear to be the more important to the system of the text. That is, the distance between Mario and Camacho is greater and more sharply drawn that that between Mario and Marito, both for the ethical reasons stated above—Camacho fails as the social gadfly—and for the literary considerations below. Taking as a cue the compound word in the title, *scriptwriter,* which forces a qualitative distinction from the commonly accepted *writer,* and considering also the novel's epigraph, an excerpt from Elizondo's *The Graphographer* that evokes an inescapable network of self-conscious writing and writing on writing, we turn to the discourse of the respective narrators for an understanding of the esthetic values that underlie the novel.

At first it might appear as if the division would lie between

147

(Mario's) autobiography and (Camacho's) radio serials, a schism that might also be stated in terms of history and fantasy. But clearly history and fantasy are descriptive generic terms incapable of fitting convincingly into a hierarchy, unless one or the other were considered a priori as superior. There is nothing inherently better about autobiography's continuity vis-à-vis the episodic nature of a soap opera, nor can the referential truth value of the former rank it above the imaginative quality of the latter.[15] The effects they create are simply different. Their relationship must be understood as dialectical, eternally articulating differences; the superiority of Camacho's or Mario's discourse thus cannot be made at the level of generality suggested here. At the level of the word, however, where the linguistic mechanisms of each narrator bare their most basic traits, a hierarchy does emerge that allows one of the interlocutors to have the last word.

Despite the obvious differences between the discourse in the odd-numbered chapters (Mario's autobiography) and in the even ones (Camacho's serialized fantasies), there are certain images and ideas common to both texts, a situation that causes a folding or overlapping in the novel's otherwise smooth fabric. In some cases a single word may be employed by both narrators and carry the same sense with each. In others the same idea is communicated via different signifiers in the respective narrations. And elsewhere the same word or phrase cuts across both narrations, but with a vastly changed meaning when taken from Mario's mouth and placed in Camacho's. But, most important, these three situations (which I shall refer to by the names of *identical signs, common signified,* and *common signifier*), as in Borges' detective story "Death and the Compass,"[16] gesture toward a fourth situation, that of the *absent sign,* where one narrator employs a key term that finds no equivalent in the repertoire of the other. It is in the last case that the power of one discourse to transcend and subsume the other becomes evident.

An example of identical signs would be the image and concept of *publication,* which has a highly positive valence for Camacho, who writes and publishes radio scripts every day, and for the mature Mario, who publishes novels less frequently (about one every three

15. In essence, I am using E. D. Hirsch's notion of "intrinsic genre" as posited in *Validity in Interpretation* (New Haven: Yale University Press, 1967).
16. Borges, *Ficciones,* 129–42.

years from 1962 to 1981) but with equal enthusiasm. Here, where the signifiers carry equivalent signifieds, regardless of who articulates them, is a strong point of concordance between the two discourses. The texts, however, begin to diverge as regards the notion of "work." Here we find a common signified, a situation where the same concept is expressed by each narrator via disparate labels. Mario's symbol for work is *coffee*. He likes the taste (another similarity with Borges; see "Borges and I"), and he never works without it. Camacho, in contrast, prefers *verbena-and-mint herb tea* as his workaday bracer. It should be noted again that both men are committed to work and define themselves largely in terms of their work. In such instances the text may be seen as a turbulent surface around a constant but concealed core of beliefs.

The inverse of this circumstance may also be found. There are cases of common signifiers, where a given word takes on a vastly different sense in the other narrator's system. Camacho's discourse is dotted with such charged terms as *rats, Argentines,* and *fifty,* all of which carry an immediate emotional charge (the first two are maniacally negative, the third ludicrously positive). While Mario uses the same words on occasion, the knee-jerk response is absent in his writing. For Mario these signifiers represent only in a literal way—a rodent, a nationality, a number—and may be positive or negative, to greater or lesser degrees, according to the particular context of their use. The text is thus deceptively calm on its surface in the case of the common signifiers, but this tranquil façade only augments the intensity of the unrest hidden beneath. At the same time, we begin to see the greater flexibility of which Mario's writing is capable, the varied tone and effects he can create at will. One situation remains, however, to determine the dominance of his voice: the absent sign.

The reason for Camacho's alienating the reader is his lack of esthetic distance from his work, his inability to play with the artistic medium. Mario, on the other hand, shows himself to be a master of distance control. He clearly delineates the border between his present and his past self and shows Julia to be uniformly engaging, both largely by means of his own keen wit. What emerges as Mario's essential strength and Camacho's greatest failing, then, can be resumed in the sign *irony*. In its multiple senses (each of which also contains an inherent plurality) irony is patent throughout Mario's discourse, both as a word in his text (see 44, 88, etc.) and as a structuring principle of that same text. Camacho's incapacity for humor, for allusion rather than denotation, and the rigid, comformist nature of his mass-produced art, in contrast, show him to be wholly oblivious of the notion of irony. It is a sign that escapes him and whose absence from his repertoire signifies in turn an acute esthetic and conceptual poverty. The absent sign irony relegates Camacho's author-ity to second division in the battle of the bards. Mario triumphs as the standard bearer, the measure of the man with respect to Marito, and the bona fide writer regarding Camacho.

The novel thus inscribes a paradox we have been leading up to for some time: the reader, by a series of rhetorical strategies, is distanced from a lack of irony (Camacho's un-self-conscious scribbling and Marito's headstrong pretentiousness) and simultaneously drawn toward irony (Mario's nuanced textual surface and Aunt Julia's humorous thrusts and parries). Where verbalization is concerned, distance breeds intimacy and immediacy promotes estrangement. In that Mario and Aunt Julia get divorced some eight years after their wedding, it is implausible to characterize the novel as the portrayal of a transcendental human relationship. *Aunt Julia and the Scriptwriter* is, rather, the tumultuous history of the reader's affair with a certain mode of writing, speaking, and thinking, one that bears the label "ironic."

CHAPTER 6

A Manual for Manuel:
Homo Lewdens

One of the most troublesome aspects of Julio Cortázar's most recent novel, *A Manual for Manuel*,[1] is the tenacity with which it exhibits its own triviality. Explicitly committed to the cause of Latin American socialism, the novel, as if captive of the inconsequential, nonetheless throughout appears to subvert that objective. Even at its most climactic moment, when the drawn-out urban guerrilla action known as the "Screwery" is about to blossom in all its erotic-political-linguistic splendor, the narrative veers away to a scene in which Manuel utters his first line. The switch is unquestionably justified esthetically, for it momentarily stalls the action and allows the suspense as to the exact nature and repercussions of this international coup to mount even higher. Politically, the change of scene sets the stage for an oracular statement, for Manuel represents the future, to which the Screwery—as well as the book that recounts its process—is dedicated. First words (and last) are always significant, especially when they come at peak moments of action. The juncture, therefore, is ripe for some inspirational augury.

As governments acquiesce to the terrorists' demands, however, and Lonstein offers his bizarre agenda for a reform of consciousness based on the principle of Fortran, Manuel utters the following labiodental, alliterative, octosyllabic locution: "Fiata, fica, fifa,

1. For the purposes of this study I exclude from the novelistic genre Cortázar's engaging collection of vignettes *Un tal Lucas* (Buenos Aires: Sudamericana, 1979). The English translation of *Libro de Manuel* (Buenos Aires: Sudamericana, 1973), is by Gregory Rabassa (New York: Pantheon, 1978). Page references to that edition appear parenthetically in the text.

151

figo" (335). Oblivious of the exigencies of the occasion, historic or literary, Manuel babbles inarticulately. He is, after all, only an infant, more interested in sucking his toes and drooling than in transmitting portentous messages. Belonging to neither the time nor the space of the Screwery's historical reality, he cannot be expected to display purposive behavior. "Fiata, fica, fifa, figo" are random, meaningless sounds a baby might emit in playing with the new verbalizing toy he has discovered. In general such experimentation eventually leads to identifiable speech.[2] But the point is that Manuel is not *trying* to master any operation; he is merely entertaining himself, passing time and avoiding boredom. This self-serving complacency (which nonetheless generates language), particularly when implanted in a revolutionary setting, threatens to cleave *A Manual for Manuel* into two novels with irreconcilably divergent tendencies. The question is whether one can work for everyone's tomorrow and play for one's own today without somewhere subverting the entire program and rendering impossible the attainment of either of those goals.

Irony and play, of course, are not identical concepts; but their points of contact are many and basic. *Intended irony*, first, belongs to an intellectual game, the object of which is to convey indirectly the insufficiency of one's collocutor's presuppositions. In order for intended irony to take place, a sense of play must be a given in both participants; play is the framework in which the ironical-dialectical process unfurls. With *objective accidental irony*, though, its other major form, things are very much the other way around. The perceived mutual incompatibility of phenomena that marks accidental irony triggers in the subject an estrangement, a vision of the world as an interplay of irresoluble contraries. Thus in the intended sense irony follows from play, and precedes it in the accidental sense—a circumstance that reflects the very contradictorily polysemic condition the word *irony* designates. Play is likewise contradictory, moreover, in that it occurs within frames of agreed-upon time and space that are isolated from those of "reality" (as Roger Caillois says, "Play and daily life are constantly and everywhere antagonistic"), and yet it cannot avoid being located also within the time and

2. Cf. Sigmund Freud, *Jokes and Their Relation to the Unconscious*, tr. James Strachey (New York: Norton, 1960), pp. 125–28.

space of that greater reality.[3] Play therefore shares in the duplicity that identifies ironic phenomena, and it is made no less ironic by its practitioner's purely internal motivation. Just as the aim of engaging in Socratic irony is only to achieve subjective freedom, "the purpose of play," Caillois says flatly, "is play."[4] Consequently, irony and play share the same marginal fate: in a production- (and consumption-) oriented society, they are tainted with the taboo of frivolity. Play—Cortázar's passion—thus occupies as fundamental a position in the scheme of irony as it does in *A Manual for Manuel*.

That Cortázar is no stranger to things ludic is well known.[5] His interest in both play and games can be traced back to the parodic drama *The Kings* [*Los reyes*], the first work he published under his own name.[6] *End of the Game* [*Final del juego*],[7] a story and collection of stories, *Hopscotch* [*Rayuela*], his masterful novelistic experiment, and *62: A Model Kit* [*62: Modelo para armar*] a spin-off from that novel, as their titles evince, are also inspired by various sorts of games.[8] His cultivation of fantastic literature, mainly in the collections *Bestiary* [*Bestiario*],[9] *The Secret Weapons* [*Las armas secretas*],[10] and *All Fires the Fire* [*Todos los fuegos el fuego*],[11] even while expressing his metaphysical preoccupations, bespeaks

3. For the antagonism between play and life see Roger Caillois, "Unity of Play: Diversity of Games," tr. Elaine P. Halperin, *Diogenes* 19 (Fall 1957): 99; cf. Eugene Fink, "The Oasis of Happiness: Toward an Ontology of Play," in *Game, Play, Literature*, ed. Jacques Ehrmann (Boston: Beacon, 1972), pp. 19–30.

4. Caillois, "Unity of Play," 105.

5. Critics who have recognized the significance of this facet of Cortázar's work include Alicia Borinsky, "Juegos: una realidad sin centros," in *Estudios sobre los cuentos de Julio Cortázar*, ed. David Lagamanovich (Barcelona: Ediciones Hispam, 1975), pp. 59–72; Doris Sommer, "Playing to Lose: Cortázar's Comforting Pessimism," *Chasqui* 8, no. 3 (1979): 54–62; and Saúl Yurkievich, "*Eros ludens:* Games, Love and Humor in *Hopscotch*," in *The Final Island: The Fiction of Julio Cortázar*, ed. Jaime Alazraki and Ivar Ivask (Norman: University of Oklahoma Press, 1976), pp. 97–108.

6. Julio Cortázar, *Los reyes* (Buenos Aires: Sudamericana, 1970 [1949]).

7. Julio Cortázar, *End of the Game, and Other Stories* (retitled *Blow-up, and Other Stories*), tr. Paul Blackburn (New York: Collier Books, 1967).

8. Julio Cortázar, *Hopscotch*, tr. Gregory Rabassa (New York: Pantheon, 1966); *62: A Model Kit*, tr. Gregory Rabassa (New York: Pantheon, 1972).

9. Julio Cortázar, *Bestiario* (Buenos Aires: Sudamericana, 1971 [1951]).

10. Julio Cortázar, *Las armas secretas* (Buenos Aires: Sudamericana, 1969 [1959]).

11. Julio Cortázar, *All Fires the Fire, and Other Stories*, tr. Suzanne Jill Levine (New York: Pantheon, 1973).

on a literal level his conviction with respect to the gaming, non-referential aspect of art. The impulse to divorce art from life is perhaps nowhere more visible than in his collage-texts, *Around the Day in Eighty Worlds* [*La vuelta al día en ochenta mundos*][12] and *Ultimo Round,*[13] whose common esthetic premise is the free interplay of textual surfaces. Writing and playing are inseparable notions in Cortázar's creative system; only in *A Manual for Manuel,* however, does that synthesis appear as problematical.

The source of the problem resides in the novel's extraliterary, specifically sociopolitical ambitions, announced in the untitled prologue. "I believe more than ever," an authorial voice asserts, "that the struggle for socialism in Latin America should confront the daily horror with the only attitude that can bring it victory one day: a precious, careful watch over the capacity to live life as we want it to be for that future, with everything it presupposes of love, play, and joy" (4). Play thus takes its place alongside love and joy as an antidote to the horror of Latin American historical actuality (and as an alternative to the monotonous cries of outrage in the literature of socialist realism).

> What counts and what I have tried to recount is the affirmative sign that stands face to face with the rising steps of disdain and fear, and that affirmation must be the most solar, the most vital part of man: his playful and erotic thirst, his freedom from taboos, his dignity shared by everybody in a land free at last of that daily horizon of fangs and dollars. [5]

The love and play proposed in the first declaration elide into a love-play in the second; as the nonprocreational, recreational aspect of sexuality, eroticism emerges as the chief form of the ludic impulse in need of defense. Assuming a radical stance in the etymological sense of the word, the author maintains that any leap into a liberated age that in the process suppresses *Homo lewdens* [*sic*], is by nature deficient and doomed to fail. And, likewise, any literary work that pretends to advance the "lewdic" cause must, in order not to subvert its own ends, do so playfully, erotically. But here the

12. Julio Cortázar, *La vuelta al día en ochenta mundos* (Buenos Aires: Sudamericana, 1967).
13. Julio Cortázar, *Ultimo Round* (Buenos Aires: Sudamericana, 1969).

dilemma underlying the whole enterprise surfaces again: the affirmative sign that the novel would constitute announces itself in a discursive passage external to the novel proper. As such, it neither practices recognizable gaming nor invokes the libidinous visage of Eros. The sober signifier effaces its giddy signified, widening rather than narrowing the gap between play and politics.

This, to be sure, is a generalization predicated on the smallest of samples—you can't tell a book by its prologue. Without abandoning totally our reservations with respect to Cortázar's avowed undertaking, perhaps we should examine the specific kinds of play espoused in the novel and the ways in which they interact. Only after analyzing the pertinent data—from which these abstractions should derive—can one diagnose to what extent *Homo lewdens* [*sic*] is or is not sic [*sic*].

Judging from the focus of the prologue, one would expect to find a greater quantity of erotic passages in *A Manual for Manuel* than in fact are present. The novel actually contains only two scenes of extended and graphic eroticism, both between Andrés and Francine (140–42, 313–15). Instead, the question of eroticism is met cursorily on a number of fronts, each angle of approach representing a variation on the theme. Rather than explore the erotic potential of each option, the novel is content to inventory alternatives through allusion and inference. Heterosexual, conjugal play, for example, finds its emblem in Patricio and Susana, Manuel's parents. A secular version of the Holy Family, they are shown "kissing and tickling" (40) as they joke about whether their son was conceived, less than immaculately, on their bed or on the bathroom floor. They doubtless enjoy each other carnally, but that delight is transmitted only through suggestion. The extramarital version of that coupling (and here we begin to stray from the straight [strait][14]) is embodied in Andrés and Ludmilla, who are relatively casual about the duration of their relation ("this one and many others were the last day even though we were still waking up together and playing and kissing" [103]). With no promise of fidelity to constrain them, they are free during the course of the novel to enter into other sexually intimate relations, Ludmilla with Marcos (216ff), and Andrés with

14. According to Johan Huizinga, "The term 'play' is specially or even exclusively reserved for erotic relationships falling outside the social norm." See *Homo ludens: A Study of the Play Element in Culture* (Boston: Beacon Press, 1955), p. 43.

Francine (140ff). Ludmilla's affair is especially noteworthy, for Marcos is at the center of the Screwery, so that as she asserts her right to an emancipated, polyfaceted erotic life she also joins forces with the movement dedicated to realpolitik. Andrés, too, seeks liberation through sex: his first extended love scene with Francine depicts elaborate preludes of cunnilingus and fellatio, and concludes with simultaneous orgasms achieved in genital intercourse. The precise phrasing of the communion, when translated literally ("we played and conjugated together in the same moan" [141]), discloses a coalescence of eros, general playfulness, and language to which I shall return later. The coupling does not satisfy Andrés, however, for Francine refuses to engage in anal intercourse, invoking what Andrés scoffingly denominates as "century-old interdictions" (152). Intent on assailing frontally the sodomistic inhibition, Andrés on another occasion takes her by force. He is only partially successful, nonetheless, in reaching the plateau of freedom he desires.[15] Like Ludmilla herself, her love scenes are simple and happy; Andrés's are drawn out and problematical. Given the erotic restraint practiced throughout the novel, the suggestion is perhaps that Andrés's lingering discontent ironically issues from his making of sex a fetish.

Allusions to other erotic possibilities include both male and female homosexuality, with respect to Lonstein and Ludmilla respectively. But neither gay alternative is portrayed as very gay: of Ludmilla's novitiate it is said that it "almost brought her to slash her wrists" (118), and Lonstein confesses plainly that "the living experiment showed me that homosexual relations didn't interest me" (209). Lonstein, whose equally indifferent heterosexual experiences have produced for him a son (210), has abandoned copulation altogether in favor of autoeroticism. But like Bustrófedon in *Three Trapped Tigers*, Lonstein exists for and through language; his masturbatory forays in the novel are thus understandably strictly verbal. In a heated dialogue with the protonarrator the-one-I-told-you, Lonstein alleges that systematic onanism can be "a total knowledge of the limits of pleasure, of its variants, of its byways" (212). He is outraged that "coitus interruptus is fine but masturba-

15. That is, he is incapable of erasing the "black stain" [*mancha negra*] or of remembering what the Cuban told him in his dream, two mental blocks that remain until he renounces his apolitical hermeticism and, albeit tardily, joins forces with the Screwery.

tion is the Onan taboo" (227). Masturbation, he contends, is "a valid erotic act on the condition that one did not turn to it as a mere replacement" (212); an art whose pinnacle resides in "the elimination of all manual help" (228).

Lonstein also serves a pivotal function in *A Manual for Manuel*: he facilitates the novel's passage from the erotic to the linguistic and political planes. His idiolectal, neophoneme-ridden speech—what he calls "a fortran of poetry or the erotic" (202)—is an attempt to escape what he sees as the subliminal yoke of bourgeois thought, necessarily bound up in language. A thoroughgoing iconoclast, Lonstein also targets the ideology of the left, charging, "They want to make the revolution and pull down all the idols of imperialism or whatever the fuck they call it, incapable of taking a real look at themselves in the mirror" (228). His interlocutor on that occasion, the-one-I-told-you, echoes Lonstein's distrust of the customary puritanism imposed by so-called movements of liberation, asserting: "It's not a matter of dirty words but what throbs behind them, the god of bodies, the great hot river of love, the eroticism of a revolution which someday will have to opt for . . . a different definition of man" (85). The novel is not so much concerned with impugning any particular state or party as with protecting humanity's erotic pulse from being stilled in the aftermath of sectarian struggle. Within or without the institution of matrimony, along or across lines of gender, alone or together—sexual play in *A Manual for Manuel* is an inalienable right.

The field of play of course encompasses more than eroticism alone. Within the novel's referential dimension three other types of play receive benevolent handling: the comic, the absurd, and a generally playful outlook. The absurd is often difficult to designate with certainty in literature, but fortunately the novel itself assists us by labeling some of its own elements absurd. The exposition of the dramatis personae, for example, occurs in a scene which has the characters both watching a movie and facing a blank brick wall: "a complete absurdity and yet those people are still there, each in his seat facing the brick wall" (11). The Screwery itself, the motivating force behind the bizantine plot (in both senses of "chain of events" and "conspiracy"), is described in those same terms. At a particularly delicate link in the action—the passage through customs of the penguin (whose thermic container is lined with counterfeit dollars, destined to be exchanged for French francs in order to finance the kidnapping of the Vip)—the enlightened Marcos remarks that "the operation was too absurd not to turn out well" (132). And incorporated in The Screwery, whose ends are decidedly pragmatic, is an appreciation for the eccentric and unproductive, incarnate in Lonstein's mushroom. In contrast with such "technocrats of the revolution" (144) as Gómez and Heredia, who scoff at frivolity, "it was good for Oscar, this absurdity" (184). In this category also belongs Oscar's fascination with lunacy (106ff), which clearly shares in the fundamental irrationality encompassed by the concept of absurdness.

The irrationality of the absurd certainly may be humorous, but it may also strike us as merely ludicrous. Humor, moreover, may derive from nonabsurdities, as Freud and Bergson, among others, have shown.[16] The novel's humor is more difficult to isolate than its absurdity because humor is both more insistently and more subtly present. The strategy behind its use, moreover, is to lend levity to questions of signal importance, as is illustrated in one of the novel's opening scenes.[17] In response to the-one-I-told-you's summary justification for armed revolution, Marcos cautions, " 'Wow . . . , you're the best there is for simplistics and tautology.' 'It's my little red morning book,' the-one-I-told-you says, 'and you've got to admit that if everybody believed in simplistics like that it wouldn't be so easy for Shell Mex to put a tiger in your tank.' 'That's Esso,' says Ludmilla, who owns a two-horsepower Citroën where the horses seem to become paralyzed with fear of the tiger, because they stop on every corner and the-one-I-told-you or I or somebody has to push it along" (9). The gravity of the potentially violent uprising the-one-I-told-you advocates is lightened consider-

16. Freud divides jokes into two categories, those which deal in nonsense (idea play) and those which exploit word play (*Jokes*, p. 138). Later he states that "nonsense and stupidity, which so often produce a comic effect, are nevertheless not felt as comic in every case" (*Jokes*, p. 194). According to Henri Bergson, the comic employs a strange kind of logic which "may include a good deal of absurdity." See *Laughter: An Essay on the Meaning of the Comic*, tr. Cloudesley Brereton and Fred Rothwell (London: Macmillan, 1911), p. 181. Both Freud and Bergson make (often inconsistent) distinctions between jokes, wit, humor, and the comic. My focus is the ludic commonality among those concepts.

17. With typical perspicacity, Freud anticipates Cortázar's strategy. "Jokes," he states, "even if the thought contained in them is non-tendentious and thus only serves theoretical intellectual interests, are never in fact nontendentious. They pursue the second aim: to promote the thought by augmenting it and guarding it against criticism" (*Jokes*, pp. 132–33).

A *Manual for Manuel*

ably by Marcos' "Wow" and by the wit of the interlocutors (Mao's quasi-divine scriptures are coupled with one of Madison Avenue's catchiest slogans of that period; Ludmilla in turn catches the-one-I-told-you in an inaccuracy). And Ludmilla's criticism is sublimated too by the narrator's evocation of her animated auto and the good-natured camaraderie occasioned by its cantankerousness. This pattern of humor is pervasive, and extends even to characters whose verbal role is relatively minor. Patricio, whose principal role is that of Manuel's progenitor, attributes the ease of carrying out of the pre-Screwery, for instance, to having the "prepaid passage in his hand and his ass on the ground" (112). Gladis, the former stewardess for Aerolíneas Argentinas and present lover of the activist Oscar, has the last (comical) word in a scene where the terrorists have suffered their first casualties. When Ludmilla asks about the fate of the escaped penguin, Oscar, stunned from a blow to his "funnybone," retorts, "They can stick it up their ass"—to which Gladis responds sensibly and with perfect timing, "It hurts" (193).

Among the more central characters is the irrepressible Lonstein, whose comicity stems from the conviction that "somebody has to fill the office of buffoon now and again" (225). A sample of his humor is as follows: Marcos relates to the skeptical Andrés how, just at the moment when a swan appeared on stage, the merry band of terrorists disrupted a Wagnerian opera. Lonstein protests, "It's not right. . . . Twisting the neck of the swan now that we've had Donald Duck for quite some time, you people have got your birds mixed up, by God" (62). As in the longer humorous passage cited above, the deployment of humor neutralizes a potentially explosive encounter (Andrés and Marcos are rivals for Ludmilla's affection). Here, additionally, Lonstein manages to evoke the Mexican Enrique González Martínez's renowned antimodernist verse as well as Walt Disney's cartoon creation, a hated representative of cultural and economic hegemony.[18] The little rabbi, as Lonstein is alter-

18. The precise wording of the opening verse is: "Twist the neck of the swan of deceitful plumage" [*"Tuércele el cuello al cisne de engañoso plumaje"*]. It is part of an Alexandrine sonnet which first appeared in *The Dark Paths* [*Los senderos ocultos*] (1911). The text I have consulted appears in his *Obras Completas*, ed. Antonio Castro Leal (Mexico City: El Colegio Nacional, 1971), p. 116. For a powerfully formulated account of the subliminal venom embodied in a cartoon character, see Ariel Dorfman and Armand Mattelart, *How to Read Donald Duck: Imperialist Ideology in the Disney Comic*, tr. David Kunzle (New York: International General, 1975).

nately called, has already been recognized as a central figure in praise of the lewdic [*sic*]. The other major exponent of that impulse is the aptly named Ludmilla, or Ludlud as Andrés fondly dubs her, who appears to be funny in spite of herself, through pure spontaneity. Andrés theorizes, for example, that Lonstein's masturbatory artistry is a rebellion that implies acceptance of the received ideas that it would abolish. Ludmilla's answer to this tenuous rationale typically deals neither with ideas nor with Lonstein, but rather relates a personal anecdote: "At the age of eleven I masturbated with a comb once. . . . God, it almost turned out bad, I must have been crazy" (171). Other phrases she is likely to launch are "Red dick and hairy snick" ["*Concha peluda y pija colorada*"] (163, etc.), whose acute obscenity escapes her, and simply "Bloop," which signifies both nothing and everything for which Ludmilla stands. Like La Maga in *Hopscotch,* and in contrast to the elaborate intellectual machinery that drives Lonstein's jocularity, Ludlud—the embodiment of play raised to the second power— exists in a permanent state of precognitive vertigo which Caillois classifies as the goal of games of *ilinx.*[19]

Ludmilla's intuitive enthusiasm cannot be contained within the boundaries of the absurd or the humorous. Her effervescent joy spills over into a general playfulness with respect to the game of life. When Marcos declares, "I can't really love anyone who at some moment of the day or night doesn't go wild with joy because the movie on the corner is showing Buster Keaton, something like that" (114), he is stating unequivocally his need for Ludmilla. He is positing also the necessity in any thoroughly revolutionary movement (of which he more than any other character is the sign) of recognizing and protecting "a bit of play, a bit of Manuel in his conduct" (185).[20] Ludmilla—a superannuated version of Manuel—is thus crucial to the success of the Screwery in spite of, or rather because of her emblematic confession, "I still don't understand anything" (304). The goal of this neo-Romantic resurgence, of course, is not the destruction of the legacy of reason inherited from the Enlightenment, but rather a fortification of that legacy by virtue of the inclu-

19. See Roger Caillois, *Man, Play, and Games,* tr. Meyer Barash (Glencoe, Ill.: Free Press, 1961), pp. 3–7.
20. Bergson, *Laughter:* "We are too apt to ignore the childish element, so to speak, latent in most of our joyful emotions" (p. 68).

sion of its limits. *A Manual for Manuel* advocates the incorporation within Western rational discourse of the suppressed unreason— from foreplay to child's play—that engenders and validates that rationality.[21]

No one need be reminded of the linguistic nature of discourse, nor of the metalinguistic nature of literature. In order to carry out the enterprise of recuperating "the reason of unreason," of defending play from unwitting charges of banality, play must thus inhabit more than the work's signified. As Barthes says in his erotics of reading, "That is the pleasure of the text: value shifted to the sumptuous rank of the signifier."[22] But the signifier itself in this case is not simple or unitary. The abundant gaming portrayed in the novel pervades not only its lexicon, which is bound to be eccentric, but also the novelistic conventions that determine its semantic configuration. Starting with the smallest units first, we see that the primary source of word play within the fiction is Lonstein, who generates neologisms with every breath. Here is a minimal sample of his logomachy:

People are like those classic torturers who end up as neurotics because all they had was their no-less-classic daughter to whom they could recount every detail of torturocomy and leadsqueal; don't you realize that in Marthe's bistro I didn't go around declining my gig as my co-pains say, and that condemns me to silence, apart from the fact that since I'm a celibate, chaste like Onan and master of my bait, there's no exutory left for me but soliloquy, except for the privybook where from time to time I defescrape a turdscript or two. [35]

Lonstein's idiolect consists in three basic linguistic tendencies: the conscription of slang, of auditorily inspired circumlocutions, and of neologisms.

In the first category we find "gig," a colloquialism that is common parlance among jazz musicians for "job" but here refers specifically to the little rabbi's solitary avocation. That activity also generates the term "master of my bait," an example of the second

---

21. Huizinga argues for the same point: "We play and know that we play, so we must be more than merely rational beings, for play is irrational" (*Homo ludens*, p. 4).

22. Roland Barthes, *The Pleasure of the Text*, tr. Richard Miller (New York: Hill and Wang, 1975), p. 65.

type of idiomatic deviation. The third characteristic of Lonstein's speech, however, is by far the most essential, for he can hardly utter a sentence without inventing new words. In general, the neologisms come about by means of the incongruous juxtaposition of existent phonemes. Thus we have "torturocomy" (suggestive of deviousness [tortuous] and sluggishness [tortoise] as well as tortures; "comy" also implies comedy and eulogy [encomium]); "leadsqueal" ("lead" as a noun suggests weightiness and imperviousness; as a verb it connotes power; "squeal" entails screeching on a literal level and in its figurative sense turning informer); "co-pains" (one's irksome associates as well as cronies [a pun on the French *copains*]); "exutory" ("exut" suggests perspiration, a form of excretion; "ory" is the thing or place used for that fluid conduction; "exutory" is also a medical procedure that involves opening an ulcer prior to curative treatment); "defescrape" (elimination and etching fused); "turdscripts" (more of the same, but made substantive); and "privybook" (a secret volume and, especially, one kept in an outhouse or latrine). Such decipherment by association, to be sure, can raise more questions that it answers. It amounts only to an initial attempt at joining in on Lonstein's ingenious word games (in spite of his announced preference to play by himself) and is in no way exclusive of other readings (except perhaps those that see no problems). More adept onomasticators might start with his "infrabatrachomiomachy" (77) and work up in difficulty.

Within the novel Lonstein's spirit infects Andrés most of all. As dominant narrator and the-one-I-told-you's successor as chronicler of the Screwery, Andrés cannot resist the urge to emulate Lonstein's verbal virtuosity. Thus he creates the verb "protogrunted" (76) and the noun "arguminsults" (81), among numerous others. Patricio, too, catches the fabricating fever and says alliteratively of the monolingual Fernando, "Chileans for the most part haven't got the gift of Gallic gab" (14, also 245). And Ludmilla carries the tendency to its most solipsistic extreme in the following description: "It was the boundary, she thought, hanging on the word, turning it over like a piece of mental fruit, boundary, rebound, raybound, boundray, roundbray, ray of the bound, bound of the ray" (241).

Many members of the radical circle and, indeed, their entire undertaking, are somehow implicated with language to an extraordinary degree. Oscar makes an intuitive connection between the occult powers of the full moon and "the implacable machinery of plays on words opening doors and revealing entranceways in the shadows" (224). Marcos and Ludmilla demonstrate their linguistic awareness when they chat at length on the regional variants of *pija*, *concha*, and *culo* (prick, cunt, and asshole respectively), obscenities whose incorporation into the mainstream of language is another integral aspect of the post-Screwery vision (285–86). The same can be said for Lonstein's dizzying fortrans (202–03) and acronyms (338–41): the consensus is that the authentic revolution is not a matter of token protests or militant confrontations but rather of radically recast thought, from which the rest may issue. And—as is well known—that mode of thinking cannot be attained through the ideologically charged, mentally shackling language of the existing power structure.[23]

But—and here the truism approaches truth—what sort of constructive alternative can one offer? The Screwery itself is its own best example of the revolutionary phenomenon to which it is dedicated, for as it conveys the sense of bringing to bear aggressive pressure, it also carries within it a sexual component.[24] The notion of paradigmatic, associative word play is also necessarily included under its sweeping rubric. Linguistic and erotic activity are thus not

23. Barthes makes several statements that illuminate *A Manual for Manuel* along different axes. "The social struggle," he avers, "cannot be reduced to the struggle between two rival ideologies: it is the subversion of all ideology which is in question" (*Pleasure*, pp. 32–33). This deep-seated iconoclasm is of course the posture represented by Lonstein. Barthes says, "there are very few writers who combat *both* ideological repression and libidinal repression (the kind, of course, which the intellectual brings to bear upon himself: upon his own language)" (*Pleasure*, p. 35, italics in original). It would appear, then, that Cortázar is in select company. When it comes to determining whether *A Manual for Manuel* qualifies as a text of bliss ("the text that imposes a state of loss, the text that discomforts [perhaps to the point of boredom], unsettles the reader's historical, cultural, psychological assumptions, the consistency of his tastes, values, memories, brings to a crisis his relation with language" [p. 14]), however, one cannot be unequivocally affirmative. At times the novel approaches this limit, but not so often, for example, as does *Hopscotch* or many novels of Sarduy or Robbe-Grillet.

24. In Evelyn Picón-Garfield's extended interview, *Cortázar por Cortázar* (Mexico City: Universidad Veracruzana, 1978), p. 59, the author contends that he intended no sexual innuendo in denominating the Screwery [*la Joda*], since that sense is lacking in the Argentine usage of the verb *joder*. We are confronted, therefore, with a prime example of the author's reading as constituting only one—and not necessarily the most fruitful—of many interpretations of the work. The novel is incomparably more interesting read in Madrid than in Buenos Aires.

cast in *A Manual for Manuel* as prostheses to a political revolution: they are in themselves forceful political acts, as is of course their advocacy.

The other level at which play occurs within the realm of the signifier is narratological. In various ways, conventions of narrative are either violated, underlined, or both, as part of a convincing demonstration of the ludic's valued presence in writing. These literary trespasses or diversions can be summarized under two main headings: *intratextual interplay* and *schizoid narration*. The seeming contradiction in juxtaposing *intra*textual with *inter*play is explained by the fragmented nature of the novel. It is a text composed of many shorter texts that restate, elaborate upon, contradict, or ignore each other. The interplay among these fragments is thus intratextual with reference to the totality of the book. Within this dynamic, the fragments have one of two basic functions, either to advance the action or to interrupt it. The interruptive texts in turn may be separated into verbal and nonverbal types. The latter category consists of assorted "mental sketches" or "organigrams" whose avowed purpose is to disclose at a glance the state of the gestating Screwery (see pp. 94, 111, 165, 196). In that they summarize what is expounded in the corpus proper, these graphics are supportive of the ongoing narrative they disrupt.

The verbal interruptions take the form of journalistic clippings in English or French, chosen, the author affirms in the prologue, randomly as he was composing the novel (4). Typographically they are at a glance distinguishable from the ongoing narrative. In contrast to the nonverbal signs, these excerpts do not always relate directly to their immediate context, especially when the play occurs in its freest form. In the main, however, when the interplay is either direct or indirect, no such discontinuity obtains. By *direct interplay* I mean to designate a situation in which the ongoing narrative and the intrusive excerpt address the same issue from sympathetic perspectives. On pp. 106–07 for instance, the discussion of Lonstein's uncanny mushroom and of the girls who run away from their reformatory under the influence of the full moon coincides with an advertisement for a magazine, *Horoscope,* which claims to have predicted the latest coup d'état in Argentina. The adjacent texts play directly with each other in the sense that they lend credence to the single notion of the extrarational.

In *indirect interplay* there is an extra step involved. In the case of the reproduced telex account of Castro's chat with Cuban students (274–77), for example, one must first generalize the text synecdochically into the context of a Third World socialist struggle before its relation to the Screwery is clear. The inverse of that same tropological process is found with respect to the testimonials of torture and other violations of human rights elicited by attorney Mark Lane (373–82), an interpolation of what the insurrection is attempting to hinder. These transcriptions also provide a salient example of the third kind of interaction, what may be called *freeplay.*

This fashionable term implies an association with another element in any other part of the text, whether proximate or not, and the relation may be positive or negative, by sound or sight as well as by meaning. An illustration of such a paradigmatic (as opposed to syntagmatic) reading is as follows: the first witness interviewed is one "Chuck Onan, from Nebraska" (373), who relates how American marines were instructed in methods of torture during the war in Indochina. The account is of course grave and condemnatory. But the witness's name precipitates an inevitable association with the Onan whose archetypal story is related by Lonstein (227). Not only is Onan the guiding figure in Lonstein's revolution-within-the-revolution, but the leap to the autoerotic sense is consistent with the little rabbi's other, linguistic facet. The multiple conceptual steps involved (tortures → Onan the witness → Onan the archetype → Lonstein → word play), as well as the contrast between the solemn beginning and buoyant end point of the associative process, justify the term *freeplay.* In that it still entails an operation suggested elsewhere by the text itself, nonetheless, such freeplay is not entirely without constraints. These finite limits are the parameters that Derrida has suggested to allow the endless de-centered freeplay of signification.[25]

25. Jacques Derrida, "Structure, Sign and Play in the Discourse of the Human Sciences," in *Writing and Difference,* tr. Alan Bass (Chicago: University of Chicago Press, 1978), pp. 278–93. The field of language is described to be "in effect that of *play,* that is to say, a field of infinite substitutions only because it is finite, that is to say, because instead of being an inexhaustible field, as in the classical hypothesis, instead of being too large, there is something missing from it: a center which arrests and grounds the play of substitutions" (p. 289, italics in original). In that Cortázar's prologue—by stating the aims of the "fiction" it precedes—attempts to stay beyond the reach of the play of that fiction, *A Manual for Manuel* reveals the orthodox foundations of certitude and immobility on which its call for insurrection depends.

Kinetic Irony

Schizoid narration denotes a variety of techniques by which narrative conventions are tinkered with, always causing a sundering of what traditionally is whole. Behind the distinction between the "protonarrator" the-one-I-told-you and the "narrator" Andrés lies the notion that the voice addressing the reader (excluding for the moment the solemn voice in the prologue) is somehow forked. By now, certainly, such a phenomenon could hardly be expected to raise eyebrows, for every novel discussed in this study so far has had multiple narrators, and rare indeed is the contemporary work that eschews this option. Yet the manner in which the narrator's doubling occurs in *A Manual for Manuel* is unique; it is not a matter of equally vocal narrators playing *off* each other but of one narrator speaking *through* the other. The ghost of the pre-scribe the-one-I-told-you—who perishes in the kidnappers' lair before the writing process begins—haunts Andrés's account from start to finish. It is the-one-I-told-you's notecards and clippings that at once provide Andrés with the raw material for his reconstruction of the history of the Screwery and explain the fragmented quality of Manuel's manual (which is what the reader has before him). In posthumous homage to the fallen chronicler, Andrés at times disappears as narrator and allows many passages to be narrated from the original perspective, with the result that Andrés is seen from without, like any other character (20ff., 168ff., 348ff.). Access to the-one-I-told-you's notes also permits Andrés to relate scenes to which he was not an eyewitness (24ff., 37ff., 295ff.), thus circumventing the major epistemological shortcoming of first-person narration. Further heterogeneity of perspectives is supplied by hearsay through other characters (Andrés: "I was missing too, but Ludmilla told me . . ." [131, etc.]), although it must be admitted that the narrational ventriloquy eventually leads to a technical breakdown. The proliferation of points of view, which responds to a need for omniscience, outstrips the novel's ability to account logically for such knowledge. Even allowing for the unlikely prospect that Ludmilla informed Andrés of her intimate sessions with Marcos (231ff., 263ff., 282ff.), how could Andrés be privy to the amorous interlude between Gladis and Oscar (224) or to the colloquy of the grotesque Vip and Vipess (253–60)? Such a criticism, of course, presupposes a mimetic theory of literature and is admittedly preempted in the prologue by the admonition that "proponents of

166

reality in literature are going to find it [the novel] rather fantastical" (3). Still, the novel *is* realistic in many ways and places, and one cannot help but wonder why the flights into implausibility occur at these particular junctures.

Further narrational bifurcation can be found in Andrés's love scenes with Ludmilla and Francine. The point of view lurches from him to Ludmilla within the same sentence ("I kissed her and tickled her, I squeezed her until she protested, still thinking, still talking, still Andrés duplicated, out of himself, kissing me, tickling me, squeezing me until I protest" [172]). It is a technique reminiscent of such early Cortazarian short narratives as "Axolotl" and "The Night Face Up," in *End of the Game* (recently retitled *Blow-up and Other Stories*). In a scene with Francine, related from a solely feminine standpoint, the dialogue is interwoven with a running description of Andrés's disrobing ("He was getting undressed, looking at me, unbuttoning his pants very slowly, letting his fingers fall asleep on each button" [290]). The simultaneous action and dialogue are distinguished by indenting the narration while permitting the conversations to extend the full width of the page. A similar technique is employed in a scene where Patricio disrupts a Bardot film (58–59). There, however, the polygraphy is threefold, for along with Patricio's antics are included the reactions of the other spectators (in boldface capitals) and the dialogue on the soundtrack (in parentheses and italics). Much of the unorthodox splintering of the text (including the erotic forays), in fact, owes to attempts at conveying simultaneity of action in ideologically disparate camps (54–71, 77–79, 252–60). The dialectic that the novel portrays and into which it is inserted thus takes the form not of a neat assertion leading to a counterproposal, but of cacophonous emission of disparate signals.[26]

In another sense, too, the text plays doubling games with narrative conventions by commenting periodically on its own nature, thus sorting itself into narrative and metanarrative strata. In spite of its constituting a ritualistic gesture of twentieth-century fiction, the inclusion of metanarration is more than routinely appropriate in *A Manual for Manuel*. For one thing, the metacomments are

26. Again we note the suitability of Barthes' descriptions: "In the text of pleasure, the opposing forces are no longer repressed but in a state of becoming: nothing is really antagonistic, everything is plural" (*Pleasure*, p. 31).

skillfully integrated, such that the self-reference tends to coincide with rather than replace straightforward recounting of the anecdote. Lonstein's statement that "it's a problem of conditioned reflexes, preventing the acceptance of hopeful [*esperables:* "predictable"] and logical structures" (203), epitomizes just such a polyvalent locution. Its immediate referent is the fortranesque utopia shared by at least some of the Screwery's proponents (Oscar, Marcos, and certainly Ludmilla if she were more articulate). At the same time, the subject of the sentence in quotes could well be "Literature" or "Writing this novel." Indeed, breaking (linear) form is one of the novel's major proccupations, and this very two-pronged sentence is a choice illustration of the means to achieve that aim.[27] Similarly, when Lonstein claims, "What counts is the execution, that's where the art lies" (228), there is no point in asking whether he alludes to the art of masturbation (as the immediate context would indicate), the art of phonemic permutation (as he practices elsewhere), or the art of "novelizing" (to borrow a coin from Cervantes). Certainly, the acceptance of one sense does not imply rejecting any of the others.

But let us not overlook what is at stake in such indiscriminate receptivity. *A Manual for Manuel* makes the case that human nature is not adequately accounted for in the term *Homo sapiens;* humanity must also be permitted to encompass Homo faber and Homo ludens. That is, writing, eroticism, and paronomasia are shown to constitute an economy in which the constituent elements are inextricably mutually implicated. Moreover, since this vision comes across through language, the novel asks especially that its bookishness never disappear from view.

Ever since the diminutive story "A Continuity of Parks" Cortázar has been campaigning against the deluded passive reader who ingests the illusion as if it were his evening cocktail.[28] To that same end this novel contains scenes—all of which occupy the metanarrational, self-referential plane—in which the extended family of urban terrorists colludes to assemble Manuel's manual. As these

27. For an account of the way in which disorder in a text triggers meaning, see Harold Bloom, "The Breaking of Form," in *Deconstruction and Criticism* (New York: Continuum, 1979), pp. 1–37.
28. I develop this notion more fully in "La continuidad en 'Continuidad de los parques,'" *Crítica Hispánica* (forthcoming).

scenes put on display the cooperative effort behind the subversive enterprise, they drive home something more essential: they are illusions, *in ludere,* part of the play, counterfeit life because authentic image. *A Manual for Manuel* thus is not so much a book about militant rebellion as it is an account of the process of compiling a book about such an upheaval. Whereas the Screwery is at best only a partial success (the Vip is rescued, allowing the Latin American governments to renege on their promises to liberate political prisoners; Marcos, the representative of "the new man," dies in the scuffle), the history of the coup survives in all plenitude. That the history is cleft along several planes only serves to put into question the univocal, military solution. Rather than an accessory to the main event, the complex play of writing emerges as the prime value, the revolutionary act supreme, the end of its own game.

This may sound like a conclusion, but it is actually only a prelude to a conclusion. Several competing notions of play are vying for dominance in this analysis. Play is portrayed at once as frivolous activity (as opposed to things done "in earnest," such as work), as an ineluctable dimension of verbalization and *poesis* (especially in the erotic sense in which Barthes incarnates the text), as the suppressed antireason necessary to the generation of rational argument, and as a gesture of profound, if disguised, political consequence. Here, without effacing any of these alternatives, we must recognize another, transcendental conception of play: what Huizinga has termed "the living principle of all civilization." That is, civilization "does not come *from* play like a babe detaching itself from the womb: it arises *in* and *as* play, and never leaves it."[29] Not only writing and other self-affecting pastimes, but also such diverse and essential social practices as law, war, and the pursuit of truth take place within this primordial playground.[30] Such is the magnitude of its terrain, says Philip E. Lewis, that "in order to conceive of the absence of play, we should somehow have to conjure up an absolute Unity, indivisible, outside of time, immune to the fragmentation of phenomena that underlies the possibility of movement, time, causation, indeed all

29. Huizinga, *Homo ludens,* pp. 100–101, 173.

30. Regarding the essential role of sports in civilization—the priority of vitality to utility, of athletic clubs to family organization—see José Ortega y Gasset, "El origin deportivo del estado," in *El Espectador* (Madrid: Biblioteca Nueva, 1950), pp. 835–59.

aspects of the deepseated relativity of our existence."[31] In a similar vein, Jacques Ehrmann asserts that "far from corresponding to a supposedly gratuitous, disinterested aspect of culture, play in the fullest sense is coextensive with culture. . . . To define play is at the same time and in the same movement to define reality and to define culture.[32]

In the fallout of this explosion of the play-form we find a curiously vibrating double-edged sword. While an arché-play undermines what Ehrmann terms the ethnocentric utilitarian and materialistic attitude that relegates play to the periphery of our culture (clearly one of the novel's aims), it also effects a leveling of the different kinds of play represented by Andrés (bourgeois, male chauvinist, yet creative), Ludmilla (puerile yet pure), Marcos (committed, yet tolerant), and Lonstein (uncompromisingly revisionistic; Barthes' text of bliss). Still, clearly these types of play are not all portrayed as equivalent, as is doubtless seen when the list is lengthened (as it must be) to include the antipathetic players Gómez and Heredia, the Gi-ant, and the Vip, with all the torture, assassinations, and disappearances they imply. So we are left with the formulation that everything is play, but not all forms of play are of like value. In so saying, of course, we are engaging in a sleight of hand that embraces neither the trivial nor the transcendental definitions of the ludic, but advocates a relentless oscillation between the significance and nonsense that inhabit all Homo sapiens' gestures.

This movement within a delimited field of play is the inconclusive conclusion to which the novel leads us. The dilemma of choosing between antithetical tendencies is reenacted over and over, in the form of individual freedom versus collective responsibility, accessibility versus accuracy, respect for tradition versus thirst for innovation, and so on. In *A Manual for Manuel,* more than in any other of Cortázar's searchings, one encounters attempted syntheses that refuse to conform to facile dialectical expectations.[33] To return

31. Philip E. Lewis, "La Rochefoucauld: The Rationality of Play," in *Game, Play, Literature,* ed. Jacques Ehrmann (Boston: Beacon Press, 1972), p. 134.
32. Jacques Ehrmann, "Homo ludens Revisited," in *Game, Play, Literature,* p. 55.
33. Barthes again: "Imagine someone (a kind of Monsieur Teste in reverse who abolishes within himself all barriers, all classes, all exclusions, not by syncretism but by simple discard of the old specter: *logical contradiction;* who mixes every language, even those said to be incompatible; who silently accepts every charge of illogicality, of incongruity" (*Pleasure,* p. 3, italics in original). In the final analysis the description applies to no text I know so well as to Barthes' own euphoric writing.

to our original question with respect to the competition between playing for today and working for tomorrow, we must answer it in this way: Cortázar's proposed marriage of the lucid and the ludic— or of the Reality and the Pleasure Principles, if you will—sometimes smacks of heroic folly. Indeed, his essay at enlisting formalism in the service of the Revolution at times gives rise to a Groucho Marxism that promises to satisfy no one. This dearth of unequivocality, nonetheless, unsatisfying though it may be, constitutes precisely the strength of his posture. It shows with painful candor not only the impossibility of finally reconciling ideological differences, but the impossibility of resolving the dismaying question of whether to maintain or abandon rational discourse itself. What remains certain is the profound superficiality of play, the inevitable, irreducible, incessant interaction of elements circumscribed by conceptual models. In view of this endless and insufficient polemic, and of the novel's avowed alliance nonetheless with the cause of socialism within that dialogue, *A Manual for Manuel* might well be characterized as *the* committed Latin American intellectual's position paper for our moment in the Ironic Age.

CHAPTER 7

The Fragmented Life of Don Jacobo Lerner:
The Esthetics of Fragmentation

The terrain between the notions of irony and of fragmentation has been charted by numerous scholars, but I shall limit myself here to one French philosopher whose name has already appeared: Vladimir Jankélévitch.[1] The "good conscience (consciousness)" whose contours Jankélévitch maps in great detail has an aversion to progression or encyclopedism. It is, rather, elliptical in nature, "a fragmentary genius" (Friedrich Schlegel's formulation) that favors recommencement over continuation. "If irony breaks up stuffy or ridiculously solemn totalities," Jankélévitch explains, "it is in order to replace them with an esoteric totality, an invisible and qualitatively pure totality" (86). Irony's de(con)structive subjectivity gives rise to a "phantom-work, in a word, that each evening returns to put itself in question" (46), a constantly composing and decomposing "Penelopean plot" (46), "a sort of embroidery, an *appoggiatura* of the *via recta*" (48, all translations mine). According to Jankélévitch, the ironic work of art is always in a convulsive state midway between being and nothingness, and its unity resides, paradoxically, in the unstinting heterogeneity of its components.

As I stated in the introduction, all the novels included in this study are in one sense or another discontinuous. That quality is a fundamental ingredient in their being formalistically charged (they

1. Vladimir Jankélévitch, *L'Ironie ou la bonne conscience* (Paris: Presses Universitaires de France, 1950 [1936]). Page references appear parenthetically in the text.

demand that the reader reconstruct a chronology or provide causal links), and therefore, given the requisite thematics, in their deserving the label "ironic." None of the books previously studied, however, appears to be "about" this formal property to quite the degree of Isaac Goldemberg's first novel. *The Fragmented Life of Don Jacobo Lerner*[2] not only employs fragmentation as a principle of its organization and applies that principle exhaustively but also "thematizes" it by making it a topic of discussion and speculation. In addition to these intrinsic qualities, however, the novel provides another instance of discontinuity, in its author-to-critic relationship. Every other novelist whose work is analyzed herein is a recognized master; Goldemberg is young (born in 1945) and relatively unknown. In placing him alongside Vargas Llosa (acknowledged dean of Peruvian novelists), for instance, I assert that criticism's role is not just to bow to recognized excellence, but also to search among the undefined mass of unheralded literature for genuine achievements. In so doing I am deviating not only from the common practice of many colleagues but also from the parameters of my present investigation. What more appropriate vehicle for such a gesture than a relatively obscure novel whose primary concern is the breakdown of integration and coherence?

Titles are to books as proper names are to people. They identify the thing to which they allude, and in so doing distinguish it from the other discrete entities of its species. Predicated upon the uniqueness and stability of the object denominated, names facilitate reference by circumventing the (infinitely) long description necessary to capture adequately the essence of a particular phenomenon. The title of Isaac Goldemberg's recently published novel, *The Fragmented Life of Don Jacobo Lerner,* is thus tantamount to its name, even as it contains within it another proper name, that of its pathe-

2. Isaac Goldemberg, *The Fragmented Life of Don Jacobo Lerner,* tr. Robert S. Piccioto (New York: Persea Books, 1976); page references included parenthetically in the text. It is by now nearly common knowledge that the novel anomalously appeared first in English and then later in the original Spanish (Lima: Libre 1, 1978; rep. Hanover, N.H.: Ediciones del Norte, 1980). The novel, unjustly I feel, has received critical attention in the United States only in the form of book reviews. Goldemberg's other publications include two poetic works: (with José Kozer) *De Chepén a la Habana* (New York: Bayú-Menoráh, 1973), and *Hombre de paso/Just Passing Through* (bilingual collection), tr. David Unger and Isaac Goldemberg (Hanover, N.H.: Ediciones del Norte, 1982). He is presently completing his second novel, *La conversión.*

tic protagonist. Between the name of the character and that of the book there appears to be a simple rapport: the latter promises an account of the existence of the former. The simplicity soon proves to be illusory, however, owing to the qualifier "Fragmented," a loose translation of the Spanish *a plazos* (installment plan). "Fragmented," it turns out, indicates that the life in question is temporally extended, discontinuous, and, most important, not entirely one's own. If we follow the implication that one whose life is not quite one's own is not quite oneself, it is apparent that a name may serve as a sort of mask. It covers the deep-seated alterity, the movement and change of the world, with a veneer of constancy. Goldemberg's novel's title, then, as it performs its onomastic, identifying function, puts into question the self-sameness of the character Jacobo Lerner and in the same gesture problematizes the principle of naming that depends on that self-identical property.

In the novel, the difficulty inherent in nomination begins with the name Jacobo Lerner, which discloses immediately a circumstance of estrangement. It is the unlikely Hispanic version of a plainly Jewish appellation. Jacobo's namesake—*Ya'akov* of the Old Testament—is the son of *Yitzchuk* (Isaac in both Spanish and English) and the sire of twelve sons who become the patriarchs of the twelve tribes of Israel. As well as a prodigious progenitor, he is a dreamer who envisages himself climbing a ladder to heaven and wrestling with an angel of God. Though his dreams are troubled, they are bounded by an implicit faith in a holy, plenipotentiary deity.

Ya'akov is derived from a word which means "supplanter" or "replacer," a sense which is consistent with Jacobo's ambitious visions. The present Jacobo's surname—Lerner—means in Yiddish "student" or "apprentice," a tag which, if it denotes subalternity, at least admits the possibility of future mastery. Within the novel's *unheimlich* Peruvian setting, however, all these labels suffer a perceptible distortion. To the extent that Jacobo learns anything, it is knowledge in its most negative sense. That is, he becomes undeceived, totally and cynically disillusioned from a lesson learned the hard way and too late. Rather than a supplanter, he is a transplantee, a displaced personage, an exile both within and without. His dreams, moreover, incoherent icons of dismal descent, have closer affiliations with the infernal than the celestial. And in stark contrast to the profuse genealogy engendered by his biblical archetype, Jacobo Lerner has but one illegitimate offspring, Efraín, who is both infirm and insane, and on whom his father never so much as sets eyes. Jacobo is thus not one with his name, which, like his life, seems also not to be entirely his own.

The fissures between the character and his proper name, suggested in the title and opened in the textual corpus, obey a single principle that manifests itself throughout the text: disjunction. Rupture and partition dominate the heterogeneous narrative on levels that range from the individual word to the most abstract textual movement. This tendency perhaps comes to the reader's attention first via the novel's many images of decimation. Efraín is obsessed with visions of his own physical decomposition, for example, as in the following hallucinatory passages: "They chop my head off and Father Chirinos throws me in the river so the crabs will eat me" (19); and "One day the're going to eat me alive. All that will be left of me is skin and little white bones spread throughout the house" (139). On a historical plane (within the fiction), Sara, Jacobo's brother's wife, recalls the suicide shooting of her brother-in-law, "Daniel with his face blown off" (130). And, in certain interpretive moves, Jacobo's "chaotic life" (167) is characterized as "a past that was quickly breaking into small fragments" (50). These are but a few samples of represented fragmentation that are "local" in scope. They are experienced in the act of reading itself, without a reconstruction that demands recourse to the reader's memory.[3]

The principle of disjunction applies on a broader scale as well. In that separations of various kinds in the plot are far more numerous than reunions, the tendency is thematized and thus available to the reader as schemata in retrospect. His family devastated, Jacobo leaves his Russian *shtetl* of Staraya Ushitza for Poland and eventually for Peru. When the potentially happy coincidence occurs that his old friend Léon Mitrani has also emigrated to Chepén, a northern Peruvian village, Jacobo must again depart for Lima in order to avoid his paternal responsibilities. He enters a shoe business in partnership with his brother Moisés (another character with an ill-fitting name), but the tandem venture dissolves in the wake of

---

3. The model of reading employed here is based on that expounded by Wolfgang Iser in *The Act of Reading* (Baltimore: Johns Hopkins University Press, 1978).

Moisés' swindling his incredulous next of kin. Formerly a devout member of the Jewish community, a jaded Jacobo makes of himself a pariah by becoming proprietor of a brothel. Late in his life, when, for all his tainted wealth, he is despairingly ill and alone, Jacobo is assessed as "a man completely unattached, cut off from his traditions, and with absolutely no sense of direction" (99).

Although Jacobo is central, his is only one of the numerous cases of disenfranchisement in the novel. His Gentile lover, Juana Paredes, receives from him no confirmation of their relationship other than a periodic allowance. She is thus subjected to a limbolike, installment-plan life of her own. More cut off still is his former lover, Virginia (Bertila in the English translation[4]), with whom he engenders Efraín. Not only does she receive no financial consideration for her trouble, but she is additionally severed in the sense of losing her mind (the popular "mental breakdown" and the slang "going to pieces" and "cracked" suggest themselves, although they all locate the schism within the subject rather than between the subject and the world). Indeed, insanity—an extreme form of divorce from communal norms—enjoys a disproportionately high incidence among those who figure in Jacobo's life story. In addition to Virginia there is her demented son, Efraín, of whom Luchting has said, "He disintegrates, almost literally, for not knowing who he is or who his father is."[5] Jacobo's lifelong friend León Mitrani and his wife are also so stricken ("If it was true that the wife was not sound and sane, it was also true that León was not far behind" [47]). Mitrani, in turn, after his death, contributes to Jacobo's mental derangement. Mitrani's body is lost en route to its interment and thus, according to lore, his spirit is condemned to roam the earth as

4. It would be ill advised to make much of this curious discontinuity between the original and the translation. According to the author, Bertila is based on a real person of the same name in Peru. He changed the name to Virginia to avoid the complications of her or her acquaintances' finding her represented novelistically in less than flattering tones. As no such danger accompanied the publication of the English version, Bertila remains herself in the translation, which, paradoxically in this lone instance, is more veridical than its less mediated twin.

5. Wolfgang A. Luchting, "Una sorpresa para la literatura peruana: Isaac Goldemberg," *Chasqui* 8, no. 2 (1979): 123. Italics in the original. The same review also appears in *La Prensa* (Lima), 31 March 1977, and in *Excelsior* (Mexico City), 8 May 1977.

an *ánima en pena*. In the last year of his life, Jacobo feels himself possessed by Mitrani's dibbuk, a condition which is alleviated only by an exorcism.[6] The ostensible conjunction with "reality" implicit in Jacobo's return to his right mind, then, is attenuated by the disintegration of souls realized in the cure. There is thus ample evidence of inter- and intra-subjective breakage throughout the referential dimension of the text.

The antidote for the ubiquitous estrangement I have been describing, of course, should be the Jewish community, the organ of cultural and religious continuity and commonality. The exiles form a synagogue, organize social gatherings, and keep in touch via the periodical *Jewish Soul,* many of whose pages are reproduced sporadically in the novel. Very revealing in this regard, however, is the term by which the community calls itself: *colony.* Enmeshed with its evocation of the displaced Italian explorer Columbus (Colón) is the notion that the colony is insular, a satellite, peripheral to some yearned-for center. The cohesion of the society is thus predicated on a shared ex-centricity, a foreignness for which compensation is sought. The solace one could hope to find among such a collectivity is consequently always already subverted, undermined by the initial loss (Lima can never be Jerusalem) that precipitates its attempt at recuperating unity.

In a way very typical of the Diaspora, the feeling of Jewry is further diluted by a tension between at times irreconcilable loyalties, for each member is split between the religion into which he is born and the nation in which he has gained asylum (see pp. 42, 115–16, etc.).[7] This division between two continuities (one implied in assimilation and another implied in cultural retention) is drama-

6. The exorcism episode, which establishes a nexus with fantastic literature, thus further fragmenting the narrative, occurs in chapter XVIII, a number (transliterated *chai*) which signifies "life" in Hebrew. That the cure does not retard Jacobo's progression toward death is entirely consistent with the novel's devaluing of life when purchased on the installment plan.

7. For a successfully ludicrous account of Jews trying to pass for *criollos*, see Mario Szichman, *A las 20:25, la señora entró en la inmortalidad* (Hanover, N.H.: Ediciones del Norte, 1981). Along another axis, the figure of a Latin American Jew whose extra displacement to Paris leaves him personally untroubled, may be found in Lonstein, in Julio Cortázar, *Libro de Manuel* (Buenos Aires: Sudamericana, 1973), studied in chapter 6.

tized through Edelman, who tempers his solitude by marrying a Christian woman, and Jacobo, who does not.[8] In addition to these and other examples of severing and dispersal in the novel, we should recognize the extent to which Judaism is primordially fragmented; that is, loss of wholeness constitutes a hallmark of its myths and ceremonies. Every Jew is pre-scribed to repeat the fate of Adam, expelled from Paradise, and of Moses, destined to strive for the Promised Land but never to pass beyond the prosaic land of Moab. Jewish life, in addition, constitutes a daily reenactment of the Circumcision which, as it ritualistically marks a male's entry into the fold, symbolizes through partition and subtraction the separation from one's origin.[9] Even the ostensible union celebrated in the wedding rite is sanctified to the accompaniment of the shattering of a wineglass. This traditional gesture would appear to signify a recognition of the impossibility of conceiving fusion without simultaneously thinking fission. The lack of development and unity in Don Jacobo's life is not to be remedied by attending dances, bazaars, or theatrical performances. The sense of ubiquitous insufficiency in him, a transcendental "not-quiteness," is a structure that has informed the Jewish psyche for millennia. The mythical underpinnings of Goldemberg's novel are thus already riddled with rupture long before Don Jacobo begins his own truncated journey.

There is still room for differences of degree, however, and Jacobo's case certainly appears to be bleak in the extreme. His piecemeal existence, in fact, "forced him to think of God as a pitiless and arbitrary tyrant" (38) and leads him to the realization that "neither the affection he feels for his sister-in-law, nor his relationship with Doña Juana, nor the satisfactory economic situation in which he finds himself have been enough to give meaning to his life" (184). But it is not the ambition of Goldemberg's novel merely to *describe* the senselessness of a particularly solitary existence. If such were the case, one could point to a few thematically comprehensive pas-

8. For identifying the Jacobo-Edelman foil I am indebted to Raymond L. Williams, "*La vida a plazos de don Jacobo Lerner*," *Journal of Spanish Studies, Twentieth Century* 7, no. 2 (1979): 230–32.

9. This sense is conveyed in Carlos Grunberg's poem "Circuncisión," whose pertinent verses are: "Aún ignoras, pobre crío,/que cuesta sangre ser judío" (You are still unaware, poor child,/that being Jewish costs blood), cited in Solomon Lipp, "Israel and the Holocaust in Contemporary Spanish American Poetry," *Hispania* 65, no. 4 (1982): 536–43.

sages and dispense with the rest of the textual minutiae. To say that the work is "about" fragmentation per se is to say that in addition to the pervasiveness of that motif in the characters' lives, the novel is composed in such a manner as to *reproduce* for the reader the acute inconsequentiality that Jacobo judges his life to embody. Such a sensation clearly cannot be reduced to a single line, no matter how pithy. Taking his cue from another displaced author, the Cuban Severo Sarduy, who in *Cobra* says, "Writing is the art of ellipsis,"[10] Goldemberg has crafted the text out of motley pieces of rent cloth. The resulting verbal collage constitutes a systematic attack on the notions of wholeness, continuity, and meaning. In such a context, an encapsuling statement would not only be insufficient to the task, but in its very pronouncement would run counter to the aims of the undertaking.

In addition to the images already described, the experience of scattering occurs at the level of language, where the fragmenting impulse is quite vigorous. Goldemberg's admirably controlled prose is sprinkled liberally with Yiddish and Hebrew, particularly in regard to Jewish holy days and the apparata of devotion: *sidurim, tfillin, yarmulka, talis,* and so forth. Beyond the heterogeneous lexicon required for the mimetic portrayal of a Jewish-in-exile thematics, there are also select passages that create a heterogeneity of syntax. Some of Samuel Edelman's locutions, for example, such as: "Thank God tomorrow I leave Chepén and no more return, since I got here everything like a dream, reliving the past again, why have to remember things give pain in heart?" (248 in Spanish, my translation), provide an insight into the rhythms and ellipses of an alien tongue spoken through a Yiddish grid.[11] Similarly, journalistic prose, advertisements, and official documents are interspersed among narrative passages to give rise to, among other things, a disparity of graphic textures. Some of these narrative sections are of striking lyricism. Among the most salient of these is the

10. Severo Sarduy, *Cobra* (Buenos Aires: Sudamericana, 1974), p. 15. The allusion to Sarduy is not as capricious as it may seem, as he, in a back-cover comment whose point of origin I have been unable to ascertain, is one of the first to have uncovered Goldemberg's novel's ironic nature.

11. It is disappointing that Picciotto's translation does not attempt to render this and similar sections in corresponding English dialect. The result is that the Spanish version maintains a burlesque edge while the English suffers from periodic doldrums.

following: "The [men] met, usually, at Jacobo's whorehouse, where they would give themselves heart and soul to the dissonant atmosphere. On these nights their lust went unbounded, and they left the marks of their emptiness on the bodies of the courtesans" (168). In short, the novel has no particular style but no lack of distinct styles.

Along what might be called an axis of decorum, one finds discontinuity in the incongruous, sporadic juxtaposition of humorous material with more solemn writing. In addition to the illness, suicide, and madness already mentioned, other misfortunes are visited upon the protagonist himself: in 1917 his parents die, his sister Judith disappears with her son, and her husband goes mad (39); in 1926 Jacobo, a traveling salesman, is hospitalized after being beaten by an irate merchant upon trying to collect payment for goods (103); in 1929, while crossing a street, Jacobo is run over by a car and left with injuries that are "not minor" (116). All this action is set before a backdrop of political unrest and antisemitism within Peru, perennial border skirmishes between Peru and Colombia, and Hitler's terrifying rise to power in Europe.

Nevertheless, passages of a clearly comic nature lighten the novel and skirt maudlin pathos. Jacobo's aspiring in-laws, for example, are drawn in caricaturesque proportions when they gullibly take him for "a kind of Count of Monte Cristo, owner of vast shining treasures buried deep in the earth, lord of enchanted palaces in distant kingdoms, consummate swordsman, and tireless traveler destined for prodigious adventures" (68). His sister-in-law Sara Lerner reveals her essential superficiality when she muses, "Perhaps this time I'd better put on my black dress. If Jacobo dies, I'm going to have to wear it to the funeral anyway. What am I going to do?" (173 in Spanish version, my translation). And Efraín, in an innocent and demented state that allows for outrageous candor, provides numerous instances of (mostly scatological) comic relief. At one point his mind wanders to a quarrel in which his grandmother scolds his grandfather as a "shitty old man. Where the hell was he when they were fucking his daughter?" (18). Later he reports that "Uncle Pedro died in the toilet. He farted, and then he died" (205). As if uniform tragedy would lend too much importance to a series of events whose significance gestures toward an ultimate meaninglessness, inconsistency in mood (and narrative mode) plays a major role in buttressing the novel's fragmenting enterprise.

The overall narrative configuration further contributes to a kaleidoscopic, mystifying effect. The mystery is actually a sort of puzzle whose key resides in Samuel Edelman's talmudic dictum: "But when man thinks he is finished then everything begins anew" (188). It is Jacobo's sense of impending death in December of 1935 (he thinks he is finished) that generates the narration of his episodic existence (everything begins anew). The search for meaning through the past's recuperation etches a roughly circular trajectory. Circular, in that the fragmentary "Chronicles" work their way from 1923, shortly after Jacobo's arrival in Peru, back to 1935, whence these memories originate. Roughly, because a preponderance of the interior monologues (interspersed with the "Chronicles," excerpts from *Jewish Soul,* and assorted documents) is set between 1933 and 1935 (weighting disproportionately the recent past and making the figure elliptical) and since it is uncertain whether the last date given ("December 25, 1935" [201]) indeed completes the return to the present. (I suspect such to be the case, however, for having Jacobo's death coincide with the birthday of the Christian Savior is too great an irony to pass over). Time is felt to be still more discontinuous through the use of the following technique: the third-person narratives, when entitled "Chronicles," are couched in the present tense, even though the action takes place in the past. Conversely, when relating the events of the novel's present, the third-person narratives make use of the past tense. The historian's conventional point of view is thus employed in a deviant, disconcerting manner. Where space is concerned (and here I refer to the point of the enunciation of the narrative) again continuity is eluded. In addition to the omniscient voices just mentioned, five different first-person narrators (Efraín, Samuel Edelman, Miriam Abramowitz, Sara Lerner, and Juana Paredes) present five radically divergent stream-of-consciousness interpretations of Jacobo and the consequences of his commissions and omissions. Of signal importance is that among the narrators Jacobo Lerner does *not* figure. His silence bespeaks eloquently the essential absence at the heart of the novel. Don Jacobo can never be known from within as a self-present *I,* a unified ego represented by a single voice. The novel that bears his name and promises an

181

account of his life in its title thus discloses structurally the nothingness implicit in that being.

One must make do with partial, sometimes contradictory reports of Jacobo from without. The possibility is raised, for example, that Jacobo and Sara Lerner, brother- and sister-in-law, may have been lovers. Innuendos to that effect are made by Sara's sister Miriam (81–82); but Sara's failure so much as to conceive of the matter in her own interior monologue would seem to indicate that such fears are merely symptomatic of Miriam's resentment over Jacobo's having canceled their wedding (28, 127). Still, in the sheer pronouncement of her words, Miriam's doubts are etched indelibly in the reader's memory. Rather than a solid, indivisible core, then, Jacobo is an interplay of shifting surfaces, a problematic series of overlapping options that never resolve themselves.

The portrayal of his mercurial identity, unquestionably abetted by the chapter he fails to narrate, attains heightened relief through another structural device. This is the journal *Jewish Soul,* the voice of the Jewish colony. Any given issue may be charged with internally contradictory or simply skewed and irrelevant material (see, for example, no. 10 [October 1934], in which a piece on the "Heroic Character of the Jewish Spirit" is juxtaposed with and made ridiculous by Jacobo's letter complaining of chronic digestive ailments, 171–74). Moreover, a particular number (or any quantity of numbers) of the publication may to varying degrees represent synecdochically the whole, but it (they) can never be that open-ended totality. *Jewish Soul* exists *a plazos,* in fractional installments, discrete syntactical units that never achieve a coherent grammar. It attains nominal integration (tautologically) only through its name, which appears to circumscribe its possibilities. The analogy between the serialized text and Jacobo Lerner, another Jewish soul, seems at this point almost too obvious to draw, but since we have returned to our point of departure (regarding the relation among titles, names, and identity), let us put it in a way that takes into account the dismantling gauntlet we have run.

Jacobo Lerner is, in one sense, internally disunified the way every soul, Jewish or not, is susceptible of deconstruction. That is, Jacobo's being is constituted by *différance,* "the spatio-temporal movement of differing/deferring which gives rise to being as presence. . . . To be proper or self-same, a thing must contain its own improper double or repetition."[12] The distortion incurred by the imposition of a proper name on something riddled with otherness and essentially improper is eminently significant because of its global application. Yet signaling his lack of self-sameness does not distinguish Jacobo's peculiar malaise. In order to appreciate Jacobo's plight and the novel's main thrust in greater dimension, we should take another, more detailed look at the notion of *a plazos,* which we have posited—in its temporal extension, discontinuity, and problematicity with respect to ownership—to be fundamental to the text.

Purchases made on the installment plan imply a curious set of give-and-take relations among the buyer, the seller, and the object. Although the seller yields at once the use of the object, he retains a claim over it—the right of foreclosure or repossession—should the buyer fail to pay in full. The buyer, in turn, acquires immediate possession and enjoyment of, and even title to, the object desired, but only gradually, with each payment tendered, does he acquire equity in it. The transferral of proprietorship, instead of occurring completely at a given instant, takes place piecemeal over an agreed-upon duration. For this convenience, tantamount to the temporary use of the seller's money, the buyer must pay interest, a surcharge tagged onto the purchase price in exchange for the granting of credit. Throughout the installment agreement the object, suspended in a commercial purgatory, belongs completely to neither party to the contract.

Principal among the buyer's motives for entering into an installment purchase agreement is the desire to gain immediate use of an item which might otherwise take him years of saving to afford. The advantage to the seller is that, just for being patient and not demanding full cash payment upon delivery of the item, he receives a total sum greater than the selling price. At the same time, he loses liquidity, for as long as the buyer withholds the seller's cash, he in effect limits the seller's freedom to dissolve his own outstanding and interest-accruing debts. But of greatest moment is the lot of the

12. This obviously Derrida-inspired quotation, which I include because of its succinctness, is from Michael Ryan, "Self-Evidence," *Diacritics* 10, no. 2 (1980): 3. For a fuller exposition of the notion of *différance,* see, among others, Jacques Derrida, *Of Grammatology,* tr. Gayatri Chakravorty Spivak (Baltimore: Johns Hopkins University Press, 1974), pp. 23, 46–47, 52–57, 62–65.

purchaser. Not only is there exacted from him a sum greater than the cash value of the object purchased, but the long-run quality of his purchasing experience is irrevocably altered.

The alteration in the credit-buyer's experience can be understood as a movement from presence to absence. First, of course, the purchaser attains possession of the object, with the enjoyment pertinent thereto. But later, after the inflated debt is liquidated and full legal ownership finally has been obtained, the new owner is likely to suffer an anticlimactic estrangement. Payment has been dissociated from possession; only in the abstract is it clear during the major part of the payback period that one is not paying for nothing. At the same time, the item is no longer new; it may be unsightly or in need of repair, and quite possibly is no longer desired at all. The fragmented, extended, and decentered transaction, whose beginning and end cannot be apprehended simultaneously, lacks the plenitude and closure inherent in a simple, unitary quid pro quo. This state of affairs—the purchaser's perennial plight—may arouse little sympathy in North American society, whose economy was founded on the tenet of caveat emptor, or in an academic community whose concerns transcend mere appropriation. But when the object desired and transacted is life itself; and when the buyer, Don Jacobo Lerner, realizes that he has been paying exorbitantly for marred, defective, and ultimately worthless merchandise—goods purchased from a seller (let us say God of the Old Testament) whose bad faith manifests itself in that He proves not to exist—the tragedy clearly touches us all. We are witness and party to a swindling, as it were, in the marketplace of existence.

The absence of meaning so ably conveyed by the esthetics of fragmentation stems from the protagonist's erroneous supposition that commercial agreements have universal, existential application. What the novel would have supplant this assumption is the considered awareness that life is not subject to ownership, no matter how good the credit terms may sound (let us not forget Don Juan Tenorio's refrain: "You gave me long-term credit!"). Don Jacobo is a slow "Lerner" and is hence incapable of marshaling the arguments here amassed against the hypothesis that business and life are coextensive. In that it doggedly insists on privileging life over finances, *The Fragmented Life of Don Jacobo Lerner* should be recognized as a novel whose poetics is at the service of its politics. Worthy of recognition, too, is its place among the leading ironic works of contemporary Spanish-American fiction, for it accomplishes its aim of persuasion with admirable restraint; which is to say, if you will, at no esthetic cost.

Epilogue:
Toward a Spanish-American Writing

The notion of a privileged link between irony and extended narrative fiction is most forcefully articulated by Georg Lukács in *The Theory of the Novel*. Lukács portrays the novel as "the epic of a world that has been abandoned by God,"[1] one where meaning and plenitude in life are no longer given. Since its inception in the *Quijote,* according to Lukács, the novel seeks to recover that lost meaning and wholeness (the sense of doubt we have attributed to subjective irony) through the construction of an organic totality. The resulting construct, however, never succeeds in being fully organic, but rather conceptual. That is, the meaning depends on the "form," which is always constituted differently by each reader's imagination, and is not "in" the work at all. The form of the novel is characterized as an abstraction seeing through itself, an eternal state of contingency, a becoming that never achieves the completeness requisite for being. The work's ultimate meaning is thus achieved negatively, by repeatedly revealing itself as absent and illusory. Lukács' vision of the novel's self-surpassing and self-consuming nature moves him to posit irony as "the normative mentality of the novel."[2]

Although it is unclear whether Lukács is speaking of the author's, the reader's, or the text's "mentality" as being ironic, his assertion

---

1. Georg Lukács, *The Theory of the Novel: A Historico-Philosophical Essay on the Forms of Great Epic Literature,* tr. Anna Bostock (Cambridge: M.I.T. Press, 1971 [1916]), p. 88.
2. Ibid., p. 84.

finds general support in Northrop Frye's observation in *The Anatomy of Criticism* that most serious fiction of the past century and a half has been ironic in mode. Bearing in mind that critical absolutes and irony are incompatible bedfellows, let us agree that the novel is not *the* ironic genre and that there are other concerns, aside from irony, that the novel treats with utter alacrity. Yet, within these parameters, the novel continues to be an extraordinarily congenial home for representing and producing irony. Studying the novel from the standpoint of irony allows us to address such traditional concerns as characterization, action, description, dialogue, theme, and style. It is also capable of putting in relief the work's negativities, its *écriture* and possibilities for generating meaning, as well as its dynamic relation to the reader. As a vehicle for literary criticism, moreover, it engenders coherent readings of challenging texts, certainly a pedagogue's prime concern.

A novel so thoroughly imbued with the spirit of irony that it merits the qualifier "ironic" must satisfy several conditions, and it may do so in many different ways. It may be expected to be replete with sundry "local" ironies, both intended and accidental. Characters and/or narrators may engage in dissembling, polysemous verbalization and may withhold relevant information from each other or the reader in order to bring about momentary disorientation or partial understanding. Novelistic entities may be confronted with conflictive or paradoxical circumstances, and there is no reason to exclude any thematics (political, mythical, psychological, epistemological, etc.) from this arena of contrariety. These conflicts, too, may precipitate within the fiction the movement of mind resumed under the heading of subjective irony. In sum, the ironic work should be rife with all sorts of represented irony, according to the nature of its subject matter. But since all these possibilities of representation—present in the seven novels under investigation here—are positivities, none alone or in combination with the others is sufficient to bring about a vital sense of irony. Required also is that the work strike the reader negatively, and to abet that coup, it must be formalistically charged. The narrative must, by the arrangement of its elements, call attention to its status as a linguistic artifact, a construct independent of the world it represents. The precise way in which it realizes such an accentuation of the negative of course differs from novel to novel. Each of these novels effects that end in its own way, yet all may be summarized under the heading of textual discontinuity.

As a thorough rehearsal of every instance of discontinuity in these novels would indeed be tedious, let us consider only significant manifestations of that principle. In *The Death of Artemio Cruz* the notion appears most emphatically as a concatenation of short narrative fragments that are regular in their length and rotation of narrators. Rulfo's *Pedro Páramo* limits its points of view to two, but the number of textual fragments is roughly double that of Fuentes' novel. The length of each fragment and the order of appearance of a given narrator, moreover, are totally unpredictable. Puig's *Betrayed by Rita Hayworth* increases the number of narrators to twelve, no two of whose temporo-spatial coordinates are identical. It is also characterized by a discontinuity of anecdote, wherein several conflicting versions of certain events are given, with no version offered as authoritative. The gallery of narrators in Cabrera Infante's *Three Trapped Tigers* is no less populous, and their monologues are far more erratic in length and uncertain in their veracity. Comparable in anecdotal discontinuity to *Rita Hayworth*, *TTT* is most easily identified by its discontinuity of signification, represented mainly in Bustrófedon's hermetic verbal paroxysms. The novel's language is at many junctures severed from any literal meaning. The distinguishing discontinuity of Vargas Llosa's *Aunt Julia and the Scriptwriter* resides in its illusion, which alternates between fictional autobiography and soap-opera scenarios (the latter a creation of a guignolesque character sketched in the autobiographical portions). Discontinuity of illusion thus signals a fissure between anecdotes rather than a point of undecidability within a given anecdote, as is characteristic of *Rita Hayworth* and *TTT*. In the case of Cortázar's *A Manual for Manuel*, the intermittency is again anecdotal, but this time it is brought about by the omission of essential data with respect to the Screwery and the police raid on the terrorists' lair. And finally, with respect to Goldemberg's *The Fragmented Life of Don Jacobo Lerner*, discontinuity assumes the form of a heterogeneous verbal collage as the reiteration of a work's title and central concern. Each of these novels, in its unique way, as Ortega y Gasset has put it, "lives more for its form than its subject matter."[3]

3. José Ortega y Gasset, *Ideas sobre la novela* (Madrid: Espasa-Calpe, 1969 [1925]), p. 180.

The upshot of all these ruptures is to effect still another breach, that between the world and the text, and to inhibit thereby the reader's naive identification with any specific image kindled in his imagination. In general, the ironic narrative does not accept passively its inherent irony but rather strives to magnify it by confronting the reader with still one more ironic phenomenon in the world. It purveys conflict and discontinuity on a local scale in order to estrange the reader and thus make of him an ironist, so that he may then apprehend the work's meaning as a form, a construct that is ultimately inseparable from himself. Ironic novels are those that manifest a meaning that is always elsewhere and a pulsating truth that can be captured only in its extinction.

In part I, "Static Irony," I applied a single novelistic model, narrative irony, to four different works. Such an imposition from without might be expected to reduce the uniqueness of the novels in question, but that does not turn out to be so. The survey of intratextual distance has elucidated an essential distinction among the works, for it can be shown that each one concentrates its ironic activity in a different zone. In *The Death of Artemio Cruz* the chief field of irony is within the titular narrator-character. *Pedro Páramo* concentrates its ironic activity both between the character Pedro Páramo and his fellow inhabitants of the village of Comala and, at first, between the reader and the character Juan Preciado. Later, the scene moves to the space between the reader and the omniscient narrator. In *Betrayed by Rita Hayworth* most of the narrative irony occurs between the reader and the many first-person narrators, as well as among all the lonely and drifting characters. And *Three Trapped Tigers* locates its irony in the same arena as *Rita Hayworth*, plus in new space created by the introduction of additional formal elements, the explicit author and explicit reader. What is most remarkable is that as the novels, in the order in which they are here presented, create narrative irony in ways that are increasingly complex, each new form of irony, rather than exhaust the reservoir of interaction, serves to open more possibilities for the generation of still more irony in a limitless fictional cosmos. In light of irony's capital role in constituting the novel, I would agree with Robert Alter that the eternal cries of that genre's demise are less sound than ever.[4]

4. Robert Alter, *Partial Magic: The Novel as a Self-Conscious Genre* (Berkeley: University of California Press, 1975).

Epilogue

In moving from static to kinetic irony in part II, I respond to certain limitations that become apparent in applying the narrative-irony method. In spite of the insights it produces, narrative irony is based on a privileged notion of the subject, a notion the fictions themselves (especially Fuentes' and Goldemberg's novels) put into question. Rather than simulacra of people, novels are universally composed of language. An approach to the novel that cannot account for our engagement with language, how we use it and how it uses us, is fundamentally deficient. The displacement of our discourse from an analysis based on the relations between who or what is represented in the novels, to the reader's stance vis-à-vis the various linguistic modes through which that representation occurs, motivates the static/kinetic distinction. The other chapters in part II, which investigate the frontiers between irony and play and between irony and fragmentation respectively, presuppose the notion of fiction as a primarily verbal phenomenon that is advanced in my analysis of *Aunt Julia and the Scriptwriter*.

In that novel the reader is barred from a facile identification either with the author-narrator Mario, a masked puppeteer, or with Marito and Julia, the engaging principal characters. The reader is skillfully steered, rather, toward intimacy with a mode of discourse. This complex, nuanced prose is thrown into high relief by the monomaniacal, univocal scrawling of the scriptwriter, Pedro Camacho. In that Camacho's writing, devoid of esthetic distance, produces in the reader an estrangement, and whereas the reader is beguiled by prose written from a more ironic outlook, the novel may be seen also to produce a dynamic that is ironic in the paradoxical sense of the word.

The view projected by *A Manual for Manuel* depends on the realization that irony and literature are to a large degree play, and on Huizinga's hypothesis that play and civilization are coextensive; that it arises *in* play and *as* play. This formulation puts into question certain basic oppositions—such as that between the serious and the frivolous, or the political and the purely esthetic; these dichotomies Cortázar's novel also systematically undermines. On the one hand, play, especially in its erotic and linguistic forms, is steadfastly defended against the forces of terror, whether from the right or the left, and whether officially perpetrated or not. On the other hand, the novel points toward the erotic and political nature

190

of *all* writing, no matter how seemingly inhibited or escapist. What is ultimately revolutionary about *A Manual for Manuel*, then, is not so much its insistent broaching of taboo subjects or its problematical advancement of armed insurrection as its call for a recasting of Western thought in order to admit contrary notions in an ironic, non-self-canceling field of interaction.

The treatment given *The Fragmented Life of Don Jacobo Lerner* derives from Jankélévitch and others' proposition with respect to the proclivity of the ironic consciousness toward ellipsis and discontinuity. The particulateness that characterizes Goldemberg's novel on so many planes constitutes a contradictory statement on the meaninglessness of a solitary and materialistic existence. In the sense that the reader is subjected to an arsenal of disparate textual fragments, the work goes beyond the mere telling about Don Jacobo's pathetic case to include a recreation of his baffling experience. And, since Jacobo's business-as-usual approach to life leads to a questioning of the continuity inherent in the very self-identity of the protagonist, the novel is seen as fundamentally political. It is an esthetically refined tract on the economically inspired disintegration of the subject and the resulting impropriety of the proper name.

Among works on contemporary Latin-American or Spanish-American fiction, this one occupies a unique niche. Whereas Fuentes, Loveluck, Ortega, and Rodríguez Monegal direct themselves only to a Spanish-speaking reader, I seek a broad public of Anglo-American readers, not necessarily specialists in Hispanic fiction.[5] In contrast to Brotherston and Gallagher, I am concerned with literary theory as an independent discipline; neither of those books addresses the important questions of the critic's role or an adequate locus for the critical discourse.[6] As sequential, linear time is one of

5. Carlos Fuentes, *La nueva novela hispanoamericana* (Mexico City: Joaquín Mortiz, 1969); Juan Loveluck, ed., *Novelistas hispanoamericanos de hoy* (Madrid: Taurus, 1976); Julio Ortega, *La contemplación y la fiesta: Notas sobre la novela latinoamericana actual* (Caracas: Monte Avila Editores, 1969); Emir Rodríguez Monegal, *El boom de la novela latinoamericana: Ensayo* (Caracas: Editorial Tiempo Nuevo, 1972). See also by the same author: *Narradores de esta América* (Montevideo: Alfa, 1963).

6. Gordon Brotherston, *The Emergence of the Latin American Novel* (Cambridge and New York: Cambridge University Press, 1977); David P. Gallagher, *Modern Latin American Literature* (New York: Oxford University Press, 1973).

the chief notions put into question by the contemporary Spanish-American novel, I have deviated from Brushwood's chronological approach, useful in a manual though it may be.[7] Bacarisse's and Harss' works are distinguished by the former's nature as a collection of essays written by a variety of contributors, and by the latter's dependence on the interview as an entry into occasional critical commentary.[8] Only Alfred MacAdam's book is comparable in over-all intent (for one thing, neither of us is concerned with "coverage" of the entire field of narrative), but there, too, the differences outweigh the similarities.[9] In the main we have treated different authors. Where we do coincide, moreover, the texts of those authors or the aspects of their texts emphasized have diverged. And most significant, the present book is unified by a specific proposition.

The thesis, it bears repeating, is that, for a variety of reasons, irony is a characteristic property of the contemporary Spanish-American narrative. All the novels studied herein are, first, examples of authorial verbal irony (of reticence, of litotes, of allegory, etc.), where language turns away from its literal dictionary sense. In addition, without exception these texts project an image of the world that is conflictive and paradoxical, and are thus thematically ironic in the situational or cosmic sense. And last, these books in diverse ways show themselves to be ironic phenomena, fictions whose profound truth resides in the revelation of their own illusory mode of being. In the final analysis, irony serves more than satisfactorily as a critical approach to these objects because of its extraordinary range and malleability: it is a world-and-self-view genre. Irony is more than just a *Weltanschauüng* on a (Third) world marked by political and cultural hegemony, adulation of authority, and widespread hunger and violence, all masked behind a rhetoric of freedom and charity. Spanish-American history does not become ironic until it is perceived as such by a subject who also views himself in

7. John S. Brushwood, *The Spanish-American Novel: A Twentieth-Century Survey* (Austin: University of Texas Press, 1975).

8. Salvador Bacarisse, ed., *Contemporary Latin American Fiction: Seven Essays* (Edinburgh: Scottish Academic Press, 1980); Luis Harss and Barbara Dohmann, *Into the Mainstream: Conversations with Latin-American Writers* (New York: Harper & Row, 1967; originally published as *Los nuestros* [Buenos Aires: Sudamericana, 1966]).

9. Alfred MacAdam, *Modern Latin American Narratives: The Dreams of Reason* (Chicago: University of Chicago Press, 1977).

terms of incongruity and contradiction. And when that beleaguered subject represents linguistically that world and self view, it is most successfully accomplished—during the past thirty years in Spanish America at least—in narrative. Open-ended and undefinable, the novel has provided Spanish America with just the stage it needed for the entire Western world to witness its uneasy emergence into prominence.

In the 1940s, when the first exemplars of the "New Spanish-American Narrative" (Asturias, Borges, Carpentier, Marechal, and Yáñez, let us say) were just making themselves heard, the term that seemed best to circumscribe their writing was "magical realism." If as a critical tool magical realism is somewhat dull edged, it certainly served at first to demarcate a zone apart from the costumbristic *novela de la tierra* and the countless works of socialist realism that dominated most of Spanish-American fiction until then. The inadequacy of that term as a generic etiquette, however, becomes readily apparent when we consider that among the novels scrutinized here, only *Pedro Páramo* is generally accepted as representing the magical realism mode. Because of the exorcism episode in *The Fragmented Life of Don Jacobo Lerner*, perhaps we may rightly include that novel under the same heading. But what of the others? A broader and more complex umbrella concept is that of the "neobaroque." Following Borges' description of the baroque as "that style which deliberately exhausts (or wants to exhaust) its possibilities and borders on its own caricature,"[10] the neobaroque focuses on Spanish-American fiction's tendency toward proliferation and self-parody. Without a doubt, each of these novels could be shown to conform to that description in one sense or another. It seems plain, also, that no novel adheres to the pattern quite so well as *Three Trapped Tigers*, which is composed largely of nontranscendental lexical permutations and frequently misleading self-references.

But if some novels fit the mold better, others require a good deal of coaxing. Least suited to the tag is *Betrayed by Rita Hayworth*. Average in length and pedestrian in diction, the novel progresses chronologically until its last chapter. If the characters come across

10. Jorge Luis Borges, *Historia universal de la infamia* (Buenos Aires: Emecé, 1971 [1935]), p. 9 (my translation).

as sad distortions of what human beings are capable of becoming, it is not because Puig's language caricaturizes itself but because it conveys so convincingly the pathetic situations of the speakers. The author has long been recognized as an accomplished mimic of the vox populi. But that talent is, after all, within the domain of literary, and more specifically psychological, realism. In a similar vein, if *The Death of Artemio Cruz* and *Aunt Julia and the Scriptwriter* are adequately accounted for by reference to the neobaroque, Fuentes' early novel *The Good Conscience* (1959) and Vargas Llosa's *The Time of the Hero* (1962) stubbornly resist such categorization. These are, on the other hand, adroitly handled in terms of irony, from verbal construct to metaphysical principle. I am not implying, to be sure, that irony can subsume the neobaroque as the neobaroque has subsumed magical realism to become the key term to circumscribe today's Spanish-American fiction. Irony, for one thing, applies as much to the North American novel as to the Spanish-American, whereas the neobaroque—outside of such practioners as Faulkner, Nabokov, and Barth—finds little resonance north of Havana. It is therefore too broad an umbrella. As the *eiron* needs its *alazon* in order to fulfill its potential, post-Romantic irony depends on the neobaroque for a structure to supplement. Neither exclusive of other means nor a central critical tool, irony is a factor without which no understanding of the nature of Spanish-American writing can be complete. I leave charting the frontiers among irony, magical realism, and the neobaroque for another occasion.

Northrop Frye has said that irony "is naturally a sophisticated mode, and the chief difference between sophisticated and naive irony is that the naive ironist calls attention to the fact that he is being ironic, whereas sophisticated irony merely states, and lets the reader add the ironic tone himself."[11] The quotation is extremely apposite: first, because it adds one more dimension to a phenomenon with which we are by now quite familiar; and second, for the paradoxical irony contained in the very passage, which affords us a performative reprise of one of our principal motifs. The paradox resides in irony's being "naturally a sophisticated mode," a state of affairs that makes naive irony less natural and therefore

---

11. Northrop Frye, *Anatomy of Criticism: Four Essays* (Princeton: Princeton University Press, 1960), p. 41.

more a product of artifice. Now, no one wishes to be considered naive, particularly no one who, fancying himself to be an ironist, views the naive/sophisticated duality as suspect. But if it becomes known that naive irony is more artful than the sophisticated sort, it may soon be fashionable to betray one's dissimulation, in order to carry it out all the more on yet another level of meaning. If this sounds like sarcasm, a mordent and vulgar perversion of irony, rather than deny it I would point to the insufficiency of all attempts (certainly mine more than Frye's) at systematically accounting for the world, thought, and art. Instead of masking the inevitable point of rupture, though, irony freely admits it, finds its origin in that breach, and builds a countersystem upon it. Unabashedly oxymoronic, irony encompasses the solemn and the ludic, literature and language, writing and reading, the self and the world. It is at once the curse and blessing of modernity.

WORKS CONSULTED

Books and Dissertations

Abramoski, Nancy Ann. "A Linguistic Approach to Literature: Three Modern Latin American Novels." Ph.D. dissertation, Cornell University, 1972.

Alegría, Fernando. *Literatura y revolución*. Mexico City: Fondo de Cultura Económica, 1971.

Alter, Robert. *Partial Magic: The Novel as a Self-Conscious Genre*. Berkeley: University of California Press, 1975.

Bacarisse, Salvador, ed. *Contemporary Latin American Fiction: Seven Essays*. Edinburgh: Scottish Academic Press, 1980.

Barthes, Roland. *The Pleasure of the Text*. Tr. Richard Miller. New York: Hill and Wang, 1975.

Bergson, Henri. *Laughter: An Essay on the Meaning of the Comic*. Tr. Cloudesley Brereton and Fred Rothwell. London: Macmillan, 1911.

Bleich, David. *Subjective Criticism*. Baltimore and London: Johns Hopkins University Press, 1980.

Booth, Wayne C. *The Rhetoric of Fiction*. Chicago: University of Chicago Press, 1961.

_____. *A Rhetoric of Irony*. Chicago: University of Chicago Press, 1974.

Borges, Jorge Luis. *Ficciones*. Ed. and tr. Anthony Kerrigan. New York: Grove Press, 1962.

_____. *El hacedor*. Madrid: Alianza/Emecé, 1975 [1960].

_____. *Historia universal de la infamia*. Buenos Aires: Emecé, 1971 [1935].

Borinsky, Alicia. *Ver/ser visto: Notas para una poética*. Barcelona: Antoni Bosch, 1978.

Brotherston, Gordon. *The Emergence of the Latin American Novel*. Cambridge and New York: Cambridge University Press, 1977.

Works Consulted

Brushwood, John Stubbs. *The Spanish-American Novel: A Twentieth-Century Survey.* Austin: University of Texas Press, 1975.

Cabrera Infante, Guillermo. *La Habana para un infante difunto.* Barcelona: Seix Barral, 1979.

————. *Three Trapped Tigers.* Tr. Donald Gardener and Suzanne Jill Levine, in collaboration with the author. New York: Harper & Row, 1971.

Caillois, Roger. *Man, Play, and Games* Tr. Meyer Barash. Glencoe, Ill.: Free Press, 1961.

Chevalier, Haakon M. *The Ironic Temper: Anatole France and His Time.* New York: Oxford University Press, 1932.

Cortázar, Julio. *All Fires the Fire, and Other Stories.* Tr. Suzanne Jill Levine. New York: Pantheon, 1973.

————. *Las armas secretas.* Buenos Aires: Sudamericana, 1969 [1959].

————. *Bestiario.* Buenos Aires: Sudamericana, 1971 [1951].

————. *Blow-up, and Other Stories.* Tr. Paul Blackburn. New York: Collier Books, 1967.

————. *Hopscotch.* Tr. Gregory Rabassa. New York: Pantheon, 1966.

————. *A Manual for Manuel.* Tr. Gregory Rabassa. New York: Pantheon, 1978.

————. *Los reyes.* Buenos Aires: Sudamericana, 1970 [1949].

————. *62: A Model Kit.* Tr. Gregory Rabassa. New York: Pantheon, 1972.

————. *Un tal Lucas.* Buenos Aires: Sudamericana, 1979.

————. *Ultimo Round.* Buenos Aires: Sudamericana, 1969.

————. *La vuelta al día en ochenta mundos.* Buenos Aires: Sudamericana, 1967.

Derrida, Jacques. *Of Grammatology.* Tr. Gayatri Chakravorty Spivak. Baltimore: Johns Hopkins University Press, 1974.

Dorfman, Ariel, and Armand Mattelart. *How to Read Donald Duck: Imperialist Ideology in the Disney Comic.* Tr. David Kunzle. New York: International General, 1975.

Dyson, A. E. *The Crazy Fabric: Essays in Irony.* London: Macmillan, 1965.

Eichner, Hans. *Friedrich Schlegel.* New York: Twayne, 1970.

Erasmus, Desiderius. *The Praise of Folly.* Tr. and comm. Hoyt Hopewell Hudson. Princeton: Princeton University Press, 1941 [1509].

Fish, Stanley. *Is There a Text in This Class?* Cambridge: Harvard University Press, 1980.

Foster, David William. *Studies in the Contemporary Spanish-American Short Story.* Columbia: University of Missouri Press, 1979.

Foucault, Michel. *The Order of Things: An Archaeology of the Human Sciences.* New York: Random House, 1970.

Works Consulted

Freud, Sigmund. *Jokes and Their Relation to the Unconscious*. Tr. James Strachey. New York: Norton, 1960.

Frye, Northrop. *The Anatomy of Criticism: Four Essays*. Princeton: Princeton University Press, 1960.

Fuentes, Carlos. *The Death of Artemio Cruz*. Tr. Sam Hileman. New York: Farrar, Straus & Giroux, 1964.

_____. *La nueva novela hispanoamericana*. Mexico City: Joaquín Mortiz, 1969.

_____. *Terra nostra*. Mexico City: Joaquín Mortiz, 1975.

_____. *Zona sagrada*. Mexico City: Siglo XXI, 1967.

Gallagher, David P. *Modern Latin American Literature*. New York: Oxford University Press, 1973.

García Márquez, Gabriel. *El otoño del patriarca*. Buenos Aires: Sudamericana, 1975.

_____, and Plinio Apuleyo Mendoza. *El olor de la guayaba*. Bogotá: Oveja Negra, 1982.

Glicksberg, Charles I. *The Ironic Vision in Modern Literature*. The Hague: Martinus Nijhoff, 1969.

Goldemberg, Isaac. *The Fragmented Life of Don Jacobo Lerner*. Tr. Robert S. Picciotto. New York: Persea Books, 1976.

_____. *Hombre de paso/Just Passing Through*. Tr. David Unger and Isaac Goldemberg. Hanover, N.H.: Ediciones del Norte, 1982.

_____, and José Kozer. *De Chepén a la Habana*. New York: Bayú-Menoráh, 1973.

González Echevarría, Roberto. *Alejo Carpentier: The Pilgrim at Home*. Ithaca: Cornell University Press, 1977.

Good, Edwin Marshall. *Irony in the Old Testament*. Philadelphia: Westminster Press, 1965.

Guzmán, Daniel de. *Carlos Fuentes*. New York: Twayne, 1972.

Harss, Luis and Barbara Dohmann. *Into the Mainstream: Conversations with Latin-American Writers*. New York: Harper & Row, 1967.

Hegel, G. W. F. *The Philosophy of Fine Art*. Tr. Bernard Bosanquet. London: Kegan Paul, Trench and Co., 1886.

Hirsch, E. D. *Validity in Interpretation*. New Haven: Yale University Press, 1967.

Huizinga, Johan. *Homo ludens: A Study of the Play Element in Culture*. Boston: Beacon Press, 1955.

Husserl, Edmund. *Phenomenology and the Crisis of Philosophy*. Tr. Quentin Lauer. New York: Harper & Row, 1965.

Iser, Wolfgang. *The Act of Reading: A Theory of Aesthetic Response*. Baltimore: Johns Hopkins University Press, 1978.

Jankélévitch, Vladimir. *L'Ironie ou la bonne conscience*. 2d edition. Paris: Presses Universitaires de France, 1950.

Works Consulted

Kierkegaard, Søren Aabye. *The Concept of Irony, with Constant Reference to Socrates.* Tr. Lee M. Capel. Bloomington: Indiana University Press, 1965.

Knox, Norman. *The Word Irony and Its Context, 1550–1755.* Durham: Duke University Press, 1961.

Lejeune, Philippe. *Le pacte autobiographique.* Paris: Seuil, 1975.

Lentricchia, Frank. *After the New Criticism.* Chicago: University of Chicago Press, 1980.

Loveluck, Juan, ed. *Novelistas hispanoamericanos de hoy.* Madrid: Taurus, 1976.

Lukács, Georg. *The Theory of the Novel: A Historico-Philosophical Essay on the Forms of Great Epic Literature.* Tr. Anna Bostock. Cambridge: M.I.T. Press, 1971 [1916].

MacAdam, Alfred J. *Modern Latin American Narratives: The Dreams of Reason.* Chicago: University of Chicago Press, 1977.

Maldonado, Armando. "Manuel Puig: The Aesthetics of Cinematic and Psychological Fiction." Ph.D. dissertation, University of Oklahoma, 1977.

Menton, Seymour. *Prose Fiction of the Cuban Revolution.* Austin: University of Texas Press, 1975.

Miller, Arthur. *Death of a Salesman: Certain Private Conversations in Two Acts and a Requiem.* New York: Viking, 1949.

Muecke, Douglas Colin. *The Compass of Irony.* London: Methuen, 1969.

―――. *Irony.* London: Methuen, 1970.

Niebuhr, Reinhold. *The Irony of American History.* New York: Scribner, 1952.

Ortega, Julio. *La contemplación y la fiesta: Notas sobre la novela latinoamericana actual.* Caracas: Monte Avila, 1969.

Ortega y Gasset, José. *La deshumanización del arte.* Madrid: Revista de Occidente, 1970 [1925].

―――. *Ideas sobre la novela.* Madrid: Espasa-Calpe, 1969 [1925].

Paiva, Maria Helena de Novais. *Contribuçao para uma Estilística da Ironia.* Lisbon: Centro de Estudos Filológicos, 1961.

Paz, Octavio. *Traducción: Literatura y literalidad.* Barcelona: Tusquets Editor, 1970?.

Picón Garfield, Evelyn. *Cortázar por Cortázar* (interview). Mexico City: Universidad Veracruzana, 1978.

Pirandello, Luigi. *Six Characters in Search of an Author.* In *Three Plays.* New York: Dutton, 1922.

Puig, Manuel. *Betrayed by Rita Hayworth.* Tr. Suzanne Jill Levine. New York: Dutton, 1971.

―――. *Boquitas pintadas.* Buenos Aires: Sudamericana, 1974.

―――. *Sangre de amor correspondido.* Barcelona: Seix Barral, 1982.

200

Works Consulted

Rivas, Duque de (Angel Saavedra). *Don Alvaro o la fuerza del sino*. Madrid: Espasa-Calpe, 1972 [1833].

Rodríguez-Alcalá, Hugo. *El arte de Juan Rulfo*. Mexico City: Instituto Nacional de Bellas Artes, 1965.

Rodríguez Monegal, Emir. *El boom de la novela latinoamericana: Ensayo*. Caracas: Editorial Tiempo Nuevo, 1972.

_____. *Narradores de esta América*. Montevideo: Alfa, 1968.

Rossman, Charles, and Robert Brody, eds. *Carlos Fuentes: A Critical View*. Austin: University of Texas Press, 1982.

Rossman, Charles, and Alan Warren Friedman, eds. *Mario Vargas Llosa: A Collection of Critical Essays*. Austin: University of Texas Press, 1978.

Rulfo, Juan. *El gallo de oro y otros textos para cine*. Ed. Jorge Ayala Blanco. Mexico City: Era, 1980.

_____. *El llano en llamas*. Mexico City: Fondo de Cultura Económica, 1953.

_____. *Pedro Páramo*. Tr. Lysander Kemp. New York: Grove Press, 1978 [1959].

Saussure, Ferdinand de. *Course in General Linguistics*. Ed. Charles Bally and Albert Sechehaye, in collaboration with Albert Riedlinger; tr. Wade Baskin. New York: McGraw-Hill, 1966.

Schlegel, Friedrich. *Friedrich Schlegel's* Lucinde *and the* Fragments. Tr. Peter Firchow. Minneapolis: University of Minnesota Press, 1971.

Sedgewick, Garnett Gladwin. *Of Irony, Especially in Drama*. Toronto: University of Toronto Press Series, 1948.

Sharpe, Robert Boies. *Irony in the Drama: An Essay on Impersonation, Shock, and Catharsis*. Chapel Hill: University of North Carolina Press, 1959.

Souza, Raymond D. *Major Cuban Novelists: Innovation and Tradition*. Columbia and London: University of Missouri Press, 1976.

States, Bert O. *Irony and Drama: A Poetics*. Ithaca: Cornell University Press, 1971.

Sterne, Lawrence. *Tristram Shandy*. New York: Signet, 1962.

Szichman, Mario. *A las 20:25, la señora entró en la inmortalidad*. Hanover, N.H.: Ediciones del Norte, 1981.

Thompson, Alan Reynolds. *The Anatomy of Drama*. Berkeley and Los Angeles: University of California Press, 1946.

_____. *The Dry Mock: A Study of Irony in Drama*. Berkeley: University of California Press, 1948.

Thomson, J. A. K. *Irony: An Historical Introduction*. Cambridge: Harvard University Press, 1927.

Turner, Francis McDougall Charlewood. *The Element of Irony in English Literature: An Essay*. Folcroft, Pa.: Folcroft Press, 1969 [1926].

Works Consulted

Unamuno, Miguel de. *Niebla (Nivola)*. Madrid: Espasa-Calpe, 1975 [1914].

Uslar-Pietri, Arturo. *Breve historia de la novela hispanoamericana*. Madrid: Editorial Mediterráneo, 1979.

Vargas Llosa, Mario. *Aunt Julia and the Scriptwriter*. Tr. Helen R. Lane. New York: Farrar, Straus & Giroux, 1982.

―――. *Captain Pantoja and the Special Service*. Tr. Gregory Kolovakos and Ronald Christ. New York: Harper & Row, 1978.

―――. *Conversation in the Cathedral*. Tr. Gregory Rabassa. New York: Harper & Row, 1975.

―――. *The Cubs and Other Stories*. Tr. Gregory Kolovakos and Ronald Christ. New York: Harper & Row, 1979.

―――. *The Green House*. Tr. Gregory Rabassa. New York: Harper & Row, 1968.

―――. *La guerra del fin del mundo*. Barcelona: Seix Barral, 1981.

―――. *The Time of the Hero*. Tr. Lysander Kemp. New York: Harper & Row, 1966.

Vidal, Hernán. *Literatura hispanoamericana e ideología liberal: Surgimiento y crisis*. Buenos Aires: Ediciones Hispamérica, 1976.

Wellek, René. *A History of Modern Criticism*. New Haven: Yale University Press, 1955. Vol. 2.

White, Hayden. *Tropics of Discourse: Essays in Cultural Criticism*. Baltimore: Johns Hopkins University Press, 1978.

Williams, Raymond L. *Una década de la novela colombiana: La experiencia de los setenta*. Bogotá: Plaza y Janés, 1981.

Worcester, David. *The Art of Satire*. New York: Russell and Russell, 1960 [1940].

Articles, Interviews, and Stories

Allen, John J. "The Narrators, the Reader, and Don Quijote." *Modern Language Notes* 91, no. 2 (1976): 201–12.

Alvarez, Nicolás Emilio. "Agonía y muerte de Juan Preciado." *Revista de Estudios Hispánicos* 13 (1979): 209–26.

Bastos, María Luisa. "Clichés lingüísticos y ambigüedad en *Pedro Páramo.*" *Revista Iberoamericana* 44, no. 102 (1978): 31–44.

Bell, Alan S. "Rulfo's *Pedro Páramo*: A Vision of Hope." *Modern Language Notes* 81, no. 2 (1966): 238–45.

Blanco Aguinaga, Carlos. "Realidad y estilo de Juan Rulfo." In *Nueva Novela Latinoamericana*. Ed. Jorge Lafforgue. Buenos Aires: Pardos, 1969, pp. 85–113.

Works Consulted

Bloom, Harold. "The Breaking of Form." In *Deconstruction and Criticism*. Ed. Harold Bloom et al. New York: Continuum, 1979, pp. 1–37.

Booth, Wayne C. "The First Full Professor of Ironology in the World." In *Now Don't Try to Reason with Me*. Chicago: University of Chicago Press, 1971, pp. 327–48.

Borges, Jorge Luis. "Borges y yo." In *El hacedor*. Madrid: Alianza/Emecé, 1975 [1960], pp. 69–70.

Borinsky, Alicia. "Castración y lujos: La escritura de Manuel Puig." *Revista Iberoamericana* 41, no. 90 (1975): 29–46.

————. "Juegos: Una realidad sin centros." In *Estudios sobre los cuentos de Julio Cortázar*. Ed. David Lagmanovich. Barcelona: Ediciones Hispam, 1975, pp. 59–72.

Botsford, Keith. "My Friend Fuentes." *Commentary* (Feb. 1965): 64–67.

Brooks, Cleanth. "Irony as a Principle of Structure." In *Literary Opinion in America*. Ed. Morton D. Zabel. New York: Harper, 1962 [1951], pp. 729–41.

Burke, Kenneth. "Four Master Tropes." In *A Grammar of Motives*. Cleveland: World, 1962, pp. 503–18.

Cabrera Infante, Guillermo. "Metafinal." *Alacrán Azul* 1, no. 1 (1970): 18–23. Repr. and tr. *Latin American Literary Review* 8, no. 16 (1980): 88–95.

Caillois, Roger. "Unity of Play: Diversity of Games." Tr. Elaine P. Halperin. *Diogenes* 19 (Fall 1957): 92–121.

Carranza, José María. "Sobre Manuel Puig, *La traición de Rita Hayworth*." *Revista Iberoamericana* 38, no. 78 (1972): 152.

Chermak, Gertrude. "The Image of the Labyrinth in *The Death of Artemio Cruz*." In *Rackham Literary Studies* (Ann Arbor) 2 (1972): 124–26.

Christ, Ronald. "Fact and Fiction." *Review* 73 (Fall 1973): 49–54.

————. "An Interview with Manuel Puig." *Partisan Review* 44, no. 1 (1977): 52–61.

Clough, W. O. "Irony: A French Approach." *Sewanee Review* 47 (1939): 175–83.

Crow, John A. "*Pedro Páramo*: A Twentieth-Century Dance of Death." In *Homage to Irving A. Leonard: Essays on Hispanic Art, History, and Literature*. Ed. Raquel Chang-Rodríguez and Donald A. Yates. East Lansing: Latin American Studies Center, Michigan State University, 1973, pp. 219–27.

De Man, Paul. "The Rhetoric of Temporality." In *Interpretation: Theory and Practice*. Ed. Charles S. Singleton. Baltimore: Johns Hopkins University Press, pp. 173–209.

Derrida, Jacques. "Structure, Sign and Play in the Discourse of the Human Sciences." In *Writing and Difference*. Tr. Alan Bass. Chicago: University of Chicago Press, 1978, pp. 278–93.

Works Consulted

Díaz-Migoyo, Gonzalo. "El Funcionamiento de la ironía." *Espiral,* forthcoming.

Ehrmann, Jacques. "Homo ludens Revisited." In *Game, Play, Literature.* Ed. Jacques Ehrmann. Boston: Beacon Press, 1972, pp. 31–57.

Embeita, María J. "Tema y estructura en *Pedro Páramo.*" *Cuadernos Americanos* 26, no. 2 (1967): 218–23.

Fink, Eugene. "The Oasis of Happiness: Toward an Ontology of Play." In *Game, Play, Literature.* Ed. Jacques Ehrmann. Boston: Beacon Press, 1972, 19–30.

Fish, Stanley E. "Normal Circumstances, Literal Language, Direct Speech Acts, the Ordinary, the Everyday, the Obvious, What Goes without Saying, and Other Special Cases." *Critical Inquiry* 4 (Summer 1978): 625–44.

Foster, David William. "Manuel Puig and the Uses of Nostalgia." *Latin American Literary Review* 1, no. 1 (1972): 79–82.

Frank, Joseph. "Spatial Form in Modern Literature," In *The Widening Gyre.* New Brunswick: Rutgers University Press, 1963, pp. 3–62.

Fuente, Bienvenido de la. "*La muerte de Artemio Cruz:* Observaciones sobre la estructura y sentido de la narración en primera persona." *Explicación de Textos Literarios* 6, no. 2 (1978): 143–51.

García Márquez, Gabriel. "Los funerales de la Mamá Grande." In *Los funerales de la Mamá Grande.* Xalapa, Mexico: Universidad Veracruzana, 1962, pp. 131–51.

González, Manuel Pedro. "La novela hispanoamericana en el contexto de la internacional." In *Coloquio sobre la novela hispanoamericana.* Mexico City: Tezontle, 1967, pp. 89–100.

González Arauzo, A. "No Other Ends than Possession." *New Mexico Quarterly Review* 1, no. 4 (1962): 269.

González Echevarría, Roberto. "Ironía y estilo en *Los pasos perdidos,* de Alejo Carpentier." In *Asedios a Carpentier: Nueve ensayos críticos sobre el novelista cubano.* Ed. Klaus Müller-Bergh. Santiago de Chile: Editorial Universitaria, 1972, pp. 124–46.

Guibert, Rita. "The Tongue-Twisted Tiger." *Review* 72 (Winter–Spring 1972): 11–16.

Gyurko, Lanin A. "Rulfo's Aesthetic Nihilism: Narrative Antecedents of 'Pedro Páramo.'" *Hispanic Review* 40, no. 4 (1972): 451–66.

Harss, Luis. "Carlos Fuentes, Mexico's Metropolitan Eye." *New Mexico Quarterly* 36, no. 1 (1966): 26–55.

Head, Gerald L. "El castigo de Toribio Aldrete y la estructura de *Pedro Páramo.*" In *Otros mundos, otros fuegos: Fantasía y realismo mágico en Iberoamérica.* East Lansing: Latin American Studies Center, Michigan State University, 1976, pp. 379–82.

Works Consulted

Jara, René. "Mito y la nueva novela hispanoamericana." In *Homenaje a Carlos Fuentes*. Ed. Helmy F. Giacoman. Long Island City: Las Américas, 1971, pp. 147–208.

Joén, Didier T. "La estructura lírica de *Pedro Páramo*." *Revista Hispánica Moderna* 33, no. 3–4 (1967): 224–32.

Leal, Luis. "La estructura de *Pedro Páramo*." *Anuario de Letras* 4 (1964): 287–94.

Lewis, Philip E. "La Rochefoucauld: The Rationality of Play." In *Game, Play, Literature*. Ed. Jacques Ehrmann. Boston: Beacon Press, 1972, pp. 133–47.

Lipp, Solomon. "Israel and the Holocaust in Contemporary Spanish American Poetry." *Hispania* 65, no. 4 (1982): 536–43.

Loveluck, Juan. "Intención y forma en *La muerte de Artemio Cruz*." In *Homenaje a Carlos Fuentes*. Ed. Helmy F. Giacoman. Long Island City: Las Américas, 1971, pp. 209–28. Also in Juan Loveluck, ed., *Novelistas hispanoamericanos de hoy*. Madrid: Taurus, 1976, pp. 249–71.

Luchting, Wolfgang A. "Betrayed by Education: Manuel Puig's *La traición de Rita Hayworth*." *Proceedings of the Pacific Northwest Conference on Foreign Languages* 28, no. 1 (1977): 134–37.

———. "Una sorpresa para la literatura peruana: Isaac Goldemberg." *Chasqui* 8, no. 2 (1979): 123–24.

Merrim, Stephanie. "A Secret Idiom: The Grammar and Role of Language in *Tres tristes tigres*." *Latin American Literary Review* 8, no. 16 (1980): 96–117.

Meyer-Minnemann, Klaus. "Tiempo cíclico e historia en *La muerte de Artemio Cruz* de Carlos Fuentes." *Iberoromania* 7 (1978): 88–105.

Miranda, Julio E. "*Tres tristes tigres*." *Cuadernos Hispanoamericanos* 74, no. 220 (1968): 201–05.

Mitchell, Phyllis. "The Reel against the Real: Cinema in the Novels of Guillermo Cabrera Infante and Manuel Puig." *Latin American Literary Review* 6, no. 11 (1979): 22–29.

Morello Frosch, Marta. "The New Art of Narrating Films." *Review 72* (Winter–Spring 1972): 52–55.

Ortega, Julio. "An Open Novel." *Review 72* (Winter–Spring 1972): 17–21.

Ortega y Gasset, José. "El origin deportivo del estado." In *El Espectador*. Madrid: Biblioteca Nueva, 1950, pp. 835–59.

Osorio, Nelson. "Un aspecto de la estructura de *La muerte de Artemio Cruz*." In *Homenaje a Carlos Fuentes*. Ed. Helmy F. Giacoman. Long Island City: Las Américas, 1971, pp. 125–46.

Oviedo, José Miguel. "A Conversation with Mario Vargas Llosa about *La tía Julia y el escribidor*." In *Mario Vargas Llosa: A Collection of Critical*

Works Consulted

Essays. Ed. Charles Rossman and Alan Warren Friedman. Austin: University of Texas Press, 1978, pp. 152–65.

Palante, Georges. "L'Ironie: Etude psychologique." *Revue Philosophique de la France et de l'Etranger* 61 (1906): 147–63.

Reeve, Richard M. "Carlos Fuentes y el desarrollo del narrador en segunda persona: Un ensayo exploratorio." In *Homenaje a Carlos Fuentes.* Ed. Helmy F. Giacoman. Long Island City: Las Américas, 1971, pp. 75–87.

Restrepo Fernández, Iván. "La cacería de Juan Rulfo." *Mundo Nuevo* 39–40 (Sept.–Oct. 1969): 43–44.

Rodríguez Monegal, Emir. "A Literary Myth Exploded." *Review* 72 (Winter–Spring 1972): 56–64.

––––––. "Structure and Meanings of *Three Trapped Tigers.*" *Latin American Literary Review* 1, no. 2 (1973): 19–36.

Rodríguez Padrón, Jorge. "Manuel Puig y la capacidad expresiva de la lengua popular." *Cuadernos Hispanoamericanos* 82, no. 245 (1970): 490–97.

Rosa, Nicolás. "Cabrera Infante: Una patología del lenguaje." In *Crítica y significación.* Buenos Aires: Editorial Galerna, 1970, pp. 175–224.

Ryan, Michael. "Self-Evidence." *Diacritics* 10, no. 2 (1980): 2–16.

Sarduy, Severo. "Notas a las notas a las notas . . . , A propósito de Manuel Puig." *Revista Iberoamericana* 37, no. 76–77 (1971): 555–68.

Sarris, Andrew. "Re-running Puig and Cabrera Infante." *Review* 73 (Spring 1973): 46–48.

Sarrocchi, Augusto C. "Sobre el narrador de *La traición de Rita Hayworth.*" *Signos* 9–16 (1973–74): 95–104.

Schaerer, René. "Le mechanisme de l'ironie dans ses rapports avec la dialectique." *Revue de Métaphysique et de Morale* 48 (1941): 181–209.

Schraibman, José. "Cabrera Infante: Tras la búsqueda del lenguaje." *Insula* 25, no. 286 (1970): 1, 15–16.

Shaw, Donald L. "Narrative Arrangement in *La muerte de Artemio Cruz.*" In *Contemporary Latin American Fiction: Seven Essays.* Ed. Salvador Bacarisse. Edinburgh: Scottish Academic Press, 1980, pp. 34–47.

Sommer, Doris. "Playing to Lose: Cortázar's Comforting Pessimism." *Chasqui* 8, no. 3 (1979): 54–62.

Sommers, Joseph. "Through the Window of the Grave: Juan Rulfo." *New Mexico Quarterly* 38, no. 1 (1968): 84–101.

Southard, David R. "Betrayed by Manuel Puig: Reader Deception and Anti-Climax in His Novels." *Latin American Literary Review* 4, no. 9 (1976): 22–28.

Suleiman, Susan. "Interpreting Ironies." *Diacritics* 6, no. 2 (1976): 15–21.

Thirlwall, Bishop Connop. "On the Irony of Sophocles." In *Remains, Literary and Theological.* Ed. J. T. Stewart Perowne. London: Daldy, Isbister, 1878 [1833], vol. 2, pp. 1–57.

Works Consulted

Tinwell, Roger D. "*La muerte de Artemio Cruz:* A Virtuoso Study in Sensualism." *Modern Language Notes* 93, no. 3 (1978): 334–38.

Tittler, Jonathan. "La continuidad en 'Continuidad de los parques.'" *Crítica Hispánica,* forthcoming.

———. "Interview: Carlos Fuentes." *Diacritics* 10, no. 4 (1980): 46–56.

———. "*La tía Julia* (historia) y el *escribidor* (ficción)." In *Actas del Simposio sobre la Historia en la Ficción Hispanoamericana Contemporánea.* Ed. Roberto González Echevarría. Caracas: Monte Avila, forthcoming.

West, Anthony. "*La muerte de Artemio Cruz.*" *New Yorker* 40, no. 25 (8 Aug. 1964): 88–89.

Williams, Raymond L. "*La vida a plazos de don Jacobo Lerner.*" *Journal of Spanish Studies, Twentieth Century* 7, no. 2 (1979): 730–32.

Yurkievich, Saúl. "*Eros ludens:* Games, Love and Humor in *Hopscotch.*" In *The Final Island: The Fiction of Julio Cortázar.* Ed. Jaime Alazraki and Ivar Ivask. Norman: University of Oklahoma Press, 1976, pp. 97–108.

INDEX

Index

Library of Congress Cataloging in Publication Data

Tittler, Jonathan, 1945–
  Narrative irony in the contemporary Spanish-American novel.

  Bibliography: p.
  Includes index.
  1. Spanish American fiction—20th century—History and criticism.   2. Irony in
literature.   I. Title.
PQ7082.N7T5   1984   863'.009'1   83-21074
ISBN 0-8014-1574-8 (alk. paper)

DATE DUE

⅄ 4 '89				
DEC 14 '89				
FEB 9 '90				

DEMCO 38-297